ADDITIONAL PRAISE FOR *TEACHERPRENEURS*

"This book gives anyone who is concerned with the education of our nation's children a great deal of hope. We should be grateful to Barr Alan Wieder for introducing us to these 'teacherpreneurs,' and innovative teachers whose stories are featured and wh These gifted individuals clearly have the ability to insp influence, and educate other teachers."

—Anthony S. Bryk, president, Carnegie Foundation for the Advancement of Teaching

"Why do I think *Teacherpreneurs* is an exceptionally inspiring book? It offers authentic teacher voices that speak volumes of truth. This book talks less about shortcomings of teachers or teaching and more about solutions that innovative teachers offer to make teaching one of the noble professions. A must-read for anyone who cares about how our schools will look in the future."

—Pasi Sahlberg, director general of CIMO (Centre for International Mobility and Cooperation) in Finland and author of *Finnish Lessons*

"*Teacherpreneurs* will be a turning point for the field. It offers 'existence proofs' of the book's central concept while bringing the concept to life. It makes the case in an easy-to-read manner. West Point trains cadets to be 2nd lieutenants but educates them to be generals. Schools of education should similarly prepare strong candidates to be effective classroom teachers and potential teacherpreneurs. While no college program can fully prepare teachers for leadership, it can shape how they think about their careers. *Teacherpreneurs* presents a vision of a career in which effective teachers shape the policies that determine the classroom environment in which they and their colleagues teach. Education professors and teacher candidates will learn how they can revolutionize teaching for the betterment of students."

—Arthur E. Wise, CTQ board chair, and president emeritus, National Council for Accreditation of Teacher Education

"The real-life stories of *Teacherpreneurs* show us the power of this hybrid model—a teacher who leads her or his colleagues without leaving the classroom, who is engaged in both pedagogy and policy, and who constantly seeks solutions. What better way to support peers and navigate the challenges confronting public schools and our students today."

—Randi Weingarten, president, American Federation of Teachers

"Strong leaders are critical in transforming schools, but too many teachers believe they must leave the classroom to make an impact. *Teacherpreneurs* profiles transformative teacher leaders who are revolutionizing teaching and learning and leading in their professions. By acknowledging that the teacher is the key element in authentic school improvement, *Teacherpreneurs* offers a roadmap for much-needed change, pointing out the institutional and cultural barriers that often stifle teacher-leadership and offering systemic measures necessary to shift the culture of school leadership."

—Dennis Van Roekel, president,
National Education Association

"Barnett Berry and colleagues have written a powerful book—offering us a powerful, new way to think about the teaching profession, now and in the future. *Teacherpreneurs* describes how eight extraordinary teachers became leaders without leaving the classroom, and provides insight into their inspiring and important work. Filled with rich narratives and research, this book is a must-read for teachers, administrators, and researchers, as well as education policy leaders who must invest in teaching to build the profession-wide expertise that our students need and deserve."
—Linda Darling-Hammond, Charles Ducommun Professor of Education,
Stanford University School of Education, California

"Hillsborough County Public Schools believes that 'teacherpreneurs,' as identified in this new book, are essential elements of a successful career ladder plan. Our best teachers want to remain teachers, but they also want to help develop colleagues, write curriculum, and have a voice in shaping educational policy at the local, state, and national level. Empowering our most effective teachers to take on broader roles should be a goal of every district seeking reform."
—MaryEllen Elia, superintendent,
Hillsborough County Public Schools, Florida

TEACHERPRENEURS

HOW TO USE THIS BOOK

This book tells the stories of extraordinary teachers who have found pathways to transformative professional leadership without leaving their classroom and students. The days of having to move out of the classroom to "move up" in your career are fading, and the teacher leaders you'll meet in these pages are proof. It is also a guidebook for other teachers, perhaps like you, who are still seeking their own leadership path.

Starting your journey is the biggest challenge. More than any other teacher leaders, teacherpreneurs must know how to connect with and create new opportunities, ready themselves with the competencies needed to lead well, and lead work among colleagues of all kinds collaboratively rather than being perpetually "out in front." Activities at the end of each chapter help you apply the big ideas you've just read about, take action, and share with others—either in your school or as a part of the Center for Teaching Quality Collaboratory, a national virtual community of teacher leaders that we invite you to join. By the time you've worked through this book, you'll have a strategic plan to prepare for and build your own future teacherpreneurial role.

Your leadership is the sequel to *Teacherpreneurs*. Let's get started.

Unlock additional content for *Teacherpreneurs* with your smartphone or tablet. Throughout the print version of this book you'll find Quick Response (QR) codes that link to video, audio, and other online content to complement your reading experience. If you don't have a smart device, you can still access content by visiting the accompanying links.

To try it out, download the free Microsoft tag reader by visiting http://gettag.mobi or searching for "tag reader" or "tag app" in your mobile app store. If you have a generic QR code reader, then you may scan the code that follows to get Microsoft Tag for free.

DOWNLOAD MICROSOFT TAG

Please download Microsoft Tag or check your QR code reader by scanning the following image with your smartphone:

We hope you enjoy this enhanced experience.

TEACHERPRENEURS

Innovative Teachers Who Lead but Don't Leave

Barnett Berry
Ann Byrd
Alan Wieder

A Wiley Brand

Copyright © 2013 by John Wiley & Sons, Inc. All rights reserved.
Published by Jossey-Bass
A Wiley Brand
One Montgomery Street, Suite 1200, San Francisco, CA 94104-4594—www.josseybass.com

Video content is available via QR code and shortened Web site links (bitly) in the print book, and through shortened Web site links (bitly) only in the e-books. If you access video content through a mobile device, message and data rates may apply. Video content may not be available indefinitely.

Jossey-Bass books and products are available through most bookstores. To contact Jossey-Bass directly call our Customer Care Department within the U.S. at 800-956-7739, outside the U.S. at 317-572-3986, or fax 317-572-4002.

Wiley publishes in a variety of print and electronic formats and by print-on-demand. Some material included with standard print versions of this book may not be included in e-books or in print-on-demand. If this book refers to media such as a CD or DVD that is not included in the version you purchased, you may download this material at http://booksupport.wiley.com. For more information about Wiley products, visit www.wiley.com.

Library of Congress Cataloging-in-Publication Data
Berry, Barnett.
 Teacherpreneurs: innovative teachers who lead but don't leave / Barnett Berry, Ann Byrd, Alan Wieder.
   pages cm
  Includes bibliographical references and index.

ISBN 978-1-118-45619-4 (pbk.)
ISBN 978-1-118-53991-0 (ebk.)
ISBN 978-1-118-54004-6 (ebk.)

1. Teaching—United States. 2. Educational change—United States. I. Byrd, Ann, 1961- II. Wieder, Alan, 1949- III. Title.
 LB1025.3.B4734 2013
 371.102—dc23

                                                                    2013018291

Printed in the United States of America
FIRST EDITION
PB PRINTING 10 9 8 7 6

CONTENTS

ABOUT THE CENTER FOR TEACHING QUALITY

The Center for Teaching Quality (CTQ) is a national nonprofit that is transforming the teaching profession through the bold ideas and expert practices of teachers. CTQ cultivates opportunities for teachers to connect, learn, and lead—for the benefit of all students.

Driving CTQ's work is the knowledge that teachers stand on the front lines of implementation for every education innovation. Because of this, they are uniquely well positioned to create practical, sustainable strategies to improve our public schools and teach and reach all students to prepare them for the global society in which they live.

Since its founding in 1999, CTQ has transitioned from a think tank to an action tank. Currently more than 20 percent of CTQ's network members are compensated to develop and use their leadership to advance the teaching profession and student learning by serving as virtual community organizers, online mentors, assessment experts, policy liaisons, writers, and speakers.

CTQ serves as one of our nation's most important thought leaders in advancing teaching as a twenty-first-century profession. At the heart of its work is the Collaboratory, a virtual community for incubating and executing educators' ideas. The Collaboratory welcomes forward-thinking administrators, policymakers, parents, and others who value teachers as leaders.

For more information, and to join the movement, please visit:

teachingquality.org

ABOUT THE AUTHORS

Barnett Berry

Barnett Berry is founder and CEO of the Center for Teaching Quality (CTQ), based in Carrboro, North Carolina.

A former high school teacher of three years, Barnett has worked as a social scientist at the RAND Corporation, served as a senior executive with the South Carolina Department of Education, and directed an education policy center while he was a professor at the University of South Carolina. In the mid-1990s he worked with Linda Darling-Hammond, then executive director of the National Commission on Teaching & America's Future (NCTAF), in developing its seminal report, *What Matters Most*. In leading NCTAF's state policy reform efforts, Barnett launched CTQ.

Barnett has authored more than eighty peer-reviewed journal articles and book chapters and published many other academic reports and articles for the popular education press. He blogs at *Advancing the Teaching Profession*, addressing today's most pressing education issues.

He frequently serves in an advisory capacity to education associations, nonprofits, and school reform organizations committed to teaching quality, equity, and social justice in America's schools. Barnett's areas of expertise include policies to advance the teaching profession, spanning from such areas as teacher recruitment and preparation to how teacher effectiveness is evaluated and rewarded.

At the core of Barnett's work is a simple and powerful conviction: our public schools will not realize their promise without drawing on the many excellent teachers we have right now. Today's expert teachers have the potential to lead the transformation of teaching and learning.

Teacherpreneurs builds on *Teaching 2030* (Teachers College Press, 2011), a book Barnett coauthored with twelve expert teachers. *Teaching 2030* depicts a provocative and hopeful future for the profession that transcends much of the current debates about teaching.

Barnett is married to Meredith, a dedicated special education teacher who just retired after thirty-five years of highly accomplished teaching. She has kept him grounded in the daily realities of public education. Barnett and Meredith are the parents of Joseph (age thirty-one), a political organizer and law student, and Evan (age twenty-six), an organic farmer, baker, and activist for sustainable community agriculture. Barnett and Meredith are very proud that both their children are dedicated to building a better world.

Ann Byrd

Ann Byrd serves as the chief operating officer and a partner at CTQ, where she leads organizational strategy, vision, and management efforts so that teachers can transform education. Her work at CTQ—and throughout her career—has been sparked and shaped by her thirteen years teaching high school English and journalism in Lancaster, South Carolina. Ann served as an instructor with the Teacher Cadet Program—run by Winthrop University's Center for Educator Recruitment, Retention and Advancement (CERRA)—for seven years while maintaining her primary role in the classroom—an experience that gave her firsthand insight into the challenges and rewards of a teacherpreneurial role. In her work with the Teacher Cadet Program, Ann sought to recruit high school seniors into education. She also served in various positions with CERRA as teacher in residence; program director; and executive director, a role she held for six years.

Ann holds a BA in English in secondary education from the University of South Carolina, an MEd in English education from Winthrop University, and an EdD in curriculum and instruction from the University of South Carolina.

She earned National Board Certification in English Language Arts for Adolescents and Young Adults in November 2000 and renewed her certification in November 2010. She also served for six years as a member of the National Board for Professional Teaching Standards board of directors. Ann continues to be energized by her efforts to ensure that teacher leaders can find ways to lead their profession without having to leave their students.

Alan Wieder

Alan Wieder is a Distinguished Professor Emeritus at the University of South Carolina who currently works as a senior research consultant with CTQ. He has also taught at the University of the Western Cape in South Africa. Besides serving twice as a Fulbright Scholar, he currently holds an appointment as Extraordinary Professor at Stellenbosch University in South Africa. His past research includes oral histories on race and education in the United States as well as on South African teachers who fought apartheid. His current book, on South African freedom fighters, is titled *Ruth First and Joe Slovo in the War Against Apartheid*, published in June 2013 by Monthly Review Books in the United States and by Jacana Media in South Africa.

Dedicated to Ann's daddy, a retired textile mill supervisor of thirty-nine years and the father of two National Board Certified Teachers, who thinks the idea of teacherpreneurs "makes a lot of sense to kinda split their time up so they can work on policy but keep teaching, too"

ACKNOWLEDGMENTS

So many teachers, with their pedagogical expertise and commitment to teaching, inspired us to write *Teacherpreneurs* and make the case for a bold brand of teacher leadership. The more than two thousand teachers in the Center for Teaching Quality (CTQ) Collaboratory keep us grounded (as much as we can be from a distance) in the daily realities—good and bad—they face in their respective classrooms, schools, districts, and states. They inspired us in countless ways. Most important, they have taught us that the number one problem in regard to teaching quality reforms of today is the lack of demand for the leadership that many, many expert teachers who currently teach could provide to transform public education. Of course, we are especially indebted to Shannon C'de Baca, Jessica Keigan, Stephen Lazar, Renee Moore, Lori Nazareno, Ariel Sacks, José Vilson, and Noah Zeichner (as well as Megan Allen, Jessica Cuthbertson, Sarah Henchey, and Ryan Kinser)—who are profiled in this book—for teaching us so much about how they developed their teacherpreneurial skills and characteristics. In telling the stories of their journeys as *innovative leaders who lead but don't leave*, we learned a lot about the soul of the teaching profession. They have taught us how to cultivate and support many teacher leaders who can do what they have done. They have motivated us even more to find ways to connect, ready, and mobilize six hundred thousand teacherpreneurs by the year 2030.

We are especially grateful to the philanthropies—the Bill & Melinda Gates Foundation, MetLife Foundation, the Rose Community Foundation, and the Stuart Foundation—whose financial support has made it possible for us to activate growing numbers of teacherpreneurs. We also appreciate the guidance and enthusiastic backing of our editor at Jossey-Bass, Kate Gagnon, who from the start saw the value of our experiences with these talented teachers and the power of sharing their stories.

Running a nonprofit and publishing a book do not always go hand in glove. Our efforts to document the leadership stories of these terrific teachers and write

Teacherpreneurs would not have been successful without our colleagues at CTQ—Kate Albrecht, Alesha Daughtrey, Teresa Durn, Eva Hardy, Ali Kliegman, Kris Kohl, Meredith Kohl, Leanne Link, Melissa Rasberry, Keshi Satterwhite, Cynthia Sharpe, Braden Welborn, Skye Wilson, and Tim Wilson. And special thanks go to Emily Liebtag, whose internship came at just the right time to keep us all (almost) sane and organized in preparing the words that follow. Every one of our board members (including Shannon and José, who are profiled herein) have been essential to the development of our organization and the advancement of teacherpreneurs—but none have been of greater importance than our chair, Arthur E. Wise, whose deep knowledge, sharp intellect, and steadfast focus on professionalizing teaching constantly frame our hopes and actions.

From Alan: I thank my wife and partner, Joanie Krug, who never wavers in her support of my work for social justice in the United States and throughout the world, and who, like Meredith Berry, is in her third decade as an educator in America's public schools.

From Ann: I thank Bobby and Shirley, my parents, and my first two teachers. Bobby showed me the value of maintaining high expectations for my students, my colleagues, and myself. And Shirley passed on a passion for reading that opened up my education and that of others in ways that would not otherwise have been possible. I am where I am because of who they are.

From Barnett: And then there is Meredith, my wife of thirty-six years, just retired from over thirty-five years of expert teaching. She shows me every day of our wonderful life together how important it is for students to have teachers who teach for a career.

PROLOGUE: WHY WE WROTE THIS BOOK

IT BEGINS WITH RENEE'S STORY

Walking into Renee Moore's classroom in Drew, Mississippi, a town of 2,500 that has had its better days, served as a pivotal moment in putting together this book on a new, bold brand of teacher leadership. We had traveled the 110 miles from the Memphis airport, driving past cotton and soybean fields as well as cinderblock penitentiaries and brazen entrances to casino compounds in the Mississippi Delta. Renee is a veteran, award-winning teacher who has deep knowledge of world literature, language, and writing. She also has an abiding faith in God, grounded beautifully in her devotion to her religion, and an unwavering commitment to the students and families of the Deep South whom she and her husband have served for over twenty-five years. Her story helped us frame what it would mean to be a *teacherpreneur*—a classroom expert who still teaches while finding time, space, and (ideally) much-deserved reward for spreading both sound pedagogical practices and policy ideas. As we watched her teach, we realized that Renee's narrative tells us much about the many innovative teachers *who lead in bold ways but do not leave their classroom*. And as we began to understand how Renee learned to lead, we realized that her story must be told if our nation's public education system is ever going to capitalize on the talents and ideas of so many teachers like her.

In her Composition I class at Mississippi Delta Community College, we watched Renee teach by responding to her students with sublime ease, similar to experts in other professions who have an intuitive grasp of complex situations. Renee, like other seasoned and accomplished teachers, "can anticipate, plan, and improvise" and "engage students in learning" while developing her "self-regulation and self-efficacy."[1] But most of all, she guided her fifteen students, ages seventeen to forty-eight, with the enormous patience and care that we soon discovered was rooted in her deep knowledge of how they learn as well as what would inspire yet *not* intimidate them.

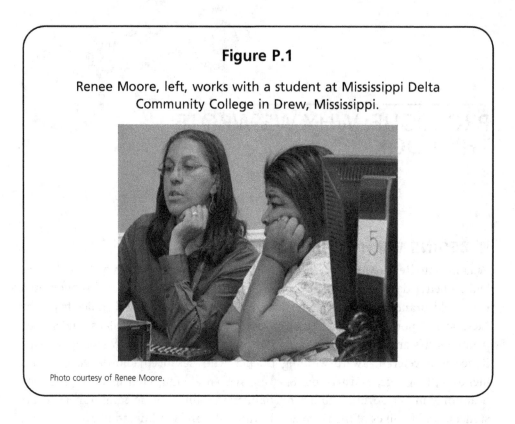

Figure P.1

Renee Moore, left, works with a student at Mississippi Delta Community College in Drew, Mississippi.

Photo courtesy of Renee Moore.

Renee had taught these students for only three classes, and they were already producing, with pride, their first two-page, polished essays, using academic as well as critical thinking and collaborative work skills that will serve them well in their future careers in nursing and palliative care, early childhood education, the military, and engineering. We watched Renee embrace the cultures her students brought to class and listened as she prepared them to code-switch—that is, to use different cultural and language patterns depending on the given situation—in the world outside of Drew.

Later, in a world literature class, we watched her gently remind her students of what was expected, drawing on well-developed scoring guidelines that clearly specified how and why her students would be assessed. She expected a great deal of them—but not too much more than she determined any given student could handle at any one time. She was expert in scaffolding their knowledge at a pace appropriate to their developing sophistication

> Successful student learning should be the basic entry requirement for anyone who leads in education.
> —Renee Moore

and limited world experiences as she opened their eyes to literacy and literature as well as hope and resolve.

As we sat down and observed her teaching, one student whispered to us, "She helps us so much; she makes everything understandable."

We saw no flashy teaching, but we did see a teacher who had intense pedagogical knowledge about which only the most rare of policymakers or policy pundits has an understanding. We saw a teacher who was patient and methodical, focused and strategic. We saw her lead a Socratic seminar, guiding her students—some of whom had never traveled the 122 miles on US-49S to Jackson, Mississippi—on a journey to ancient times through the epic poem of India *The Ramayana*, helping learners connect its philosophical and devotional elements to their lives and relationships with their own family. Renee's teaching style is not one of a drill sergeant making students march to orders, but more like that of a maestro of jazz music, with all its tightly connected polyrhythms and syncopation, born of African American culture in the South.

As we reflected on what we witnessed in our visit to Mississippi, we considered the distance between the efforts of today's education reformers to ratchet up teaching quality and what Renee does and means for this rural Delta community, which is beset by severe poverty and overt racial discrimination and in which public schools still are segregated tightly and teachers are expected to deliver a narrow curriculum defined by those who know too little about the students and their academic, social, and emotional needs.

In our visit to Renee, after observing her teach one evening, she offered up one poignant point after another. This one stood out:

> No one is arguing that a few children do escape poverty through education, but why should poor students have to go to poor schools; and why should their teachers have to go through so many unnecessary obstacles to help the neediest students achieve that escape? If we are so convinced that education is the way out of poverty, then why do we make the way so cluttered and so hard?

Amid the wars between school reformers who say "no more excuses about poverty" and teacher union leaders who call for "better working conditions," in *Teacherpreneurs* we profile Renee and seven other innovative teachers who lead but do not leave—Shannon C'de Baca, Jessica Keigan, Stephen Lazar, Lori Nazareno, Ariel Sacks, José Vilson, and Noah Zeichner. Their work stands in stark contrast to conventional wisdom about teaching quality today that says our schools will improve if we recruit brighter people to teaching who work harder. The eight we profile and so many more are "brighter people" who already are teaching and having tremendous impact in and out of their classroom. Their teaching and leadership skills—and those of many others—offer new ways to think about and act on school reform.

Richard Elmore made the compelling case that many education policies and practices often wither—primarily because reformers fail to "develop organizational structures that intensify and focus" on the new reforms, which are supported by too few "intentional processes for [the] reproduction of successes."[2] His research pointed out that reform is about learning—and for humans to learn they must have "encouragement and support, access to special knowledge, time to focus on the requirements of the new task, [and] time to observe others doing it,"[3] but these conditions rarely are in place.

THE POWER AND PROMISE OF TEACHER LEADERSHIP

Ariel, Jessica, José, Lori, Noah, Renee, Shannon, and Stephen are eight of the over two thousand teacher leaders who are part of our **Collaboratory** at the Center for Teaching Quality (CTQ),[*] a virtual community of classroom experts who seek to remain in teaching while transforming public education far beyond the reaches of their school, district, state, and nation. They work to change teaching and learning for their students and many others; they take advantage of circumstances that come their way as well as those they create. And although American policymakers continue to divide the worlds of teachers and reformers, these eight teachers (and so many others) do much of what Peter Drucker attributed to entrepreneurs many decades ago: they "search for change, respond to it, and exploit it as an opportunity."[4]

We offer a simple proposition: these eight teachers are exceptional—but they are not the exception. There are many, many others like them who want to lead without leaving the classroom. A 2013 MetLife study found that 23 percent of American teachers are "extremely" or "very" interested in serving in a hybrid role as a teacher and leader. (And the vast majority of them—84 percent—are "not very" or "not at all" interested in becoming a principal.)[5] So the space between what they want and what they don't want is just waiting to be filled by the teacherpreneurial role.

---

[*] Wikipedia has defined a collaboratory as a "center without walls" where "researchers" (or other professionals) can work together "without regard to physical location" while "interacting with colleagues" and "sharing data" and "accessing information" in a digital space (Collaboratory. [n.d.]. Retrieved from http://en.wikipedia.org/wiki/Collaboratory). CTQ has become such a place for teacher leaders with its online community—formerly named the Teacher Leaders Network, now the Collaboratory.

However, this book is not just about that 23 percent; it is for all teachers—those who want to lead now as well as those who may want to lead later. And it is for educators and others who want to support them in realizing their potential to lead. Our public schools, and the students and families served by them, deserve more of their leadership, grounded in classroom realities.

This book has everything to do with the challenges facing our public schools in the second decade of the twenty-first century and how to address them. And it has everything to do with building demand for those who teach to continue to do so regularly *and* have the time and space to lead reforms and incubate and execute bold new ideas (while being rewarded for doing so).

Renee put it bluntly:

> Anyone who can't teach well has no business setting education policy, designing curriculum, or training teachers—at least not having the predominant say in those activities. Successful student learning should be the basic entry requirement for anyone who leads in education.

When we talk about the teacher leadership we want to see, we are not referring to the kind that is often represented by teachers' unions, which in our estimation have had to fight oppressive working conditions of the past (that in some cases are still present today). But we are also not talking about the leadership often represented by technology and textbook companies, and by well-heeled advocacy groups who seek to control teachers (and their costs) in efforts to influence who gets taught what and by whom, and then get their hands on the potential profits that can be found in the $600 billion public education enterprise.

Instead we are talking about leadership from teachers in at least three contexts.

First, we are talking about teacher leaders who work with parents in creating deeper learning opportunities for their students and who are "innovation ready,"[6] while making their own school a place of democratic deliberation and authentic connectivity, as well as stability and inspiration.

Second, we are talking about teacher leaders who take advantage of emerging technology tools to lead the personalization of learning, using digital files to rapidly spread pedagogical expertise worldwide, and who will soon be using ubiquitous smartphones to keep track of their students' progress and transform accountability systems.

And finally, we are talking about teacher leaders who would have kept us, the authors of this book, in the classroom. Like so many others of both yesterday and today, we should not have been forced to make a choice between teaching and leading.

THIS BOOK IS PERSONAL

For Barnett it began in 1980, his second year of teaching, when he was struggling to figure out how to engage 167 high school students, many of them reading far below grade level, and educate them on a vast array of social studies content, including U.S. history, consumer economics, civics, and "freshman seminar."

I sought help from both my department chair and principal, but to no avail. Then one day they walked into my third-period economics class, with a university professor, to assign a student teacher to me—because, as they told me, "I was doing the best job of anyone in my department." I then realized that if American education policy leaders had tried to create the most dysfunctional system of teacher development, then they could not have done a better job.

During my graduate school years, the heyday of *A Nation at Risk*, I immersed myself in what scholars Howard Becker, Dan Lortie, and Amitai Etzioni concluded

Figure P.2

Barnett Berry in 1979, in front of the blackboard at Eau Claire High School, Columbia, South Carolina, tries to teach his students how to write a coherent essay.

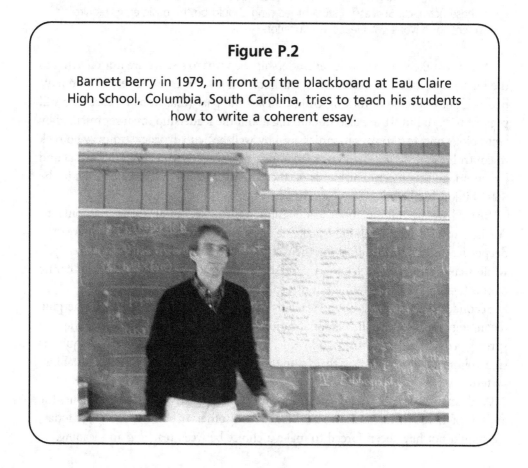

about teaching and professionalism. I learned how teaching lacked a codified body of knowledge that was developed, spread, and enforced by teachers themselves. Then my deep ethnographic studies of teaching began to surface how distant the expertise, careers, and ideas of teachers are from those of the individuals who make the rules and regulations that govern teachers' work. Over the last three decades, as my career shifted from think tank researcher to top-level state education agency bureaucrat to professor and now advocate, I have seen little closing of the gap between policy and practice. And I have seen the stakes get higher and higher for the kids while the reform rhetoric about teachers increasingly becomes more negative and divisive. I can think of so many examples, but following are three touchstones.

First, in 2004, just a year after we at CTQ launched our virtual community of teacher leaders, Rod Paige, then secretary of education for President George W. Bush, made the case (later recanted) that the National Education Association, the nation's largest teachers' union, was a "terrorist organization."[7]

Second, after releasing CTQ's inaugural TeacherSolutions report on performance pay in 2007, the eighteen classroom experts who penned the white paper were rebuked for their provocative and "third-rail" ideas in separate venues by two very different camps: (1) a group of union leaders criticized the report because the teachers were "getting ahead of them" and using a term (performance pay) they did not like; and (2) a well-positioned leader of a "progressive" Washington DC–based think tank dismissed the report because teachers were "not capable of developing new compensation policies." In these cases, the representatives of the union and the leader of the Democratic-leaning advocacy organization, respectively, made these claims with several of the teacher leaders present in the conference room as if the teachers were invisible to them.

Finally, in 2009, in our effort to recruit a teacherpreneur, a principal refused to answer our phone calls to consider the hybrid position (50 percent release from the classroom), which called for teaching as well as national policy work, because he expressed concern that he would not know what "his teacher was doing in the afternoons." It was then that I became convinced it was time to get much more serious about cultivating teacher leaders to serve as teacherpreneurs.

For Ann it began in 1983, her first year of teaching eleventh and twelfth graders in the blue-collar mill town of Lancaster, South Carolina.

As a teacher, I soon found myself feeling obligated to commit to the classroom for my career. Anything less than that would begin to tug at my teaching conscience and remind me of my self-imposed need not to feel like I was abandoning my students. I thought for sure I would do what teachers who had inspired me to teach had done: stay in the classroom for at least thirty years and then retire. The choice between serving teenagers as a teacher or managing school bureaucracy as a principal was—well—no choice at all for me. But after thirteen years in the classroom, I was feeling a bit burned out from teaching a full load, serving as senior class sponsor, and managing the high school literary magazine and the classes that produced it, among many "other duties as assigned."

> The conversations about leadership always stopped once I shared my unwavering refusal to become an administrator. I realized that this one option would never be enough, and I have been on a path to do something about it ever since.
>
> —Ann Byrd

I was so conflicted about leaving the classroom that it took me two years of serious consideration to decide to leave temporarily as a teacher in residence in a state agency dedicated to supporting leadership from the classroom. During my time (ironically) out of the classroom, I learned much about how other teachers taught and why and how I could be an even better teacher when I returned to working with students. I found many kindred spirits: other classroom teachers who "wanted it all"—teaching students daily, the magnet that pulled us into our profession, while also "teaching our colleagues" (that is, leading). And, although I did not know it at the time, my first jaunt out of the classroom is where this journey, the story of this book, began.

When I returned to the classroom after three years of residency, I sat for and earned National Board Certification. I became even more motivated to share what I knew about accomplished practice as well as to learn more about what I did not know. During my time "on the outside" I had also learned so much about what my profession could be and what it was not—not yet. I realized then that I did not recall even once during my teaching career having a conversation with any of my colleagues about *teacher leader* roles (real ones—not department chair or textbook committee or test coordinator roles). The conversations about leadership always stopped once I shared my unwavering refusal to become an administrator. I realized that this one option would never be enough, and I have been on a path to do something about it ever since.

In 1999, when I left the classroom for (what was probably) the last time (except when I renewed my National Board Certification in 2010), I was searching for a teacherpreneurial role—an option that did not yet exist. After a six-year stint as executive director of a state agency focused on teacher leadership that never quite reached the level of impact I had hoped for, I made my way to CTQ. I have been focused on paving the way for teacher-preneurs for many years now—and the next best thing to being one myself is knowing and working with the eight featured here and the many more like them I learn from daily. The secret sauce to being really smart in this profession has a simple recipe: listen to, learn from, and share what practicing teachers talk about and do.

Figure P.3

Ann, right, in spring 1988, discusses a term paper with one of her seniors at Lancaster High School, Lancaster, South Carolina.

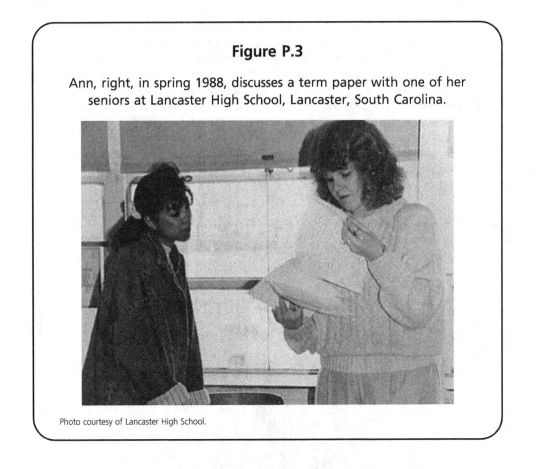

Photo courtesy of Lancaster High School.

For Alan it began in 1971, when he was a progressive history teacher in Cleveland, Ohio. Deeply interested in social justice and race, Alan entered teaching without formal preparation and came to believe that he could be more effective as someone who engages in the analysis of the teaching profession and its role in our democratic society. He left teaching after one year, and then began to flourish as a scholar, critic, and teacher educator at both the University of South Carolina and the University of the Western Cape in South Africa.

In both countries, I worked with teacher candidates and classroom veterans to develop awareness of and actions toward social justice—the fight against class disparity and racism. But it was actually in South Africa, interviewing teachers who had fought the apartheid regime, that I met with teacher elders, who if they were still teaching today might be referred to as teacherpreneurs. These were women and men who were totally committed to teaching academics with powerful pedagogy, while at the same time possessing leadership roles in their school and community—and in the struggle against the apartheid regime.

It was very difficult for me to imagine how a teacher like Richard Dudley, who began teaching in the 1940s and had the highest academic credentials, could not formally hold the position of "principal" teacher because of the color of his skin. Dudley taught, managed, and led, and he collaboratively guided a school that somehow enabled black students to attend the University of Cape Town, a segregated university, while at the same time leading a teachers' union that never divided pedagogy and politics. This union not only represented the voices of teachers but also helped facilitate teacher and student protests against the oppressive regime.

Figure P.4

Alan Wieder prepares for his undergraduate teacher education class at the Ohio State University in 1976.

Photo courtesy of Bernie Mehl.

Needless to say, Dudley and his colleagues profoundly affected Alan. And the teachers profiled in this book possess many of the same teaching skills as well as values concerning social justice that Dudley held. But most important, like Dudley, teacherpreneurs continue to teach and lead. As the context for school reform becomes more complicated, we will need more of those who teach to also lead. We understand the challenges, but we must, as the teacherpreneurs do, look to the future.

ALWAYS LOOKING FORWARD

Truly transforming education here in the United States is one of those "wicked" policy challenges because so many of the solutions are poorly defined, open to multiple interpretations by competing interest groups, and resistant to resolution.[8] Transforming teaching and learning in ways that have deep meaning for students and families will require a close look at the profession's past and a bold reach toward its future. Further, because the day-to-day realities of how students are taught (the pedagogy) as well as the distant rules and regulations that govern those who teach (the policy) are closely intertwined, altering these realities is a complex undertaking.

Power relationships must shift, which most in today's reform space often see in solely zero-sum ways, with one party losing control because another one gains more influence. This does not have to be the case. We believe that when more teachers lead, more administrators can do their job more effectively. Indeed, the 2013 MetLife survey also revealed that 75 percent of today's principals feel the job has "become too complex."[9]

Teaching is our nation's largest college-educated occupation (one in one hundred Americans is a practicing classroom teacher), and we know, also from the telling MetLife survey, that at least seven hundred thousand of these teachers are ready to lead much like those we describe in *Teacherpreneurs*.[10]

This book is not just about why teacherpreneurs must lead but also about how they can do so.

This book is about the empirical and moral case for why America's public education system should embrace transformative leadership from the classroom.

This book is about the information policymakers and practitioners need to make the dramatic shift from seeing teaching as a bureaucratically controlled occupation to understanding it as a sophisticated profession led by not a few "effective" teachers but legions of classroom experts. It is about the stories of teacher leaders whose personal narratives show that the job of leading the schools is too complicated to be held primarily by those who are not directly reminded on a daily basis of why children are or are not learning.

This book is not just about teacher leaders; it is also for them.

First, we dig deeper into the concept of teacherpreneurism—and why it is so critical for our nation's public schools (Chapter One). Then we tell, in part, the stories of eight teacher leaders (Chapters Two through Six) and how they have come to lead outside of the classroom. We share how their journeys have unfolded in the context of teaching's past and present, and in doing so we surface key attributes of teacherpreneurism. Of the eight teacher leaders, Noah and Jessica have been formally supported by our organization, CTQ, as teacherpreneurs, teaching in the mornings for their respective school districts—and leading policy reforms in the afternoons and evenings.

Yet we make it clear that their stories embody only a small fraction of what teacher leaders across the United States and worldwide are doing now and could do in the future. These teacher leaders are vanguards in forging classroom-led teaching policy reforms as well as in online learning, curriculum development, global networks, and new student-centered school designs. But there are many more teacher leaders, including those in CTQ's virtual community, who are breaking new ground in these teacherpreneurial spaces, and also those in the worlds of teacher education, student assessment, educational games, and community partnerships.

Next, we address the cultural, organizational, and political barriers that get in the way of bold teacher leadership (Chapter Seven), sharing stories from other teacher leaders with whom we have worked. We focus on resistance from today's threatened administrators and teaching colleagues who cling to top-down, rigid school cultures; proponents of pyramid-shaped organizational charts; and inflexible reformers with narrow policy agendas. Frankly, our nation will not cultivate and use the teacher leaders required for tomorrow's schools without unveiling these more troubling but rarely recognized obstacles.

But we point to these barriers with an eye toward solutions, highlighting what we can do today to address the challenges that beset us. We then turn to the *how-to* of selecting, supporting, and sustaining teacherpreneurs, offering pragmatic advice for teachers and administrators as well as policymakers and the public (Chapter Eight).

We are buoyed by the fact that somewhere on this planet, if not in the United States, everything we imagine for bold teacher leadership has begun to take hold. Many teacher leaders in our network are hopeful and energized by the prospects and possibilities suggested by the reality in Finland, where policymakers of various ideological stripes work together to invest in the teaching profession (Chapter Nine). Our growing community of teacher leaders includes those from top-performing nations—and we capture conversations among them and those from the CTQ Collaboratory to frame a way forward.

We conclude with an eye toward the year 2030—a marker for CTQ and our mission to support a high-quality public education system for all students that is driven by the bold ideas and expert practices of teachers. Here we speculate on the progress we will have made—and how (Chapter Ten). We suggest, in somewhat provocative fashion, what we anticipate will happen between 2013 and 2020 that will lead to the enormous growth of teacherpreneurs, totaling over six hundred thousand by the fourth decade of the twenty-first century. We will be seventy-four (Barnett), sixty-nine (Ann), and eighty (Alan); we point to what will have been accomplished, or not, and why. Ariel, Jessica, José, Lori, Noah, Renee, Shannon, and Stephen will then range in age from forty-eight to seventy-eight; projecting seventeen years into the future, in Chapter Ten they describe where they will be in 2030 and how *teachers will have transformed teaching.*

At each chapter's end, readers will be invited to dig deeper into what they are learning by thinking about their own experiences as teachers and leaders. By Chapter Ten, readers should have a road map for becoming the teacherpreneurs they aspire to be—for joining forces with the eight featured here.

We ask you to unite with us as we seek to create a high-quality public education system for all students that blurs the lines of distinction between those who teach in schools and those who lead them.

We know that the journey to cultivating and connecting teacherpreneurs will not be easy. We also know what must come first: we must make the case for the importance of—*and advocate for*—innovative teachers who lead but do not leave.

TEACHERPRENEURS

Advocating for a Bold Brand of Teacher Leadership

● *Teacher leaders must be producers of solutions rather than just implementers of someone else's.*

—Lori Nazareno

Almost a decade ago, Jennifer York-Barr and Karen Duke put together a comprehensive review of teacher leadership, a new field of inquiry at the time of this review's publication. It is a *must-read,* even for those who are not inclined to read academic journals. They describe a great deal about the dimensions and characteristics of teacher leadership, but point out that although the literature is "relatively rich" in regard to classroom experts' potential to lead, it is light on the "evidence of such effects."[1] Nevertheless, York-Barr and Duke thoughtfully outline how teacher leadership has evolved over time, pointing to three distinct waves.

In Wave 1, teachers served in formal roles as grade-level chairs, department heads, or union representatives and took on managerial roles designed to "further the efficiency of school operations."[2] This means that teachers did the work that administrators did not want to perform.

In Wave 2, teachers took on instructional roles, helping to implement the mandated curriculum, leading staff development workshops, and mentoring new recruits or showing them the ropes as "buddies." These teacher leader roles have become a bit more commonplace today, especially with the formalization of induction programs for new recruits. But as other researchers have made clear, few school districts implement these programs with much fidelity. For example, although more new recruits have access to induction programs, few programs have the qualities (that is, mentoring by trained veterans, a reduced teaching load, and so on) known to improve the retention of teachers in the classroom.[3]

And in Wave 3, teachers began to lead what are now called professional learning communities (PLCs) in an effort to support collaboration and continuous learning among themselves. But as Andy Hargreaves has noted, "many professional learning communities can be horrifically stilted caricatures of what they are really supposed to be."[4] Most administrators do not know how to embrace the "P" of PLC. They do not understand or know how to cultivate professionalism inside their school, and teachers often do not, as a collective, know what high-functioning PLCs look like.

York-Barr and Duke do point out that "professional norms of isolation, individualism, and egalitarianism" often undermine teacher leadership.[5] But they do not address the fact that for most of teaching's past, administrators and other powerful political and policy leaders of our nation's public school system have wanted all of those who teach to play the same roles. For example, a National Board Certified Teacher (NBCT) from the Center for Teaching Quality (CTQ) Collaboratory, whose recent essay describing a school of the future garnered a national award, shared with us that her principal directly told her not to pursue anything outside of her classroom. The reason is simple, but also troubling: if all teachers do primarily the same thing, they are easier to manage.[6]

A NEW WAVE OF TEACHER LEADERSHIP

Examples like those just given are why we are advocating for a *Wave 4* of teacher leadership—in which those who teach have time and space to lead, and are rewarded for leading, well beyond their district, state, and nation. As Lori Nazareno (whom you will get to know in Chapter Six)—an NBCT who incubated a teacher-led school in Denver, pushing both her district and her union to think differently about reform—reminded us, "In Wave 4, teacher leaders must be producers of solutions rather than just implementers of someone else's." We must make this happen—and here are a couple of compelling reasons.

First, powerful evidence speaks volumes about how teacher leadership can make a significant difference for students. Almost twenty-five years ago Susan Rosenholtz's landmark study concluded that "learning-enriched schools" were characterized by "collective commitments to student learning in collaborative settings . . . where it is assumed improvement of teaching is a collective rather than individual enterprise, and that analysis, evaluation, and experimentation in concert with colleagues are conditions under which teachers improve."[7] Other researchers have found that students achieve more in mathematics and reading in schools with higher levels of teacher collaboration.[8] And economists, using sophisticated statistical methods and large databases, have recently concluded that students score higher on achievement tests when their teachers have had opportunities to work with colleagues over a longer period of time and to share their expertise with one another.[9] Teachers themselves put an exclamation point on these empirical findings: in a 2009 Met-Life survey of American teachers, over 90 percent of teachers reported that their colleagues contribute to their own individual effectiveness.[10]

> The current crisis in education should bring us to reexamine the essential core of teaching and learning for all students.
> —Shannon C'de Baca

Second, the challenges facing our public schools cannot be met with all teachers serving in the same narrow roles designed for a bygone era. Consider the complexity of teaching to our nation's Common Core State Standards and the personalized learning systems required to prepare a diverse mix of fifty-five million (and growing) students for career and college in a global economy. Then think about today's one in five students who do not speak English as their primary language; by 2030 the number will double to 40 percent. Almost 25 percent of our nation's public school students, because of their families' devastating economic situations, are at risk of not meeting the higher academic standards imposed by the new economy. One in ten of our nation's children live in what sociologists call *deep poverty*.* And deep poverty creates early life stresses in children—a fact proven by neuroscientists who have shown how anxiety and tensions can "disrupt the healthy growth of the prefrontal cortex," inhibiting the cognitive development that is critical to academic learning.[11] Effectively addressing these out-of-school issues requires more *teacher solutions*—a special brand of pedagogical and policy ideas generated by classroom practitioners who regularly serve students and families.

And finally, such top-performing nations as Finland (see Chapter Nine) and Singapore have built their success on reducing standardized testing and increasing curriculum flexibility. Both of these nations promote, explicitly through national policy, more teacher professionalism and greater connectivity between those who teach and those who make policy. In Finland and Singapore, which invest heavily in

---

* The United States Census Bureau has created a category labeled "deep poverty" that applies to individuals more than 50 percent below the official poverty line (approximately $11,000 for a family of four, excluding food stamps or other noncash support) (Poverty in the United States: A snapshot. [n.d.]. Retrieved from http://www.nclej.org/poverty-in-the-us.php).

teacher education, there is no such thing as a shortcut into teaching. Unlike in the United States, these nations do not focus mainly on recruiting more talent into teaching for a few years and statistically identifying those who generate student test score gains. Instead, they invest *deeply* in preservice preparation and demonstrate *serious* respect for teachers by promoting the importance of teaching for a career. Finland and Singapore also, through the way teachers organize themselves into PLCs, capitalize on teachers' capacity to lead.

And their results are real.

But there is more.

Futurists claim that U.S. schools will face more, not fewer, economic disparities among the students they serve, and must organize themselves differently—including more expansive leadership, new forms of assessment, and "diverse learning agent roles."[12] Individual school principals, even with a small band of assistants, do not have the know-how or the capacity to do all that must be done as schools morph into 24/7 "hubs" for integrated academic, social, and health services. The kinds of roles teacher leaders must play include building and scoring new assessment tools tied to internationally benchmarked standards, integrating digital media into a more

Figure 1.1

Finland's and Singapore's Program for International Student Assessment (PISA) results far outpace those of the United States.

PISA 2009 Results		
Reading	**Mathematics**	**Science**
Shanghai–China (556)	Shanghai–China (600)	Shanghai–China (575)
Korea (539)	Singapore (562)	Finland (554)
Finland (536)	Hong Kong–China (555)	Hong Kong–China (549)
Hong Kong–China (533)	Korea (546)	Japan (539)
Singapore (526)	Chinese Taipei (543)	Korea (538)
Canada (524)	Finland (541)	New Zealand (532)
New Zealand (521)	Liechtenstein (536)	Canada (529)
The United States (500) is 14th out of 40.	The United States (487) is 31st out of 40.	The United States (502) is 27th out of 40.

Data courtesy of the Organization for Economic Cooperation and Development.

relevant curriculum for constantly wired students, and partnering with community organizations. And although technology can allow students to engage in personalized learning experiences like never before, it will take well-prepared, expert teachers to offer them deep educational opportunities. A special brand of teacher leader—one who has skills in spanning organizational boundaries—will be required to meet the demands posed by twenty-first-century schooling.

MOVING PAST OUTDATED STRUCTURES AND INADEQUATE SOLUTIONS

Dramatically improving public education for all will take both collective action and the discretionary judgment of many expert teachers, not just a few. Teaching and learning, now and in the future, are as complicated as the work of a federal judge who is issuing a decree on immigration law in contentious communities in Arizona and South Carolina; or the efforts of doctors who are interpreting an array of blood tests, MRI results, and family medical histories to determine how to treat a brain tumor. To best serve children and their families, we need far different approaches to organizing our schools—and we must enlist the help of our 7.2 million educators in both the K–12 and higher education sectors. And we should call on teacherpreneurs in particular.

However, today's conceptions of America's teacher leaders remain too narrow—often upholding the existing, and quite archaic, school structures. Educators rightly have called for teacher leaders to serve as *resource providers* (helping novices set up their classroom); *instructional specialists* (studying research-based classroom strategies and sharing findings with colleagues); *curriculum experts* (helping colleagues use common pacing charts and develop shared assessments); *classroom supporters* (demonstrating a lesson, coteaching, or observing and giving feedback); and *school leaders* (serving on committees or acting as grade-level or department chairs).[13] These are important roles, don't get us wrong, but they barely get us out of Wave 2 teacher leadership. Teachers are sometimes given a chance to lead, but they are expected to do so only inside the confines of their school or district. Granted, our public education system still needs to develop future Wave 2 teacher leaders. But students and their families and communities need teacher leaders who initiate change, much like today's reformers who are calling for education entrepreneurs to improve teaching and learning. Unlike the teacherpreneurs featured in this book, however, education entrepreneurs are not necessarily required to have deep, successful classroom experience or knowledge of students and their families.

Granted, teacher leadership has become more popular of late. Several years ago, a group of educators pieced together a string of domains and standards for teacher leaders—the Teacher Leader Model Standards—designed to delineate the knowledge, skills, and competencies that teachers need to assume leadership roles in their school, district, and profession. And some universities have taken steps forward by using these standards to create innovative programs—as is the case with UCLA's Center X, which created a Lead Teacher Certification Program that advances more ambitious leadership from the classroom, with social justice and action research at its core to solve immediate problems of practice.

UCLA's approach may very well inspire more universities to begin building demand for teacher leaders by preparing them. But most approaches to teacher leadership training, found in a hodgepodge of higher education programs and school district workshops, can be lacking in depth and breadth and often mark teachers as targets of reform, as opposed to championing teachers' efforts to lead reform themselves. These programs promote roles and expectations that are typically defined either by administrators in response to external guidelines or by those who do not teach and remain stuck in public education's long-standing, top-heavy bureaucracy, with all of its administrative levels.

Shannon C'de Baca, an award-winning science teacher (whom you will get to know better in Chapter Five), made a powerful point as we talked about leadership in the classroom:

> The current crisis in education should bring us to reexamine the essential core of teaching and learning for all students. Rather, it has brought a host of new Band-Aid approaches that reinforce a system that is broken in deeper structural ways. In our education system here in America we let go of nothing, and this leads to an overload of work for teachers that undermines their capacity to lead.

In leading an online conversation inside the CTQ Collaboratory, Shannon called for teachers to get "out in front" by establishing learning structures for students and colleagues alike. This brand of teacher leadership calls for teachers who are "connectors." Later, at a CTQ retreat, Shannon led a brainstorming session that defined more clearly what it meant for teacherpreneurs to serve as connectors who have a wide knowledge of local and global policy issues, so they can prepare their students for an interconnected world. (See Figure 1.2.)

There is much more discussion today of leadership from those who teach. Reformers talk of developing a teaching profession with simplistic policies that focus on firing bad teachers and rewarding a few good ones, as well as promoting charter schools to compete with so-called traditional ones. However, their solutions, captured in documentaries like *Waiting for Superman*, do little more than lionize a few Hollywood-ized "superteachers"—such as Jaime Escalante, played by Edward

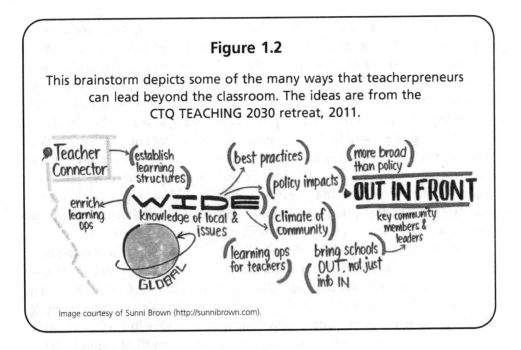

Figure 1.2

This brainstorm depicts some of the many ways that teacherpreneurs can lead beyond the classroom. The ideas are from the CTQ TEACHING 2030 retreat, 2011.

Image courtesy of Sunni Brown (http://sunnibrown.com).

James Olmos in *Stand and Deliver* (1988), or Erin Gruwell, played by Hilary Swank in *Freedom Writers* (2007).

Often reformers talk of supporting teachers, but many of their policies suggest that the profession is overrun by pedantic teachers like Ben Stein's character in *Ferris Bueller's Day Off* (1986), or other awful ones, like Cameron Diaz in *Bad Teacher* (2010), whose movie poster is too unseemly to reproduce in a book honoring and elevating America's teaching profession. There is just no evidence to suggest that school reform can succeed if it is carried solely on the backs of hero teachers portrayed by Olmos and Swank—or only if we get rid of the types of classroom practitioners represented by Stein and Diaz.

It is as if we have only two paths to good teaching: gush over a few extraordinary teachers who work overtime to create miracles in their own classroom, or mock or vilify those who do not teach as they should.

In a brilliant *New York Times* essay from September 14, 2012, Elizabeth Alsop unpacks the cinematic portrayal of the teaching profession as "shorthand for a character's dysfunction or even cosmic disenfranchisement" and teachers as either "psycho" or "saint."[14] She cites film scholar Dana Polan, who has identified the "problem of the pedagogue's embodiment," in which the media sources that portray teachers, the journalists who lambaste them, and the policymakers who make rules for them have difficulty "imagining the teacher as a real person."[15]

But we also know there are great challenges in educating a growing and diverse group of public school students in the "flat world," portrayed by Thomas Friedman as one in which the historical and geographical divisions in the global marketplace have become increasingly irrelevant.[16] In some respects, the "flat world" economy, driven by interdependency among people, complex systems of information, and outsourcing, will demand the power of professional capital in our public schools—a textured concept developed by Andy Hargreaves and Michael Fullan to explain that individual talent is not enough to improve schools for twenty-first-century student learning.[17] But teacherpreneurism is not just about growing numbers of classroom experts incubating and executing their own individual ideas. Instead, teacherpreneurism is about finding grounded solutions to vexing problems that have the power to redesign archaic school routines and scale up systemwide improvement.

To drive systemic change that will serve *all* of America's public school students, it will take far more than haphazardly continuing to recruit almost anyone to teach—and preparing new recruits through 1,200 different versions of university-based programs and 600 truncated training regimes that shortcut serious preparation. It will take far more than rewarding or punishing teachers on the basis of an annually administered standardized achievement test. And it definitely will take more than the efforts of a cadre of education entrepreneurs from outside the system. It will take the careful cultivation of teachers who can lead without leaving the classroom. And it will take more than the inclusion of "teacher voice" in school reform conversations.

TEACHER LEADERSHIP AND "VOICE" AND THE SLOW MARCH TO PROFESSIONALISM

Since the mid-1800s, teaching as an occupation has been on a long, slow, and wavering march to professionalism. For every step forward for teachers—drawing on a codified body of knowledge, enforcing standards among their ranks, and leading in the best interests of the students they serve—there seems to be almost three-quarters of a step backward. For most of the history of education in the United States, teachers have worked at the bottom of the school organizational chart. They are expected to do as they are told with little or no opportunity either to make their effective teaching practices visible to their colleagues or to have their ideas about smarter and more innovative ways to implement policy reforms sustainably known and embraced by school board members, state legislators, and researchers.

For the last two decades, America's public education system could have systematically used accomplished teachers as leaders. But it has yet to do so. The best opportunity began to emerge in 1987, when the National Board for Professional Teaching Standards (NBPTS), under the leadership of its founding president Jim

Kelly, was established and began developing an advanced certification system built around high standards of teaching practice.

With the launch of its first certifications in the early 1990s, NBPTS used "state-of-the-art" assessment tools that went "far beyond multiple choice examinations" and "[took] into account the accumulated wisdom of teachers."[18] Designed for twenty-four different subject areas and student developmental age levels, the NBPTS assessment process includes a portfolio mirroring the rigors of an Architect Registration Examination as well as an online battery measuring a teacher's content knowledge. Teachers who sit for the relatively expensive performance exam (more than $2,500) must demonstrate—through analyzing digital recordings of their teaching practice and student work samples—that they "know their subjects and how to teach those subjects to students" and "think systematically about their practice and learn from experience" (see the NBPTS Five Core Propositions: http://www.nbpts.org/five-core-propositions).

Despite some mixed empirical findings on the impact of NBCTs on student learning, the research evidence has been positive—including the gold seal of approval from the National Research Council.[19] And slowly, but surely, increasing numbers of states and districts began to offer incentives for teachers to sit for and earn the advanced certificate.

By late 2012, NBPTS had certified more than 102,000 K–12 teachers across the United States. A large share of NBCTs can be found in North Carolina (19,799); Florida (13,635); and South Carolina (8,435)—three states that had in place for some time comprehensive incentives for teachers to participate in the assessment process, meet its standards, and use their acknowledged expertise in their practice.[†]

Kelly believed NBCTs would be offered "enhanced professional roles" that would enable them to use their expertise while remaining in the classroom.[20] And he began to organize his staff's work to do so. But Kelly's vision was never realized before he retired as NBPTS president in 1999. Researchers have found that leadership from NBCTs has been undermined by: (1) administrators who lack knowledge of the assessment process, (2) too little time for teachers in general to work with one another, and (3) the critical need among NBCTs to learn how to lead.[21]

[†] North Carolina awards its NBCTs a 12 percent salary supplement (along with significant incentives to take the exam). And Florida at one time offered both a 10 percent salary increase for achieving National Board Certification and an additional 10 percent bonus if the NBCT agreed to mentor new teachers. South Carolina paid NBCTs a $7,500 salary supplement for the life of the certificate (Berry, B. [2008]. The National Board for Professional Teaching Standards and the future of a profession. Washington DC: National Board for Professional Teaching Standards).

And without any evidence that NBCTs were spreading their expertise, it was easy for those who resisted the advanced certification process (and investments in teaching as a fully realized profession) to gain ground. The number of states offering financial incentives for teachers to earn National Board Certification decreased from thirty-nine in 2005 to twenty-four in 2012."[22]

Critics claimed the assessment process was too "time-consuming and expensive"[23] and focused too much on how teachers make decisions and what they do to improve learning rather than on the test scores of their students.[24] And although both national teachers' unions supported NBCTs, and the National Education Association (NEA) sought to have their policy ideas embraced,[25] there was never any systematic attempt at scale to elevate these classroom experts and differentiate them seriously from other members. The NEA did not capitalize on NBCTs as a special brand of teacher who could promote quality control within the ranks. As Arthur Wise and Mike Usdan pointed out, because the unions "have failed to advance professional accountability . . . there is an insufficient basis for public trust in teachers as a group."[26] Teacher leadership, especially a bold brand, requires greater trust of the profession writ large.

High-ranking education officials, including U.S. secretary of education Arne Duncan, have *called for* support of NBCTs as leaders, and recently called for more "respect" for teachers in general, creating new venues to "elevate [their] voice in federal, state and local education policy."[27] However, we have seen little action (at the time of publication).

Granted, more policy groups and think tanks are turning to teachers, or at least to a select few of them, to hear what they have to say. And this increase is a good thing as well, even if some of these teachers have been chosen because they will agree with policy groups' and think tanks' predefined strategies, and not necessarily for how they teach.

Although the rhetoric suggests that teachers, especially expert ones, should *lead* reforms, most often these classroom practitioners are not much more than the targets of them. At a policy meeting late in spring 2012 in Washington DC, we sat in a room full of nonprofit staff members, state education agency employees, and administrator trade association representatives to discuss the Common Core State Standards and their implementation.

The standards have been designed to be "robust and relevant to the real world"[28] and to guide teachers toward teaching strategies that will "give students a deep understanding of the subject and the skills they need to apply their knowledge."[29]

But we were the only organization to take a practicing teacher to the meeting. And when the question of who should be involved in building global competencies into the Common Core State Standards was raised, teachers did not make the top three. The administrators and nonprofit leaders in the room seemed to think that textbook publishers, after-school program directors, and higher education faculty should be included in this competency-building process before classroom teachers. We were disappointed by the lack of

> Truly engaging with "teacher voice" means taking seriously the collective and individual expression of teachers' professional opinions based on their knowledge and classroom expertise.
>
> —José Vilson

priority given to the practitioners who would actually be implementing the Common Core State Standards, yet unfortunately we were not surprised. A recurring focus of the meeting was how to make sure that "principals get the information they need" and "stay ahead of their teachers." (See more about this story in Chapter Seven.)

At another meeting in New York City, this one hosted by an organization promoting teacher voice that was spurring conversations about tenure and evaluation reforms and attended by several CTQ virtual network members, we learned that to participate one had to "sign on" to a set of "principles" before any discussion took place. For us, *teacher voice* suggests placing limitations on the extent to which those who teach inside public schools are involved in making major decisions on how students are taught and assessed, as well as restricting how they view themselves. José Vilson (whom you will get to know better in Chapter Five) was there in New York City and warned that teachers, if they are not careful, can be used:

> Sometimes, "teacher voice" means that the convening group or individual actually wants meaningful input from educators. But more often than not, teachers are being asked to complete a project or support an agenda that needs little more than their reluctant signatures. Truly engaging with "teacher voice" means taking seriously the collective and individual expression of teachers' professional opinions based on their knowledge and classroom expertise. Anything else is just a "teacher nod." Like we're all bobble-head dolls.[30]

Policy leaders and think tanks may reach out to teachers so these teachers can *say things* but not *do things*. Teachers may *sit* at the table but may not *set* it. The powers that be may call a few teachers in to be heard, but not to be embraced as a collective. It is time to connect, ready, and mobilize teacherpreneurs, especially because of their commitment to social justice and skills, to spread their pedagogical and policy know-how in transforming their profession. And it is the

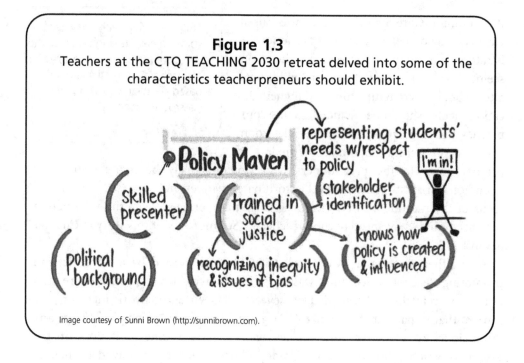

Figure 1.3
Teachers at the CTQ TEACHING 2030 retreat delved into some of the characteristics teacherpreneurs should exhibit.

Image courtesy of Sunni Brown (http://sunnibrown.com).

policy maven-ness of teacher leaders, as information specialists and connectors, that *really* defines them as teacherpreneurs. Next we turn to defining this concept more fully, exploring the "right stuff" of a bold brand of teacher leadership.

● Chapter One Selected Web Sites

Following is a list of online resources that relate to the discussion in this chapter. If you find that any of these links no longer work, please try entering the information in a search engine.

Common Core State Standards: http://www.corestandards.org

PDF of the Teacher Leader Model Standards:
http://www.teacherleaderstandards.org/downloads/TLS_Brochure_sm.pdf

UCLA's Center X Lead Teacher Certification Program: http://centerx.gseis.ucla
.edu/for-educators/lead-teacher-certification

Activity for Chapter One

Now What?

Create Your Map for Leading Without Leaving

Goal

You've learned about four different "waves" of teacher leadership in this chapter. Wave 1 management roles are meant to help other teachers become more efficient or compliant with existing policies. Wave 2 instructional roles focus on coaching peers to become sharper practitioners within their class-room. Wave 3 collaboration support roles are designed to help colleagues work in more effective teams inside their school. Finally, Wave 4 teacherpreneurial positions give space for teachers to develop and enact transformational approaches to challenges in their school, in their district, and beyond.

The numbers assigned to the waves reflect the order in which these types of roles evolved within our profession, but none of these kinds of positions has "expired." Roles that fit in each of these waves all exist in public schools today. And the journey among these roles isn't a linear progression. Some teacher leaders start out as mentors to new teachers (Wave 2), are then asked to move into a very circumscribed department chair position (Wave 1), become teach-erpreneurs (Wave 4), and then return to their building full-time as transforma-tional leaders of their school's team (Wave 3). Your own journey is just that: your own. The only common thread is that all these roles start at a "Wave 0" mastery of accomplished teaching practice!

You can't map your way forward as a leader until you know where you have been. This activity and the ones that follow in each of the other nine chapters suggest strategies for reflecting on the unique "map" of your career as a teacher leader and envisioning what routes you'll take next. Prompts at the end of every chapter will help you think about—and act on—ways to develop yourself as a teacherpreneur.

Think

By now, you may already be imagining a future role for yourself as a teacherpreneur. Let's start by seeing how your past has prepared you for it. Use the template provided to map the journey of your teacher leadership up to this point in your career.

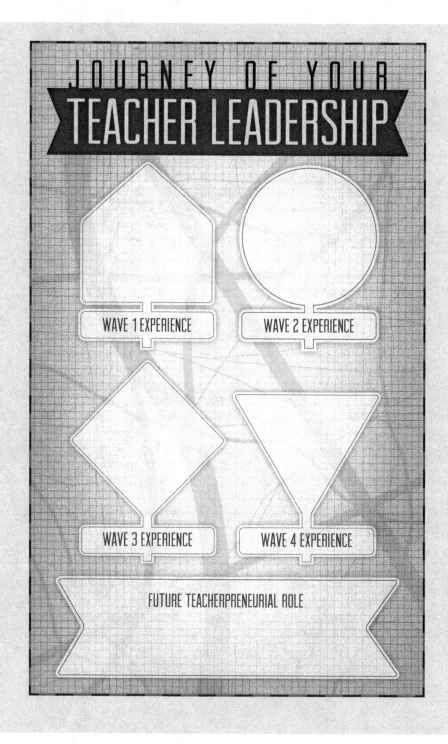

In the space shown for each wave, note the titles for the roles you've held, along with a one-sentence position description for each. (You can map your Wave 0 opportunities to develop pedagogical mastery in the space surrounding the other waves!)

Now reflect. Of which waves have most of your prior roles been a part? Which waves might you want to explore more? Add notes to each wave about additional experiences you'd like to cultivate. (You may want to use a different color of ink or star these roles for the future.) Ultimately, what would your ideal teacherpreneurial role look like? Develop a one-sentence job description and add that to the space given at the bottom of your map.

Act

Think of one person who could help you learn more about the teacherpreneurial role you imagine for yourself, if it is similar to roles that already exist in your district, or who could help you create such a role if no Wave 4 positions are in place. Make time to speak with that person about what it would take to develop the role or to be selected for it.

Share

Follow the link to the CTQ Collaboratory (http://www.teachingquality.org) to join our online community, if you aren't already part of our network, and share your ideas with other teacher leaders there. As you engage in the activities in this book, we'll continue to prompt you to post ideas to our online gallery of teacherpreneurial plans.

Defining the Teacherpreneur

● *Teacher leadership is the present. Teacherpreneurism is the future.*

—José Vilson

I f you Google the term *teacherpreneur,* you'll get about 17,500 results. So the word, a combination of *teacher* and *entrepreneur,* has some "lexiconic" lift. For us, the word *teacherpreneur* represents the bold concept that teachers can *continue to teach* while having time, space, and incentives to incubate big pedagogical and policy ideas and execute them in the best interests of both their students and their teaching colleagues. It is a word expressing our hope that teachers will no longer be isolated in individual classrooms with the doors closed, a phenomenon often characterized by sociologists as schools' "egg-crate" organization. It is also a word communicating our expectation that teachers will no longer be controlled by meddlesome advocates and rigid bureaucrats.

For the last several years, our ever-expanding vision for teacherpreneurism has been growing, in large part due to ideas from and increasing interest in our previous book, *Teaching 2030.* The animated video linked in the following paragraph highlights the big ideas of the book. Written by Barnett and twelve expert teachers from the Center for Teaching Quality (CTQ) Collaboratory, the book transcends the typical debates among today's school reformers, union leaders, and politicians while carving out powerful solutions for how to best organize teaching, learning, and schooling.

TEACHER + ENTREPRENEUR = TEACHERPRENEUR

Teaching 2030

http://bit.ly/Q2AM25

Deliberating in our conference room back in 2009, the word *teacherpreneur* captured our imagination. It is a word that brings together concepts from what are usually entirely separate lines of thinking—the dedicated, student-focused teacher and the innovative, ambitious entrepreneur.

We all were comfortable with the word *teacher*. And why not? Among the thirteen coauthors, only one of us (Barnett) had not taught for many decades. Everyone else was a practicing teacher, and the combined pedagogical experience in the room was well over two hundred years. So what about the word *entrepreneur*, a term foreign to many who teach and work in the public sector? A common dictionary definition refers to "one who organizes, manages, and assumes the risks of a business or enterprise."[1]

Most teachers readily proclaim that they teach because of their commitment to students, not their pay. As *Teaching 2030* coauthor José Vilson wrote:

> What if accomplished educators' jobs could be restructured, enabling us to use and spread our expertise in innovative ways while also keeping one foot in the classroom?
>
> —José Vilson

> Right now, teachers across the nation are going above and beyond our responsibilities to benefit our students: developing online professional learning communities, fine-tuning our schools' curricula, and connecting students' families to community resources. What if accomplished educators' jobs could be restructured, enabling us to use and spread our expertise in innovative ways while also keeping one foot in the classroom?[2]

We were quick to recognize that entrepreneurs take risks in making decisions about what to do and how it is going to be done. They launch new initiatives and accept full responsibility for the results. The coauthors all agreed, "We do this all the time." Entrepreneurs are self-reliant and highly optimistic. They are idea generators. They work outside the lines. They are mobilizers.

Figure 2.1

In *Teaching 2030*, written by Barnett Berry and twelve teacher leaders, teacherpreneurs are considered integral to the transformation of our nation's public schools.

TEACHING 2030

What We Must Do for Our Students and Our Public Schools...

Now and in the Future

THE BIG IDEAS

BARNETT BERRY and the TeacherSolutions 2030 Team:
Jennifer Barnett • Kilian Betlach • Shannon C'de Baca • Susie Highley
John M. Holland • Carrie J. Kamm • Renee Moore • Cindi Rigsbee
Ariel Sacks • Emily Vickery • José Vilson • Laurie Wasserman

Cover image © Teachers College Press, 2011. Used with permission.

Two famous entrepreneurs, living in two distinct eras, point to the heart of entrepreneurism. Thomas Edison made the point that entrepreneurs focus on "what the world needs, then . . . [proceed] to invent it."[3] Steve Jobs's entrepreneurism has been characterized by his ability to make connections as well as create "insanely different experiences" and master the message.[4] The creative process of entrepreneurism demands some definitive degree of rule breaking.

What if we took the best thinking and imagery of the two worlds and literally illustrated what the teaching profession could be—and how we could get there, with teacherpreneurs as the centerpiece of the transformation? What if we, unlike the 2013 South by Southwest Education Conference, jettisoned the idea that the worlds of teachers and entrepreneurs are distinctly divided?[5]

Much of what we discussed at our TEACHING 2030 retreat (from which the graphic note taking shown here emerged) focused on shifting away from the current one-way conversation in school reform between school reformers and those in the classroom who must implement their mandates. With teacherpreneurs in the mix, this no longer would be the case. They would finally disprove the myth that teachers are born and not made—and lead a revolution in how America invests in those who teach young people. We know of and work with many teacher leaders who use their knowledge of students as well as teaching and learning to dream, think, plan, act, and react like entrepreneurs—and turn the rigid, pyramid-like organizational structure of schools upside down.

Rick Hess reminds us that the work of education entrepreneurism requires a mix of "seasoning and experience" on the one hand, and "energy and a fresh perspective" on the other.[6] But unlike education entrepreneurs so in vogue today, teacherpreneurs still work with students on a regular basis, always drawing on their everyday experiences with children and adolescents as they design and develop as well as mobilize and transform systems of teaching and learning. As we wrote in *Teaching 2030*:

> We see teacherpreneurs, not primarily as marketers [of their own ideas], but as expert practitioners who are paid to spread their ideas and approaches as virtual mentors, teacher educators, community organizers, and policy as well as action researchers. The purpose in creating teacherpreneurs is not to identify "super teachers" who will make a lot more money, but to empower expert teachers who can elevate the entire profession by making sure that colleagues, policymakers, and the public know what works best for students.[7]

Ultimately, teacherpreneurism is not so much about establishing a new income stream for individuals as it is about promoting and spreading a new culture of collective innovation and creativity in a sector—education—that has been woefully lacking in one. What is more, it is about calling on a group of professionals who have been vastly underused—teachers—to establish that culture.

Figure 2.2

As this mindmap suggests, teacherpreneurs would be the designers, knowledge brokers, system thinkers, talent maximizers, and bridge builders in the transformation of education.

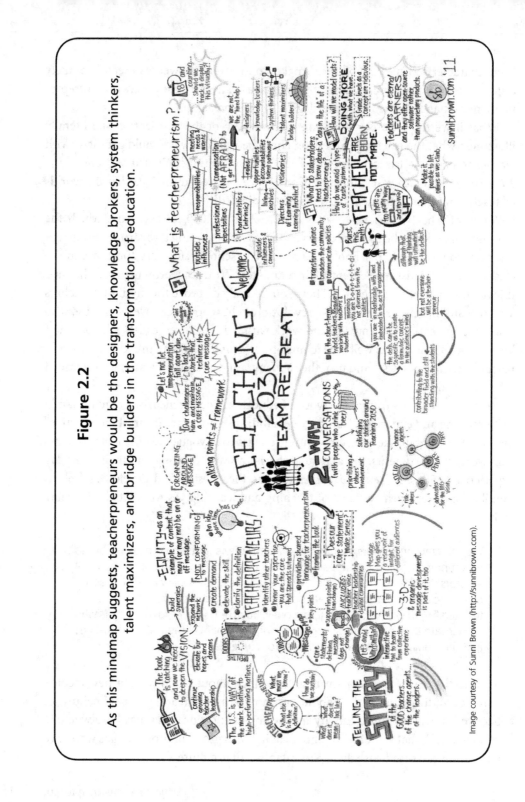

Image courtesy of Sunni Brown (http://sunnibrown.com).

We know very well that the history of the teaching occupation includes long-standing control by laymen, a lack of clarity and rigor in the process of becoming a teacher, and limited prestige and income—restricting the professional possibilities for its members.[8] When it comes to fostering teacherpreneurism, teachers should not have to face the dilemma of choosing either to teach as hired hands or to lead as professionals.

Over the last ten years, as our virtual community of teacher leaders in the Collaboratory has grown (from forty in early 2003 to over two thousand in 2013), we have come to know many who have the "right stuff" to be teacherpreneurs. What follows are the faces of teacherpreneurism.

THE FACES OF TEACHERPRENEURISM

We could shine a spotlight on almost any of the thousands of teacher leaders who have been engaged with CTQ over the years. This book focuses primarily on eight of them (including two, Noah Zeichner and Jessica Keigan, whom we supported as teacherpreneurs in the 2011–2012 school year).

We chose these eight because they teach in some of the most challenging urban and rural school systems in America (see Appendix A for a group résumé). They are terrific teachers and have results, measured in a variety of ways, to show it; they are experienced, and have used that experience to deepen and widen their expertise. All of them care deeply for their students and their profession. But above all, we chose them because they are representative of so many other teacher leaders like them who can and should be given more opportunities to lead.

These teachers have started their own teacher-led school; designed and fueled new performance pay systems; hosted a public television show on math and science; spread bold pedagogical and policy ideas through award-winning blogs; led efforts to globalize curricula for schools and districts; created powerful peer review programs to revolutionize teacher evaluation; founded grassroots youth development initiatives; launched a vanguard effort to share digitally recorded images of teaching for others to view online and critique; engaged in efforts to transcend cantankerous teacher evaluation debates; and served as directors of boards of venerable nonprofits, such as the Carnegie Foundation for the Advancement of Teaching.

> The purpose in creating teacherpreneurs is not to identify "super teachers" who will make a lot more money, but to empower expert teachers who can . . . [make] sure that colleagues, policymakers, and the public know what works best for students.

They range in age from their early thirties to their early sixties. Collectively they blow away so many of the myths that fill today's school reform space, such as the thinking that older, more experienced and traditionally trained educators can neither lead reform nor take a good idea to scale. As one foundation officer, whose organization promotes education entrepreneurs (but not CTQ's work), told us as we began writing this book: "Career teachers have no alternative vision, and at best can only lead change efforts from the middle of the school reform enterprise." This book proves her wrong. In fact, these eight teacher leaders all fit Hess's definition of an education entrepreneur, but they know and do much more. They have deep knowledge of teaching and learning as well as of students and families. They have commitments to their classroom and community.

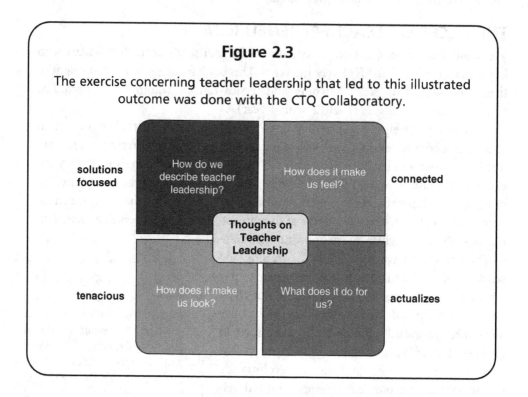

Figure 2.3

The exercise concerning teacher leadership that led to this illustrated outcome was done with the CTQ Collaboratory.

These teacher leaders—and a number of their colleagues whose voices we elevate—exude creativity, spirit, and relentlessness as well as profound knowledge of and skills in regard to how to teach. When we ask members of the CTQ Collaboratory about teacher leadership, first and foremost, they don't see obstacles. In facing a challenge with a troubled student, recalcitrant colleague, self-righteous reformer, or rigid-minded policymaker, they say, "What now?" instead of "Oh well." As teacher leaders, they are proactive, student centered, and solutions focused.

As they lead, they feel connected and appear tenacious. As a result, they become self-actualized with the confidence and tools necessary in shedding teaching's historical challenges and complications to drive the transformation of their profession. We begin to unpack the right stuff of teacherpreneurism with Noah, whose *well-traveledness* and intelligent humility play a central role in his approach to leadership.

NOAH: THE RIGHT STUFF

Once we got to know Noah (now thirty-five years old) and his teaching, we knew he would be an ideal fit for one of our first teacherpreneurial roles, working with students in the morning and serving as a policy advocate later in the day. We knew he had the right stuff to serve as a test pilot to rocket-power teaching toward the professional status that students and teachers deserve. We could see Noah—and many, many other classroom experts like him—shaking up the teaching profession and the public's image of teachers, much like John Glenn, Alan Shepard, Gus Grissom, and others shook up the flying fraternity and altered NASA's concept of the astronaut.[9]

Noah's teaching and his relationships with his students personify thoughtful citizenship with a robust vision for the kind of public education that a healthy American democracy requires, both today and tomorrow. The United States has always been a nation of immigrants from every continent and culture. And as America becomes even more diverse, its public schools are needed to help glue those cultures together in ways that unite our society. Noah has a big, global view of what public education must be for every one of his students and his district.

His teaching of social studies exemplifies what classroom practice should look like in a democracy: Noah's students learn how to apply and interpret knowledge and participate actively in building a strong community, locally and globally. The way Noah teaches, and why, have a lot to do with his success as a teacherpreneur who led teaching policy reform efforts in the afternoons and evenings in his local district, in the state of Washington, and nationwide.

Deeply Connected

As we walked into Noah's classroom in January 2011, we could feel its collaborative spirit and academic focus. The classroom had eight tables with four seats at each table. There were two teacher desks because Noah shared the room with a social studies colleague. There were political posters on the wall, and above both desks were photographs of Noah with students and family members, including a picture of him with a group of students in Chongqing, China. The classroom also had a bookcase along the windowed wall. The classroom book collection included biographies of Nelson Mandela and Bill Clinton, *Fast Food Nation*, and other political and

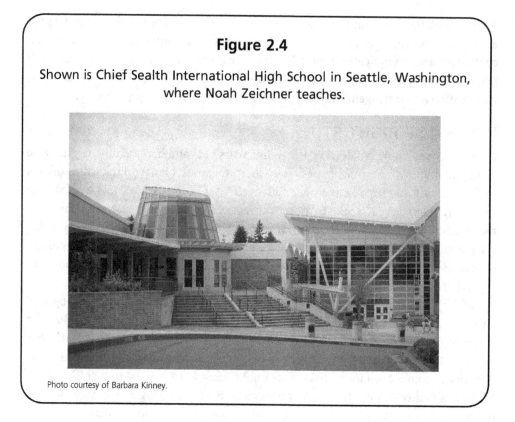

Figure 2.4

Shown is Chief Sealth International High School in Seattle, Washington, where Noah Zeichner teaches.

Photo courtesy of Barbara Kinney.

environmental titles. There was also a small magazine rack with *Time, Yes*, and *Earth*, in addition to six computers, a few printers, and whiteboards. One wall held clocks with times set for different places in the world.

As Noah explained later in the day, he built the class on a Freirean, democratic model, whereby community building is important, with students having both rights and responsibilities. The next day, his class on global leadership—one that he designed in collaboration with a nonprofit called Global Visionaries—was putting into action what they learned through community service. Noah's students had prepared to teach a group of younger students at nearby Roxhill Elementary School. We returned to the school to observe—and we saw a lot. An hour before leaving for their one-mile walk to Roxhill, Noah had his students engaged in small groups, fine-tuning their presentations and curricular activities on consumption and the environment. We could easily determine how much they had learned from lessons Noah had taught a month earlier, including an amazing array of facts and concepts from *Stuff: The Secret Lives of Everyday Things* by John Ryan and Alan Durning. Each group had its own personality, and Noah adapted his teaching and cajoling as he moved around the room, multitasking (including making last-minute cell phone calls to parents to ensure his students had permission to leave Chief Sealth for a few hours to teach over at the elementary school).

The groups came together for their quick practice runs, with Noah nurturing and encouraging them to slow down their presentations. He praised their work for the breadth of content they were bringing to their teaching, reminding them that they must not "dumb down" their lessons. When there was side talk in the room, he softly and gently stopped the class, and the disturbances quickly ended.

Part of Noah's responsibility on the mile walk to the school was to make sure that his students arrived safely, without any stops or diversions. He taught for the entire walk.

Once inside the school, both Noah and the fourth-grade teacher were almost entirely observers as the high school and elementary students interacted and learned from one another. Noah's students appeared confident in their tasks, and the elementary students engaged deeply with them in both the content and the process.

On the walk back to Chief Sealth, Noah e-mailed his colleagues at the high school to notify them that they were running late while also framing the next assignment for his students, which would include an analysis of what they learned while teaching at the elementary school.

Several months later, we had a chance to meet Molly Freed, whom Noah taught in three different classes. "All of his classes were very focused and interactive," Molly told us. "He taught me how to think and refused to ever tell me any answers that I didn't deduce on my own. Zeichner would have us wage carefully guided, discussion-based 'wars' on our fellow classmates around controversial issues."

Molly, who is now at Scripps College in Claremont, California, gave us some of the most powerful evidence of Noah's effectiveness as her teacher and as a leader:

> As a college student, I have found that Zeichner has helped me in many ways. He taught me how to think about many issues, from a historical standpoint as well as an ethical standpoint. I'm much more skeptical of any teacher that simply teaches the "right" answers and expects us to accept it. I try to hold him as an example for myself in applying yourself to what you truly love, and putting your absolute all into it. His passion and intelligence inspire me to do well in everything I do, and I only hope that one day, if I work hard enough, I may be in a position to do as much good and touch as many lives as he has.

Through every interaction with administrators and students as well as his teaching colleagues, we could see Noah's strong ties to his students as well as his school community. We soon learned of his leadership at Chief Sealth as the chair of the school's Family Engagement Committee, through which he helped develop a

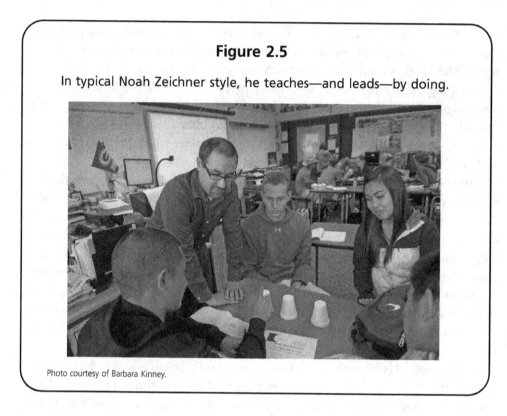

Figure 2.5

In typical Noah Zeichner style, he teaches—and leads—by doing.

Photo courtesy of Barbara Kinney.

sophisticated program for coordinating home visits among faculty to connect more deeply with the school's ninth graders. These connections help explain why he struggled with giving up some of his teaching time to work as a teacherpreneur. Paul Fischburg, who teaches with Noah, told us, "It is ridiculous how engaged he is with students; they come to see him all the time. I believe it is because understanding and respect and dialogue and conversation are the holy grail of his classroom." And Noah's deep connections extend well beyond his work with students in the classroom to interactions with union leaders and other community members who see his influence firsthand. Through the time and scheduling afforded to Noah in his hybrid role, he has developed a strong relationship with local and state union leaders, among them Jonathan Knapp, president of the Seattle Education Association. Jonathan understands the profound potential of teacherpreneurs of Noah's caliber.

> [Teacherpreneurs like Noah] have a soft place in their heart for ideals like equality, justice, and opportunity, but they also have . . . a hard head for building what works.
> —Jonathan Knapp

Motivated by Teaching and Learning

Noah is serious about a teaching career and the role teachers play in serving students and families. His drive to teach has been there for much of his life, but was catapulted by his work in summer camps during his high school and undergraduate college years, and then later when he taught as a volunteer in Quito, Ecuador.

Figure 2.6

Shown is the city of Quito, Ecuador, where Noah Zeichner taught early in his teaching career.

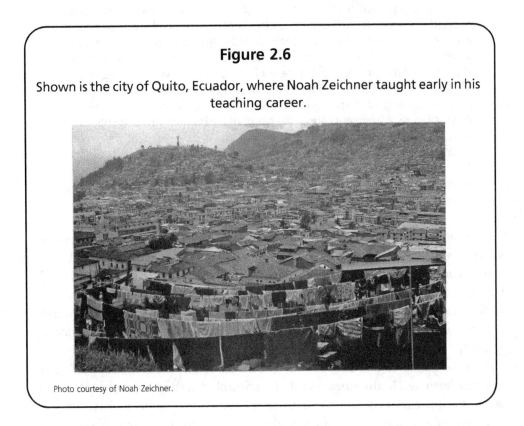

Photo courtesy of Noah Zeichner.

Quito, burrowed in a long, narrow valley in the Andes Mountains, is a capital city of over two million people, one-third of whom live well below the poverty line. Noah told us that in Quito he learned a great deal about motivating children who grew up very differently than he did. The school in which he taught, which also trains teachers, provided him with "endless support" and "constructive feedback and encouragement that kept [him] going." Further, working in Quito, Noah began to deeply understand how to tap into young people's "desire to learn," even in a culture so different from his own, and how to teach those who lived under the "most overwhelming economic hardships." But most important, when Noah talks about his experience of working with children in Quito, he focuses not on the abject poverty, but rather on the richness of the culture and the human spirit. Noah told us:

> In the southern outskirts of Quito, I taught history to high school students. My class had twelve students, ages twelve to eighteen. The school is unlike any I have ever encountered. The school, run by a local nongovernmental organization, embraces progressive teaching methods that create independent and civic-oriented learners. In addition to serving the impoverished neighborhood's children, the school serves as a community health care center and provides adult education classes for the students' families in the afternoon and evening. The history of the community and the students' culture are viewed as assets and are incorporated into the school's curriculum. All of the teachers share responsibility for teaching all students in the school. All of the teachers share the belief that the future of their country is in the hands of the children. The students, most of whom come from broken homes and eat their only meals at the school, proudly wear their uniform and more often than not have a smile on their face. The positive energy in the school is contagious. Those kids taught me that year. They taught me the power of education, and they convinced me that I was going to be a teacher.

In a later visit with Noah in spring 2012, he greeted us with news about his students who had been debating the brief annexation of the Philippines by the United States in one of his classes earlier that day. With a wide grin, Noah shared, "I had kids arguing about history as they were walking out the door today. It was great."

Noah takes on a noticeably different tone about his "day job" when the topic turns to the "preneur" side of being a hybrid teacher. He is deeply committed to his students, and despite his growing expertise in policy, he has difficulty finding the desired time outside the classroom and school day that he wishes he could spend supporting his students' learning. He also struggles with the concept of the teacherpreneur, because it is easy to equate with education entrepreneurs whose focus on themselves, competition, and individual rewards trumps what is needed to create an equitable system of public education that serves all students and embraces all teachers.

Despite his passion for unpacking policy research, new learning, and professional development opportunities, Noah's "joy meter" goes off the scale when he is working with both his teenage students and his teaching colleagues at Chief Sealth. It is clear, however, that Noah does see the larger picture of the impact of his teacherpreneurial work outside of his school and district. And he is able to think about the value this work is bringing to others in his school, especially as he focuses on what he has learned from being part of a virtual community of teacher leaders in which both pedagogical and policy ideas are shared and vetted. He is compelled to spread what he is learning. "I want more time to share with colleagues in my building," he reminds us often.

Committed to Advancing the Profession

Noah also excels at policy work, complementing his impressive classroom pedigree. He does his homework and respects diverse perspectives, but he never deviates from his deeply held values about the role public education plays in a democratic society—and about the kind of teaching profession that is needed to support students, families, and communities. Serving on Washington's Professional Educator Standards Board, he has worked to stave off attempts to devalue teaching experience as a qualification for prospective school principals. And his low-key approach to leading helped district administrators and union leaders come together in launching a much-needed Teacher Advisory Council to assist the Seattle Public Schools in implementing its new teacher evaluation system.

Noah defines what it means to be a teacher leader. He is a skillful teacher who reaches his students in ways that are abundantly apparent when you visit his classroom. He is committed first and foremost to his students, but he is also committed to advancing his profession. He has taken on leadership roles while still remaining in the classroom. We all have much to learn from Noah and should be grateful that he has chosen teaching as his profession. Our students—and the profession of teaching—are the better for it.

Noah absorbs sophisticated research reports with relative ease, although he never would admit it. His quiet leadership was felt in the work of a small group of early career teachers, collaborating as part of CTQ-Washington's[*] efforts to elevate and advance the

Noah Zeichner on Assessing Teachers

http://bit.ly/UYk18p

---

[*] Since 2009 CTQ has been supporting teachers in specific communities as they draw on their classroom expertise and understanding of research evidence to advance policy and pedagogical reforms. In early 2013 CTQ-Washington, with over 150 teachers from the Puget Sound region, represented one of those communities.

reform conversation about how best to assess teaching. He was quick to analyze a number of studies to inform his team's case for greater teacher accountability without the misapplication of value-added statistics (in vogue at the time).

He pointed out that the statistical models that reformers in Washington State proposed to use did not seem to account for the fact that teachers team-teach, or that some students receive after-school tutoring and summer school instruction whereas others do not. He drew on his "international mindedness" in suggesting that teachers could develop, like they do in Ontario, their own performance assessments that could be built into more sophisticated models of measuring teacher effectiveness.

Over the last year, he has used his global mind-set to carve out a new teacher-preneurial role for himself. He told us: "I think the more funders let teacherpreneurs drive the nonteaching part of the work, the better. That makes it much more 'entrepreneurial,' right? Every role will look different and will have a different focus." Soon Noah began to realize that he "craved" the hybrid role he was defining and expanding, and crafted his own message for *Educational Horizons Magazine* on how teachers can advance in their career without leaving students.[10]

Funded by MetLife Foundation, Noah, in his second year as a teacherpreneur, is bringing his external work with CTQ even closer to his colleagues at Chief Sealth and integrating it throughout his school district. Noah's focus has shifted to codifying a global curriculum, applying an international lens to varied subject matter, which he is now helping his district spread systematically.

In 2012–2013 Noah also began to help his Washington State teaching colleagues learn more about how top-performing nations (such as Finland and Singapore) invest in their teachers. He worked with CTQ in developing a concept paper and plan for launching a virtual community of teacher leaders from several locales in Asia and North America, including his own district. Partnering with the Asia Society, Noah built a case for the community-based lessons he learned throughout his career from teachers in other countries, beginning in the late 1990s when he taught at the Instituto de Investigación, Educación y Promoción Popular del Ecuador (INEPE), the school run by the Quito-based nongovernmental organization for which he worked. Noah shared in the concept piece, "I can credit much of my own teaching philosophy and skill to lessons I have learned throughout my career from teachers in other countries and, just as importantly, to the process through which I learned with them."[11]

As a teacherpreneur, Noah is a force that shapes the mission and the vision of Chief Sealth and the district's focus on globalization and international education. He is now working closely with Karen Kodama, a leading (and very progressive) district administrator, to spread global competencies throughout the district. Or as Noah put it, his aim is "to reignite the collective consciousness of being an international school." From our perspective, he is blurring the lines of distinction between those who teach in schools and those who lead them.

Figure 2.7

Noah Zeichner stands proudly in front of Chief Sealth International High School in Seattle, Washington.

Image courtesy of Barbara Kinney.

Noah is becoming better known, locally and nationally, but he remains a humble man. He struggles with some of the "celebrity status" he has earned as a policy leader, and he keeps one foot firmly in the classroom with students. And it is his humility that, in part, makes him the effective teacherpreneur that he is. His colleagues trust him. No wonder. Noah explained in his low-key voice, "I will only serve as a teacherpreneur if I fully maintain credibility among my fellow teachers who teach full-time."

John Boyd, former Chief Sealth principal, signed off on Noah's initial teacher-preneurial assignment. Now serving as a central office administrator in a nearby district, John explained to us, with a dry sense of self-deprecating humor, the core of Noah's teacherpreneurism:

> Noah really has a deep commitment to being in the classroom. The truth is, wherever he wants to go, he will; whatever he wants to do, he will. He is still young. He has a lot ahead of him. I don't see him being a school administrator. I think he has too much integrity for that.

But it was Jonathan Knapp who said it best in regard to Noah's teacherpreneurism:

> In every school system there are many teachers who are fully satisfied to put their skill into practice while working with peers to do their best to teach kids. They are the bedrock of public education. Happily for all of us, though—parents, students, and educators alike—there are a few rare individuals who are not just satisfied with teaching students. They aspire to move us to higher ground. They want to be agents of change. They want to make manifest the values that brought them into the profession in the first place. They want to move public education down the road to becoming a force for a fairer and saner world. They have a soft place in their heart for ideals like equality, justice, and opportunity, but they also have—and this is the most important thing—a hard head for building what works to move us all down that road and for avoiding what doesn't. Noah Zeichner is one of these rare individuals.

Noah is indeed special, but so are many other teachers who have taught us much about teacherpreneurs and how to prepare more classroom experts for the teacherpreneurial role. We turn next to stories of Jessica Keigan and Ariel Sacks to demonstrate how teacher education can begin to connect, ready, and mobilize teacherpreneurs—now and in the future.

● **Chapter Two Selected Web Sites**

Following is a list of online resources that relate to the discussion in this chapter. If you find that either of these links no longer works, please try entering the information in a search engine.

PDF of the *Teaching 2030* Visual Handbook: http://www.teachingquality.org/content/teaching-2030-what-we-must-do-our-students-and-our-public-schools%E2%80%A6now-and-future

Global Visionaries (nonprofit): http://www.global-visionaries.org/

Activity for Chapter Two

Now What?

Develop Your Own Teacherpreneurial Résumé

Goal

You've recorded where your career as a teacher leader has taken you, and where it may take you next as you grow toward a future role as a teacher-preneur. Now it's time to build a more specific résumé that can help you make the case to decision makers for the value of that role and guide you in seeking opportunities for professional growth to make the vision a reality.

Think

Using the lists you created at the end of Chapter One as a reminder of key leadership roles you may wish to highlight, create a teacherpreneurial résumé that emphasizes your knowledge, skills, and dispositions for leadership. We suggest that you do this exercise *without* looking at your current, perhaps more traditional résumé so that you don't constrain your thinking. In fact, we encourage you to use section headers on this résumé that are as fresh as the idea of teacherpreneurism itself. You may wish to refer to Appendix A to get a sense of some of the experiences of the eight teacherpreneurs you'll be reading more about in the coming chapters, or to scan ahead as noted on our list that follows. Here are our suggestions for categories:

- Professional objective (draw on your one-sentence teacherpreneur job description created in the activity at the end of Chapter One)
- Evidence of "intelligent humility," the ability to own and assert what you know humbly and while acknowledging what you do not yet know (discussed in this chapter)
- Evidence of making great teaching visible, by both practicing and articulating what makes classroom practice effective and masterful (Chapter Four)
- Evidence of well-traveledness, the capacity to connect your own local experiences to a broader landscape of challenges and solutions (discussed in this chapter)
- Experience with reciprocal mentoring, supporting the professional learning of other teachers as a community of peers (Chapter Three)
- Evidence of the "right stuff" for teaching and leadership, with a mind-set for continuous growth, openness to new ideas, and strategic innovation (discussed in this chapter)

- Evidence of cultivating other teacher leaders by sharing what you know and practicing collaborative rather than solo leadership (Chapter Six)

Now review your résumé, with an eye to the competencies needed to be successful in the teacherpreneurial role you envision. (Assume that the position exists!) What additional experience and expertise might help you be a stronger candidate for that position? What steps might you take to obtain that experience or expertise? Sketch into your résumé what you might do in the next year, three years, five years, ten years—as long as you think it will take to prepare yourself for your role. Look at this "future state" version of your résumé again carefully. Are you a more informed candidate now? Review and revise as needed throughout your reading of and reflection on this text.

Act

Choose one preparation step from your résumé that you can take this year . . . and then take it. If you are interested in building knowledge and skills that are specific to teacher leadership, or that you can't find a way to gain elsewhere, CTQ offers webinars and other online learning materials to help you. Follow this link for more information: http://www.teachingquality.org.

Share

Consider sharing what you learn by participating in an online conversation within the Collaboratory. If offline conversations feel more natural to you, sit down with a trusted mentor or colleague to show him or her your new résumé. What learning goals might he or she share? How can you support each other in the next steps of your journey?

CHAPTER 3

Preparing for Teacherpreneurism

● *[My Bank Street College of Education professor and mentor] Madeleine was so important to my development as a teacher. She taught me how to know children and not to lose my practice.*

—Ariel Sacks

The eight teachers profiled in this book entered teaching through various pathways, with some having serious preparation, but others not. This may come as a surprise to the casual observer of America's teaching profession. Unlike in such top-performing nations as Finland and Singapore, policymakers in the United States have never expected all teachers to meet the same high standards before entering the profession. There never has been a systematic and consistent effort to prepare all teachers deeply for teaching, much less cultivate them as leaders and teacherpreneurs. The American way has been to opt for inexpensively prepared teachers who are readily replaceable, exemplifying the early-twentieth-century factory model of teaching and learning still in place today.

SHARED EXPERIENCES

The stories of these pedagogical powerhouses and their development as leaders jolt our nation's current policy structures. Without question these eight teacher leaders took different routes to arrive at classroom teaching—everything from an internship as an instructional assistant to a fifteen-month master's degree in education; a five-week alternative certification program; and, in one case, no training whatsoever. But they had a number of common experiences that set them on a path toward developing the pedagogical "right stuff" of teacherpreneurism that speak volumes about how our nation must begin to invest in the teaching profession.

All of them had powerful K–12 teachers whom they revered and wanted to emulate. They all took seriously the need to learn about child development—either as part of their university-based teacher education program or on their own, with assistance from their own professional libraries and constant contact with colleagues who held similar values. Along the way they acquired a deep respect for the multilayered learning required to teach all students at high levels. All but one of them entered formal teacher training after earning an undergraduate degree in a subject matter discipline. Further, most had terrific teacher educators who deepened their pedagogical know-how, but they all, except Lori Nazareno, experienced intensive working relationships with senior colleagues who mentored them in their first few years of teaching. Finally, perhaps most important, all are effective as leaders because of how they have learned from colleagues, because of how they embrace ambiguity, and because of their unwavering commitment to classroom teaching.

All too often, today's policy talk and action further reinforce the false choice between the questionable merits of traditional university-based teacher education—which often disconnects research and theory from the realities of school practice—and alternative certification programs that take shortcuts past serious pedagogical know-how and much-needed clinical training.

Yet each of these eight teacher leaders, with the kinds of pedagogical skills they have developed and used, reminds us of how childish these dysfunctional debates have become. Each has acquired substantial technical know-how—demonstrated, for example, in using a student's culture to teach academic concepts, adapting the curriculum to reach second-language learners, and orchestrating classroom life to instill deep learning. And these teaching skills, learned over many years under the guidance of expert teacher educators and mentors, frame their effectiveness as teachers and explain why administrators and colleagues invite and embrace their leadership.

The right stuff of teacherpreneurism begins with and demands sophisticated pedagogical expertise, the vast majority of which can be learned systemically in a redesigned teacher education system—one that transcends today's debates and leverages the best of what works today and what students need tomorrow. We envision Teacher Preparation 2.0, with a look toward 3.0—whereby pre-K–12 and university resources are fused, cohort-based residencies are the norm (not the exception), varied pathways into teaching are embraced (with performance assessments used), and teacherpreneurs are positioned as education professors and researchers as well as organizational boundary spanners in interlocking virtual communities.

Our relationships with these eight teachers have taught us much about what it takes to develop a deep understanding of children and adolescents and maintain an expansive repertoire of teaching skills while also acquiring leadership skills in connecting classroom to community, and policy to pedagogy. We could write an entire book on these dimensions, drawing on the lessons we learned from all eight. Here, however, we focus on two of our teaching colleagues, Jessica Keigan and Ariel Sacks, who in part due to their own diligence in selecting their respective university-based education programs, had preservice pedagogical training that clearly enhanced their teacherpreneurial talents. Jessica served as a Center for Teaching Quality (CTQ) teacherpreneur in 2011–2012; and they both pushed the boundaries of controversial teaching policies from their vantage points in Colorado and New York, respectively. We discovered from Jessica and Ariel that in both of their teacher education programs—Jessica's at the University of Colorado–Denver and Ariel's at Bank Street College—they learned the importance of *reciprocal mentoring*.

JESSICA AND RECIPROCAL MENTORING

"Jessica Keigan is a woman full of ideas," Tom Fitzpatrick told us.

Back in Jessica's rookie year of 2003, Tom, who was closing out his thirty-year career, cotaught an interdisciplinary course with her in English and history at Horizon High School, located in Adams 12 district in the sprawling suburbs north of downtown Denver.

"She was young and had minimal teaching experience, but she was well prepared and was very dynamic and creative," Tom said.

He then let us know how Jessica impressed him with her rich descriptions of how she would design project-based lessons and her insight into what makes fourteen- to eighteen-year-olds tick in a classroom.

Jessica and Tom had a profound impact on each other, and their collaborative teaching made them better teachers, setting the stage for Jessica to flourish as a leader and policy advocate and for Tom to transition from his thirty-year teaching career into becoming a successful teacher educator.

Large high schools like Horizon, serving two thousand students, are well known as places where teachers, in isolated egg crates called classrooms, teach subjects, not students. But Horizon, which opened in the late 1980s, is built on the principles of

> I recognize that I cannot ever hope to be successful without the help and guidance of those who are smarter than I am, and hope to pay that forward by helping those who have less experience.
>
> —Jessica Keigan

personalized learning for students and distributed leadership among administrators and teachers. Walking into Horizon, the place feels warm, even with its huge foyer and long hallways. And after meeting administrators and teachers, and the receptionist who signed in visitors at the front door, there's clearly a sense that this school is one in which the students and teachers work collaboratively with one another.

Figure 3.1

Jessica Keigan chose Horizon High School in Thornton, Colorado, to be the setting of her first teaching job in 2003.

Photo courtesy of Barbara Kinney.

Jessica vividly recalls her first meeting with Tom, wearing his archetypal Colorado uniform of blue jeans and a flannel shirt, during the hiring interview, which took place almost a decade ago. "He was smart and open minded," Jessica noted. "I knew I wanted to teach with him." She then pointed to how he mentored her, and what he expected of her, even when she was a novice teacher:

> He was so good at helping me navigate the politics of our school when I was so young in my career. I never thought I had second-class status as his junior teaching partner. He treated me like an equal and celebrated my successes as

well as pointing out several areas in which I needed to grow as a teacher. He encouraged me to develop my voice. Even though I was a newbie, and he was a veteran of three decades, he never even implied throughout our teaching partnership that I "had a place" or that I needed to keep my mouth shut.

There was more than a one-way, learning-to-teach relationship, according to Tom:

> Jessica was great for me. I remember our partnership was an excellent mix of youthful ideas and seasoned routines in the classroom. Every time I tried to do something that was sort of by habit, Jessica would question the process and ask what was taking place. In a sense she would make me go back and reexamine what we were trying to do in the classroom and how well it fit into the curriculum for that particular year. She also brought in such new, fresh ideas and identified so well with students. I learned from her as well, especially in how she engaged with the kids.

Jessica's current teaching partner, Dave Cialone, explained a similar relationship the two of them share today: "We have the kind of collaborative teaching relationship where we can really critique each other."

The teaching partnership Jessica had with Tom and has with Dave, as well as her learning experiences with her professors at the University of Colorado–Denver, fostered what we call *reciprocal mentoring*—a fundamental building block of teacherpreneurism whereby the mentor expects the protégé to teach as much as to learn.

In reflecting on her teaching partners, Jessica told us, "With the ever-growing need for accountability, being in a classroom with another teacher allows for constant reflection through a more organic process of critiquing each other."

Building Relational Trust

Jessica also has had support from excellent administrators, who were expert teachers themselves. Joan Watson, a teacher of thirty-two years before she became the principal of Horizon, remembers Jessica's first years of teaching and her leadership.

"She came in with knowledge and confidence from her teacher education program and put herself in a position to learn from her fellow teachers," Joan said. "And if she saw that she wasn't going to learn much from one of her teaching colleagues, she would take the lead."

For Jessica, more than anything else, it's important that Tom and Joan, and now Dave and her current principal, Pam Smiley, all share a deep level of trust in her ideas and abilities. Listening to them talk about Jessica, we were reminded of the concept of *relational trust*, defined by researchers Tony Bryk and Barbara Schneider as an "interrelated set of mutual dependencies" in their efforts to uncover what it takes for serious school improvement and the closing of the achievement gap.[1] Trust, in Jessica's mind, is tied to not just her core competencies in teaching but also the personal integrity and regard she brings to what she does. Jessica is trusted deeply because of her moral compass and the degree to which she extends herself to serve students and the school community.

Explaining why Jessica has been able to be so effective, Joan told us, "It's not because she is a control person; it's not because she wants to be the boss of things; it's because she feels by leading, by thinking, and by getting into the mess of things, you can really get into the system and improve it."

Figure 3.2

Jessica (at right), in collaboration with the CTQ-Colorado team, particularly Allison Sampish (left) and Dana Tucker (who served in hybrid roles), led policy conversations on the Common Core State Standards, school redesign, and teacher evaluation.

Photo courtesy of Jessica Keigan.

Jessica on PBS #1

http://bit.ly/WtynhF

Until we met Jessica in 2010, when she joined the CTQ Collaboratory, she had not thought much about getting involved in influencing the policies that shaped her teaching. But it did not take long for Jessica to get deeply involved in her state's controversial approach to reforming teacher evaluation. Jessica—along with growing numbers of her teaching colleagues—stood in contrast to reformers who sought to punish teachers who did not improve standardized test scores and union leaders who resisted change. Jessica supported the evaluation law that required student growth to account for at least 50 percent of a teacher's rating. But she made the case that "no one is more qualified to comment on a student's achievement than the person who works with that student every day."[2] Soon she was testifying before the state board of education and advising the Colorado Department of Education on the implementation of the Common Core State Standards.

Jessica on PBS #2

http://bit.ly/XGRkK5

Early in fall 2011, while participating in a Rocky Mountain PBS talk show, Jessica pointed out how important it is for "teachers to be well aware of what is happening [in policy]," but also touched on how those who teach inside a classroom all day long tend to have "tunnel vision."[3]

"But this does not have to be," Jessica asserted.[4]

"We have some solutions," Jessica noted in the interview on the PBS talk show.[5] Jessica and her colleagues have brought much more sense to what could have been a disastrous piece of state education policy by developing clearer definitions of the multiple measures of student learning as well as developing scenarios to show administrators how evaluation can be a helpful process rather than an "event" that happens once or twice a year.

"My teaching of students adds so much gravitas to my policy work," Jessica told us. And Michelle Exstrom of the National Conference of State Legislatures could not agree more: "I heard Jessica speak at a conference, and she was terrific. She had policymakers in the audience really listening to her. You could see how they trusted her voice."

Principal Pam Smiley encouraged Jessica to take on the teacherpreneurial role so she could help lead much-needed teacher evaluation reforms back at Horizon. In describing Jessica's leadership persona, Pam pointed out that "what many see as another assignment, Jessica often sees as an opportunity to learn something that allows her to know her students better, to teach more effectively, and even to become a better person."

Figure 3.3

Jessica Keigan at Horizon High School in Thornton, Colorado, shares instructions for a jigsaw activity in her Advanced Placement (AP) U.S. history and literature and writing course.

Photo courtesy of Barbara Kinney.

The Role of Teacher Preparation

Jessica's pedagogical and policy ideas are not born solely of talent, gumption, and energy, although she has plenty of all three. University of Colorado–Denver teacher education professors Stevi Quate and Karen Hartmen capitalized on Jessica's mind and mind-set. These two master's program professors prepared Jessica to use a range of pedagogical strategies to engage adolescents in literature and writing. Stevi and Karen, both of whom had extensive experience teaching high school, did a lot more than just help her with pedagogical strategies, some of which Jessica still uses ten years later.

"Stevi and Karen modeled leadership for me," Jessica noted, "and they pushed me." Jessica reflected on the number of times they "volunteered" her for numerous committees and projects after she graduated. "They gave me the confidence to try new things in my teaching and take on leadership roles outside of the classroom. In retrospect I see how they encouraged and showed me how to think about policy."

Stevi embraced the opportunity to answer our question about her first memories of Jessica, describing Jessica in one of her writing classes:

> She really stood out. She took risks in class, and she posed hard questions. She always wanted to get better. And she pushed her classmates as well as her professors—and she could do so while being so diplomatic about it. No wonder she is good in communicating policy ideas to both her teaching colleagues and policymakers.

Stevi taught Jessica in several courses on the pedagogy of English and writing, using a variety of methods but always expecting the future teachers under her wing to demonstrate knowledge of teaching methods by using them in real contexts. Stevi told us that if we want teachers to effectively teach young people to write, and to develop their thinking skills through writing, then they must do it themselves—a lot of it.

Jessica confirmed this theory of practice: "The same processes I use to develop my own professional writing I use with my students to help them think and compose. This all stems from Stevi and Karen's mentorship."

"Jessica was always willing to share her writing when other teacher education students could not. She would not hide her academic vulnerabilities," Stevi added. Many of Jessica's classmates were fearful of being inadequate. Jessica embraced the possibility of "not looking good" with the first and second drafts of her academic papers.

And Jessica gives Stevi and Karen credit for helping her "embrace failure" and work well "with those above" her in the traditional school hierarchy. Much of Jessica's teaching and leadership moxie emerges out of her formal teacher preparation, of which she is highly appreciative to this day. Contrary to conventional myth, university-based teacher education can develop talented recruits into expert teachers and leaders—and it does *not* always disconnect research and theory from the realities of school practice as critics like to claim. But teacher education faculty must know how to identify and capitalize on talent, curiosity, and well-traveledness like Jessica's.

When we asked Jessica about the literature that has most influenced her, she immediately spoke about one of Anne Lamott's memoirs, *Traveling Mercies*:

> I am drawn toward powerful women who have compassion. I think Lamott exhibits those characteristics. She is very opinionated. She has a lot of political leanings, but she also lets her faith guide her in terms of how she deals with humanity. Her memoir was influential for me in terms of how I look at my students. I can't ever judge them based on an action or the way that they come across. I can always see their potential. This has worked really well for me as a teacher—and I guess now in my work outside my school, district, and state.

Many Americans believe that teachers are born and not made. And Jessica, no doubt, was born with some solid pedagogical DNA. She is a *very* proud member of a multigenerational family of teachers—including her great-great-great-grandpa, who taught in an Iowa "country" school, and her grandmother, who inspired her and had a double degree in English and elementary education with a minor in French. But Jessica's story is not about some teaching gene she inherited. It is about her commitment to teaching as a career and her constant quest to get better at her teaching and find experienced colleagues who can help her do so. And this drive is what makes up much of her teacherpreneurial skill and spirit.

"I recognize that I cannot ever hope to be successful without the help and guidance of those who are smarter than I am, and hope to pay that forward by helping those who have less experience," she shared.

Throughout her ongoing pursuit of learning, Jessica has absorbed many leadership opportunities, but her embrace of them seems to emerge from reciprocal mentoring that has fueled her confidence.

However, over the course of her 2011–2012 teacherpreneurial work, Jessica struggled with "being pulled by too many masters." After she returned to full-time teaching, she told us:

> As a teacher and policy leader, you have to shift gears rapidly in the middle of the day, from working with teenagers to working with adults on matters of very different content and pace. I soon felt disconnected from my peers at Horizon.

When you are not in the building all day, you miss out on the organic collaboration. It is almost like robbing "Peter to pay Paul." The hybrid role allows you time to lead policy and pedagogical reforms, but it cannot alone allow for your heart to be balanced in your work with students and colleagues.

That said, Jessica reminded us, "Since I returned to full-time teaching I have had the best professional conversations with my colleagues—and much of it is because of what I had learned as a teacherpreneur."

And although Jessica has returned to the classroom full-time in 2012–2013, she continues to find a way to lead. She does this even while teaching 150 students a day (and because she is so good at teaching, the administration assigns her some of the most needy teenagers in the school). For example, early in fall 2012 she had already taken the lead in her school's efforts to fine-tune implementation of teacher evaluation reforms, consulted for the Denver Writing Project (and advocated for its federal funding), served as a classroom expert for textbook publishers around the Common Core State Standards, and began her term on the Learning Forward–Colorado board of directors. In addition, Jessica continues to serve as a blogger and virtual community organizer for the CTQ Collaboratory, and has taken on the informal role of mentor for all the new teacherpreneurs. She said: "I am still a teacherpreneur in spirit, but I just do not have the time, contract, and compensation for it."

ARIEL AND HER "NIMBLE TEACHING MIND"

"Ariel Sacks has a very nimble teaching mind," according to Craig Cetrulo, chair of the English and language arts department at Brooklyn Prospect Charter in New York City. Craig has tremendous respect for Ariel as a teacher and colleague. "A lot of teachers have the ability to hone in on what a particular student needs in the moment, but Ariel has developed very special skills in drawing on her knowledge of adolescents, academically and emotionally," he said.

Everyone we talked to at Ariel's charter school—the CEO, the principal, the department chair, teaching colleagues, and students—deeply respects her and how she teaches. And virtually everyone there knows the role that Bank Street College has had in developing Ariel into the teacher and leader she has become. She has amassed six years of teaching experience in the city's public schools (some functional and others dysfunctional) and three years in a dynamic progressive charter school in which teacher leadership is embraced.

Ariel's teaching is paramount in this charter school, which is unlike most others in urban America, designed to serve students from varied racial, ethnic, and

Figure 3.4

Ariel Sacks has been teaching in the New York City public schools for six years.

Photo courtesy of Ariel Sacks.

socioeconomic groups.[6] Many charter schools are highly segregated, and their students are quite homogenous. This is not the case at Brooklyn Prospect, however, where teachers need to know a great deal more about teaching and learning, given that students' reading skills in their classroom can span many grade levels, and considering that all students are expected to meet twenty-first-century academic standards of global citizenship.

"Ariel knows so much about adolescent development," Craig continued. "She can pick up so much about what kids need to know academically or what may be going on in their lives from a piece of writing or a comment they make in class."

"She knows a lot more than I do about kids," Craig said.

In addition, Ariel has learned a great deal about how to translate her knowledge of students and sound pedagogy into leading students as well as leading adults.

"Ariel is a great teacher," said Dan Rubenstein, a Teach For America alum, National Board Certified Teacher, 2002 recipient of the Presidential Award for

Excellence in Mathematics Teaching, and founder and executive director of Brooklyn Prospect. "She is not an 'in front of the room lecture' kind of teacher, not at all, but she is in charge, and that does not fundamentally change for her."

As founding principal LaNolia Omowanile noted,

I see her growing a lot as a teacher leader, especially as we think through twenty-first-century learning in the school. Of all of the faculty, she is one of the leaders in that regard, as far as her knowledge and ability to implement new reforms, whether it is new teaching techniques or a different way of assessing and paying teachers. And I believe she leads so effectively because she respects students, and also admires the teachers and colleagues she has here.

Knowing Students and Their Families Well

Ariel is relentless in getting to know her students well, and at Brooklyn Prospect the range of academic prowess among students varies enormously. In her eighth-grade classroom of twenty-five students, one can find reading levels ranging from second-grade to first-year-college proficiency. Although she teaches in a highly diverse school, her students' proficiency rates on state tests are 50 percent higher than the district average—and have been increasing steadily each year she has taught. But Ariel believes that the state and district assessments are not accurate enough and do not tell her enough about what her students really know and can do.

At Bank Street College

http://bit.ly/WV4rZl

Ariel has reminded all of us who want to improve the quality of teaching and learning, "You must start with the children and who they are." In one of her many blog posts, informed by Edutopia's video of how Bank Street College empowers new teachers,[7] she wrote:

As the video shows, at Bank Street, I learned how to observe, understand and build relationships with students through a combination of reading and discussing developmental theory, and supervised field work through the advisement program. In my course work and student teaching, I learned to take and identify developmentally appropriate content and determine the key concepts students need to understand within it. I practiced designing curriculum that provides students with experiences, language, reflection and application opportunities to really grasp those concepts. Through what Bank Street calls the developmental-interaction approach, students do not learn skills in isolation. We introduce skills as they are relevant to students' experiences and questions.[8]

Ariel told us,

I know my one hundred students really well. I have relationships with their parents. They trust my teaching. They understand there is a reason for everything. In meetings I ask how reading is going and ask what they are thinking. I give them lots of opportunities to voice their learning, and they see me make adjustments.

Ariel learned how to teach by teaching, but under direct and close supervision. She was not expected to teach independently until she had demonstrated what she could do. "There were so many parts of my, or anyone's, teaching job that could not be fully anticipated through preservice work," Ariel said. "But in my preparation, I learned the importance of planning engaging, appropriate curriculum for my students, of creating long-range, in-depth studies, as well as detailed daily lesson plans with objectives that build toward the long-range goals."

As executive director at Brooklyn Prospect, Dan marvels at Ariel's pedagogical skill learned at Bank Street College and its impact on the school he founded—no less profound than the impact on students and parents. Dan has seen firsthand Ariel's immense talent in using her teaching to reach all members of her school community. For example, she built a poetry unit that truly connected her students' creative expression to all those who care about them. Ariel told us:

In this unit, I had students investigate their own cultural backgrounds, from today's youth culture to the cultural heritage of their grandparents and ancestors. They interviewed the oldest living member of their family and used this and other investigative activities as inspiration to write poems celebrating their complex identities.

"Her poetry unit was so moving, we had to upload a video on our Web site," Dan told us.

Ariel learned a lot about middle school students at Bank Street College. She was also taught about many highly complex, technical aspects of teaching. "I learned a great deal about how to teach reading and literature but also how to create critical learning

"I Am" Poems

http://bit.ly/14puqOr

Video courtesy of Brooklyn Prospect Charter.

communities among many types of kids." Her poetry unit is a stellar example of how she brings all she has learned to her classroom and to everyone connected to her students—from her colleagues to her students' family members to others in the community.

Lessons from Bank Street College

Dan told us,

> When you are leading your colleagues, it is a very different dynamic. You forget that being a teacher does not teach you how to build a coalition and manage all the politics. But Ariel has learned how to do this—and do it well. She's so reflective and really open about what her strengths and weaknesses are, and seeks mentorship, guidance, and advice, which are critical pieces. She is also ambitious and self-assured.

"I think Bank Street College taught me a lot about expecting the unexpected," Ariel told us. Ariel's pedagogy is highly adaptive, and her training has prepared her to strategically adjust her lesson plans. But there is more to her expectations:

> I have often thought about getting away from expecting only slow, incremental growth in students—often, we see what may look like stagnation (but is actually gestation), and then a sudden, surprising leap forward! My Bank Street College training in experiential learning has been conducive to my creating the "aha" moment of synthesis for students.

Bank Street College has a long history of research-based, progressive education that prepares future teachers and administrators who know students well. With deep roots in the ideas and actions of Lucy Sprague Mitchell, an early-twentieth-century educator, the "Bank Street way" has been built on investigations of how children learn and "what kind of environment is best suited to their learning and growth."[9]

In many ways Bank Street College has been the mother ship of teacher education that puts children at the center of preparing new recruits to teach. The small college, nestled a few blocks from Columbia University on the Upper West Side of New York City, has for almost one hundred years been home to a progressive K–8 school as well as graduate-level preparation programs for teachers and administrators.

Ariel, who earned an undergraduate degree in English from Brown University and taught in Providence, Rhode Island, for eight months as a substitute teacher without any pedagogical preparation, has considerable appreciation for her graduate-level training at Bank Street College, as it afforded her the opportunity to "integrate direct experience with children, teachers, and families; exploration and examination of theory; and observation and reflection."

Jon Snyder, chief academic officer of Bank Street College, who has worked with Ariel during her program and in the years since she graduated, said, "She came to Bank Street College after entering teaching without preparation. She really wanted to learn to teach and lead."

Figure 3.5

Ariel Sacks approaches her work with students knowing that "you have to start with them." Her preparation at Bank Street College and continued support from professors inform her evolving practice.

Photo courtesy of Ariel Sacks.

On the Shoulders of Giants

Ariel recalls that in one of the first courses she took at Bank Street College, under the tutelage of Madeleine Ray, she learned about how to conduct neighborhood studies to get to know students, families, and communities. Madeleine also taught her how to take risks in the classroom (and expected her to do so), even under the specter of high-stakes testing and narrow accountability metrics so common in the New York City schools in which she has taught. Ariel took us deeper into the relationship between her preparation and mind-set about teaching and learning:

> Madeleine was so important to my development as a teacher. She taught me how to know children and not to lose my practice. As Craig and I worked on our school's expert teacher framework, we landed on the idea that part of it has to do with the teacher's ability to say, "This is my practice. This is what I do, why I do it, and how it works for kids."

Creating Critical Learning Communities

http://bit.ly/1258GYC

Smiling broadly, Ariel told us more about what teacher education, and Madeleine, taught her:

> Madeleine planted a different concept in my mind: let students read novels in their entirety. Then let them talk about what *they* find interesting in the book, facilitating the group's exploration of the text. She convinced me to do away with prescribed comprehension and discussion questions and let the students lead the way. I first tried this "whole novels" method as a student teacher in Bank Street College's own private lab school and really learned a lot in doing so. I have been building this method ever since—and am now drafting a book manuscript for publication so I can share what I have learned how to do with other teachers who are looking for a different way of teaching literature.

Unlike many teachers who enter teaching with only modest training, Ariel has brought deep preparation that pays off for students. Craig noted, "Her design of curriculum and preparation of materials are made to allow students many ramps to access the content."

Ariel, unlike most new entrants to the teaching profession, had an opportunity to try out progressive teaching techniques at both high-functioning as well as high-need schools. She was part of an experiment (Partnership for Quality), funded by a federal grant, to establish internships in several types of schools that had varying needs and diverse students, but never without strong support from higher education faculty. Ariel reflected on her internship experience:

> Throughout my internship I received support and continued advisement from Bank Street College faculty members who understood the context in which I was teaching. They helped me to sort out what my role as teacher was; to solidify my opinions about my school; and, finally, to begin to understand how I could purposefully help my students develop as learners. With this level of support, I learned to implement progressive pedagogy where many people thought it was neither possible nor worthwhile.

"Every time she faced a challenge," Jon noted, "she had a cohort of peers and faculty there to help her solve the problem and continue to pursue her pedagogical ambitions."

Ariel described her development as a teacher and leader:

> I look to the "giants" in my life, on whose experience and wisdom I rely. One such person is Madeleine. She taught me—and reminds me often—that a teacher is, first and foremost, a group leader. As a leader in my own classroom, it's my job to know my students as thoroughly as I can and to put their needs first. In the face of difficult conditions, which often seem to ask that I push aside or downplay the needs of my students, I must demonstrate the courage to stand up for them and for what I know to be true.

She does stand up for her students and her beliefs in this way—and her ethical commitment to students carries over into how she works with adults to share her expertise on policy as well as pedagogy. She has led a design team for the transformation of teacher education for Bank Street College. Ariel has also become a prolific blogger.

Bringing Practice to Policy

As a result of her writing, Ariel has a growing presence on the national education policy circuit. At a 2011 Education Writers Association (EWA) meeting in New York

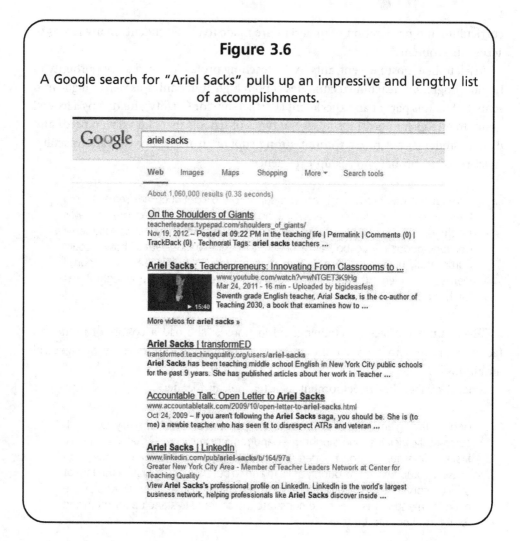

Figure 3.6

A Google search for "Ariel Sacks" pulls up an impressive and lengthy list of accomplishments.

City, Ariel was one of several teacher bloggers asked to attend but not to formally speak to the journalists assembled (our colleagues Stephen Lazar and José Vilson were invited as well). Researchers, think tank analysts, journalists, and "reformers" officially were given the microphone. But the lack of a recognized role for teachers did not muffle Ariel's voice. One participant noted that Ariel made "the critical observation that the conversation should really not be about the recruitment of teachers, but rather about the *retention* of effective teachers."[10]

Ariel has become quite at ease—in front of the camera at the Big Ideas Fest,[11] or in front of journalists like those at EWA. It is not that Ariel is an extrovert; she has developed a deep sense of confidence in her ideas, without any hubris. In part, this is why she was asked to revolutionize the way teachers are paid at her school. Dan and others have embraced the idea she came up with and contributed mightily to it, and the school is committed to implementing the proposal. No wonder. With only three years of teaching under her belt, Ariel penned a *New York Daily News* op-ed on why teachers need the *right kind* of merit pay.[12] And now Dan and LaNolia have asked her to help lead the design and implementation of their school's "career cycle" for teachers and connect it to plans for both a residency program and a 360-degree evaluation system.

> [With] support, I learned to implement progressive pedagogy where many people thought it was neither possible nor worthwhile.
> —Ariel Sacks

Ariel, a contributor to our book *Teaching 2030*, has much to say about why teacherpreneurism is so important for many teachers who want to continue to teach students while leading reforms in and outside of their school, district, state, or, now in her case, charter network. "There is no career trajectory for teachers," Ariel said, "and all too often the only way to move up is to go do something else." Ariel wants something more for herself as well as for *all* teachers.

Despite the fact that Ariel and most of her colleagues have not been formally supported by CTQ as teacherpreneurs (Ariel has, however, had CTQ support for five years as a blogger), it is evident that her involvement with like-minded teacher leaders has greatly contributed to her development. LaNolia pointed out how the CTQ Collaboratory has cultivated Ariel's teacherpreneurism:

> Your [CTQ's] network has been instrumental. The conversations and the hard-edged sharing of teaching practices and policy ideas have given her additional tools she needs to reflect on her teaching. She is always bouncing her ideas off other teachers in your online community—and this makes her better at it here at our school.

We talked to Ariel about her leadership from the classroom—and as usual, she wrote publicly about her thinking in her own distinctive and powerful voice in an Education Week Teacher essay:

> Six years ago, when I first joined CTQ's Teacher Leaders Network [now Collaboratory], I couldn't have even told you what teacher leadership was. Through conversations on TLN's online forum [then a listserv], I learned about this powerful concept, which was developing in response to several pressing needs. Teachers were looking for avenues to share their knowledge and provide input into education beyond their classrooms. At the same time, we felt frustration

Figure 3.7

Ariel Sacks and the other eleven expert teachers on the *Teaching 2030* writing team pushed us hard (and still do) to think about teacherpreneurs and how they are different from other teacher leaders. Ariel drew this sketch of a teacherpreneur's career path when the concept was in its early stages.

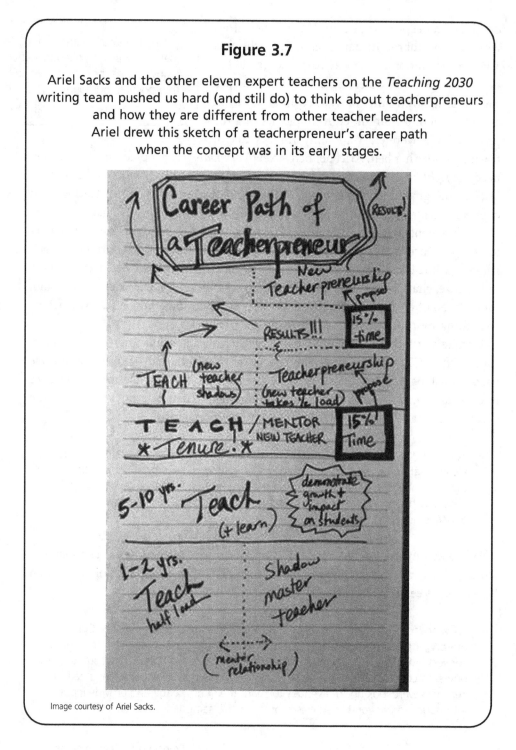

Image courtesy of Ariel Sacks.

with decisions made by education leaders from principals to politicians that so often reflected a lack of understanding about teaching and the realities of students' lives. Teachers who served unofficially in leadership capacities lacked formal recognition and compensation for their contributions, while many early-career teachers were leaving the classroom for professions with greater mobility.

The crucial question for teachers is no longer, "What is teacher leadership?" Rather, it is, "What kind of teacher leadership is worthwhile for me?" Teaching students is the single most important thing that happens in education every day. That is where teachers make their biggest impact. So a leadership opportunity must provide a compelling reason to step away from the classroom—even for a day—or give up our valuable personal time. It must help teachers use their knowledge to empower their colleagues and school communities rather than present yet one more obstacle for effective teaching and learning.[13]

Both Ariel and Jessica, unlike many young teachers who leave teaching after just a few years to go into education policy, have learned how to do more than just build on their (limited) teaching experience. They also understand the world of teaching students and act in integrating their classroom know-how into the world that governs the public school enterprise. Much of what they do now as leaders relates to how they learned to teach. Through their stories, we begin to understand how teacherpreneurs can be systematically developed through not just traditional course work and internships but also cohort-based residencies and virtual communities. But what they teach us most is the importance of teacherpreneurs who never "lose their practice"—in the classroom or at the Capitol. As young teachers who will not yet be fifty years of age in the year 2030, Ariel and Jessica help us think about how to prepare for teacherpreneurism and how classroom experts can make themselves and teaching more visible—the latter being the topic we address next.

● Chapter Three Selected Web Sites

Following is a list of online resources that relate to the discussion in this chapter. If you find that either of these links no longer works, please try entering the information in a search engine.

Teaching 2030: Leveraging Teacher Preparation 2.0:
http://www.teachingquality.org/teacher_prep_2.0

Ariel Sacks's Education Week Teacher essay on the Teacher Leaders Network (now the CTQ Collaboratory):
http://www.edweek.org/tm/articles/2012/10/17/tl_sacks.html

Activity for Chapter Three

Now What?

Examine the "Why"

Goal

In Chapters One and Two, you've had the opportunity to explore your leadership broadly, but with a sharp visionary eye on the future. Sections of these activities, especially the experience you have listed under the résumé heading of "evidence of making great teaching visible," have helped you to zoom in on the ideas and mind-sets modeled by the teacherpreneurs discussed in Chapter Three. It's now time to consider the philosophies and pedagogical approaches that underlie your teacher leadership practices. And, perhaps more important, it's time to examine the roots of these beliefs.

Think

Reexamine the lists of experiences in various teacher leadership "waves" and the résumé you created following Chapters One and Two, respectively. As you review these documents, consider the greater themes around teaching and learning that are represented there. We recommend that you use the following guiding questions to support your thinking and analysis:

- What role(s) do you believe you play in the lives of your students?
- Under what conditions do you believe students learn best?
- How does your role as a teacher extend into your school's community beyond your individual classroom (including relationships with colleagues, parents, local partners, and other community members)?
- What's your vision for the teaching profession as a whole?

(*Note:* We encourage you to jot down responses or key ideas relating to the preceding questions as you reflect. This will help you identify themes and patterns within your beliefs.)

Next, review your responses to the questions and identify key themes that emerged. For example, the importance of both individual roles and a community of relationships is touched on in this chapter.

Use a T-chart like the one that follows, outlining your themes on the left-hand side. Then, on the right-hand side, write down the "why" of these ideas. Are your beliefs rooted in your previous professional experiences, relationships with mentors, formal and informal preparation as a teacher and teacher leader, or other areas of your life?

Philosophical Themes	Roots (the "Why")

Act

Review your T-chart and choose one or two themes in your beliefs about teaching and leadership to explore further. Research these topics to discover what others say. Consider investigating various disciplines, including neuroscience and psychology, in your search. All the while, reflect on the implications of this information for the teaching and learning taking place within your classroom.

Share

Seek out an opportunity to talk about your philosophical themes with a colleague within your school or via CTQ's virtual network (http://www.teachingquality.org). Use this dialogue as a chance to continue to process and refine your thinking (and to update your chart as you see fit).

CHAPTER 4

Making Teachers—and Teaching—Visible

> *I am not afraid to make my teaching visible; I am not afraid to make views on teaching heard.*
>
> —Renee Moore

Almost forty years ago, sociologist Dan Lortie made the case that teaching, as a profession, was beset by its cellular organization, which isolated teachers from each other and the public. For Lortie, the status of America's teaching profession hinged on teachers' being able to "document their statements that their work was dynamic rather than static, that collegial judgment played a key part in decision-making, and that teachers acquired arcane, indispensable training to prepare them for the high demands of teaching."[1]

Both Stephen Lazar and Renee Moore do all of this—and much more—in advancing teaching as a profession. They know how to not only identify problems but also lead with solutions. Their long-term commitment to teaching and serving our nation's highest-need students, in inner-city New York and the rural South, respectively, is profound.

IDENTIFYING SYSTEMIC DEFICIENCIES

As we sat down with Stephen for the first time, it did not take him long to express his strongly held views about his commitment to engaging and challenging students, his teaching of critical inquiry, his passion for history, and the wrongheadedness of our nation's student assessment policies.

Sipping a cup of coffee at Grounded, a café in New York City's West Village, Stephen said, "We will not let the Regents be our religion."

He is highly critical of the state's high-stakes testing regime (like others across the nation), and for good reason. Teaching in New York State, the geographic heart of high-stakes accountability, Stephen often cites the evidence of how narrow-minded standardized testing—exemplified by New York's Regents exam in history—undermines quality teaching and learning. He talks about the breakneck pace of the Regents curriculum that does not allow for teacher creativity or flexibility in response to student interests. He talks about a better way of teaching and assessing, as well as documenting what and how students are learning. But he doesn't just have ideas: he also has been a part of developing valid and reliable tools to hold teachers accountable for the right results.

He is not alone. The Regents exam in history, which Stephen's students have taken routinely, was found to be "a peculiar mix of the trivial, the self-evident, and the historically inaccurate" in a formal review.[2] In addition, there are scathing critiques of how New York City's education leaders of late (including former chancellor Joel Klein) have blatantly misused student test score data to assess teachers and their effectiveness.[3] In fact, Mississippi Delta teacher Renee, whom we introduced earlier, also points to reams of research as she laments how U.S. policymakers glom onto high-stakes accountability systems built from low-quality standardized testing. "These tests can cause students to regress rather than progress intellectually," Renee said with the same conviction found in the best of Sunday morning sermons in the Deep South.

Stephen told us,

> I learn exponentially more about my students' capabilities from the performance assessments they regularly complete in my class than I do from the mandated standardized exams like the Regents. Furthermore, the work I give them is authentic and requires more intellectual work on their part in the discipline I am teaching.

In a March 2009 post on her *TeachMoore* blog, "Test to the Teach(ing)—Not Vice Versa," Renee reminded school reformers so smitten with high-stakes accountability of the inequities created by systems purported to close the student achievement gap:

> It's a harsh reality that some students in this country receive a rich, challenging curriculum which allows them to perform consistently well on tests and other evaluations; while other children—particularly the children of the poor—are more often in schools focused on control and remediation. Ironically, many of

those who insist on forcing teachers and students to spend inordinate amounts of time drilling basic skills believe they are helping "close the achievement gap." In fact, they may actually be making it wider.[4]

Stephen and Renee, like others we profile in *Teacherpreneurs*, teach students every day (and often into the evening), yet they also find time to build their knowledge of research and policy. They readily cite a range of studies (for examples, see http://www.fairtest.org/reports-high-stakes-testing-hurts-education) showing that constant testing can actually widen, not close, the achievement gap. They often note, from their own experience as well as from research evidence, that many assessments from the current crop of high-stakes tests include unimportant topics and produce a classroom climate that actually "turns off" students and disengages them from learning. They are very good at making their ideas visible.

In this chapter, Stephen and Renee offer us powerful examples of the impact of teacherpreneurs—and shed light on why we must find ways to cultivate and elevate their talent, and formally acknowledge the leadership roles they now play.

REDESIGNING SCHOOLS FOR AUTHENTIC TEACHING AND LEARNING

We could see and feel Stephen's expertise in performance assessment as soon as we walked into his classroom at the Academy for Young Writers, nestled in the Williamsburg neighborhood of Brooklyn, New York. He was right in the middle of small-group work, whereby students were learning about the nexus of economic principles, personal finances, and mathematics. After the lesson, one of Stephen's students said this:

> I would say he is a great teacher, a very talented teacher, and he is very attentive to you. He keeps good control of the class. He doesn't do the same thing over and over again. He makes it interesting, so kids actually attend and are active in the class . . . He builds a relationship with you that most teachers wouldn't build with students. Students are more comfortable to be around him and in class with him. It makes for a better environment . . . He stepped up and made us more college bound and ready.

"He treats the kids like intellectuals," Thandi Center, who worked with Stephen when she led professional development for the Institute for Student Achievement (ISA), told us during a phone interview. "It is the first message that kind of comes across when you step into his room."

Thandi, who has extensive experience in supporting and transforming underperforming urban high schools, understands the connections between teaching

Figure 4.1

Stephen Lazar, center, a proponent of project-based learning, talks with students at his Brooklyn, New York, school.

Photo courtesy of Alan Wieder.

conditions and teacher effectiveness. Researchers have made it clear that teachers are the most influential in-school factor affecting student achievement.[5] Effective teaching is not just about teachers' knowledge, skills, and dispositions, but also about the context of instruction and the conditions under which they work (for example, whether there is time to collaborate with colleagues on matters of instruction; access to information, materials, and technology; and helpful feedback on teaching).[6] Thandi told us that Stephen has always been involved in helping create these conditions in the schools in which he has taught.

Gerry House, named the 1999 National Superintendent of the Year when she led Memphis Public Schools, and founder and CEO of ISA, had a lot to say about Stephen:

> We have always turned to Stephen to lead our reform work. Many teachers don't know how to ask, "What do you want kids to know, and how will they demonstrate that?" Stephen does. Not only is he great in the classroom but

also he is so analytical about what he does—and articulate about what he knows—and so what he knows is very accessible to other teachers and administrators.

Stephen has been teaching for less than decade, and all three of the New York City schools in which he has taught have been launched by ISA. He is one of the go-to teacher leaders for ISA and its efforts to transform underperforming public high schools by drawing on distributed counseling, extended-day and extended-year schedules, and proven strategies for engaging parents. He leads as if he were a twenty-five-year veteran.

Implementing and Sharing Expertise

Stephen's blog, *Outside the Cave*, captures the attention of educators and policy leaders nationwide, and his writing is now featured by Gotham Schools, an independent news source covering the New York City public schools. Stephen addresses head-on what works and what doesn't in New York City public education. He also has been a leader inside of the United Federation of Teachers, using his deep pedagogical expertise to mediate the usual divides on matters of what to do when teachers are not treated fairly by administrators and when teaching is not up to standard. He has leveraged his know-how to influence the pilot of the state's new teacher evaluation law, which must be implemented in a contentious environment in which student test scores have historically been misused in judging teachers.

But perhaps most important, Stephen has drawn on his teaching expertise to lead assessment reforms—for both students and teachers alike. He has been deeply involved in a national effort, centered in New York City, with the Stanford Center for Assessment, Learning, and Equity to design more authentic student assessments (performance tasks) and support teachers in using them—such as the ones he created on the topics of "democracy in America" and "sociological identity and media."

Too many of today's school reforms continue to create disconnects between what students are expected to learn; what teachers teach; and how achievement is measured, scored, and reported. And Stephen works hard to ensure the connections among these critical elements exist. When visiting Stephen at the Academy for Young Writers early in May 2012, we saw him put curriculum, teaching, and assessment together—despite barriers presented by federal and state education policy. We also ran into Gerry, who had brought ISA board members and funders to the school to hear Stephen's students present their work with Project Citizen, a program sponsored by the Center for Civic Education that promotes responsible participation in local and state government. Stephen has embraced the Project Citizen approach because of its focus on students' conducting research, using evidence and reasoning, and taking a stand.

In a Gotham Schools article highlighting Stephen's teaching, Stephen pointed out, "I want my students to be ready for college—and I want them to vote and be part of our democratic process as citizens of the United States."[7] And most of Stephen's students move on to higher education, including his current seniors, who will be attending such institutions as Howard University, Nyack College, the University of Vermont, and the University of Wisconsin–Madison.

Stephen's skill in developing assessments based on Project Citizen principles pays off for students. Amani, one of Stephen's students, presented her analysis from her policy project, "The Gentrification of Williamsburg and Public Education," in which she demonstrated her knowledge of history, sociology, and political science as well as her research and public speaking skills. She, like her peers, made a big impression on classmates and classroom visitors.

Figure 4.2

Stephen Lazar's students present their group project on gentrification.

Photo courtesy of Alan Wieder.

Gerry said,

> After watching Stephen's students, we could see that inner-city kids can learn from more than just the KIPP Academy [and its more scripted and narrow] approach to teaching and learning. They can learn a lot without the uniforms and test prep. They can learn a lot when they have a voice in their own education.

Teaching as Thinking

During our impromptu coffee klatch, we spent several hours talking with Stephen about how he became the teacher he is and his current after-hours efforts (with his new colleague Kate Burch and several other classroom experts) to open Harvest Collegiate High School, which is now up and running near Union Square. Stephen's influence is clearly present in this new school, which is focused on the pragmatic, the personal, and the political.

Stephen writes:

> At Harvest, so many of my selves get the opportunity for fulfillment. The 18-year-old me gets to prove his English teacher wrong; the 20-year-old me gets to be a Sizer [one of America's most prominent progressive educators] apostle; the 22-year-old me gets to focus on teaching. The teacher gets to create the environment in which he teaches. The school designer gets to apply the lessons he learned from Bronx Lab [my previous school]. The professional developer gets to support teaching and learning. The advocate gets a platform to show, among other things, how a school that focuses on essential skills and understandings better serves all students than test prep factories. The writer will have plenty to share. I, all of us, get the biggest challenge of my life.[8]

Stephen told us,

> I grew up in Cleveland and went to Agnon [a Jewish progressive school]. I was amazingly well educated through eighth grade. It was only ten years later that I realized it was progressive and student centered and inquiry based and interdisciplinary. At the time I just thought I went to a weird Jewish school where teachers really knew you well.

> He honestly wanted to know what I thought about his teaching, but also was coaching me through my learning as a teacher.
> —Stephen Lazar, on his first mentor, Ben Bruder

He continued, "And then I went to a very traditional high school and was never challenged." Stephen's high school was one of the best in Ohio, with high test scores, soaring college-going rates, and the like. "But for me, with the exception of a couple of teachers, it was a joke, an absolute joke,"

Stephen said. "There was nothing I did in four years of high school that was nearly as challenging as the eighth-grade final project I had to do to graduate from Agnon."

Agnon impressed on Stephen the need to think, care, and question. And he did. As the editor of the school newspaper, Stephen wrote what he now calls a "less-than-nuanced" article about teaching and learning and the teachers at his school. "I was really put off by distant, conceited, and 'never-listen-to-kids' teachers," Stephen said.

Later, at Brown University, Stephen took a philosophy of education course, and when reading Ted Sizer's *Horace's Compromise*, he had an epiphany:

> I felt like I was reading about my old high school. I discovered that a famous professor at Harvard made a similar argument about teaching and learning and teachers, but his writing was much more nuanced than mine. I think that is when I thought a lot about being an education reformer, even before I decided to teach for a career.

And like Ariel Sacks, profiled in Chapter Three, Stephen had a powerful experience in his student teaching internship. He started cutting his teeth on how to teach at the MET School in Providence, Rhode Island, where the curriculum empowers students to take ownership of learning.

Stephen told us:

> So there I got the experience of first seeing as radical a different school model as you can in a public school. I also worked with this brilliant guy named Ben Bruder. The first time meeting me, he asked right away, "What could I have done better?" I'm like, are you serious, I've never been in a classroom before. That humility taught me something from day one. He honestly wanted to know what I thought about his teaching, but also was coaching me through my learning as a teacher.

Stephen, at thirty years of age, has embraced his eight years of teaching—including at the Academy of Young Writers and the Bronx Lab School—and wants to teach for decades to come. But he has more ideas to pursue and execute, and more leadership to muster and exert.

In our coffee shop meeting, as Stephen described the curriculum of Harvest, which will be part of the New York Performance Standards Consortium, we learned more about his teacherpreneurism and got to know Kate, one of the school's founders who will serve as a teaching principal.

Stephen described the Harvest curriculum, designed to push students to discipline their thinking on topics of moral or aesthetic significance while helping them develop

Figure 4.3

Stephen Lazar stands with a student, who came in second place in New York City's National History Day contest.

Photo courtesy of Stephen Lazar.

self-efficacy and ensuring that they feel a powerful sense of belonging to the school. We soon realized that Stephen was describing not just the school curriculum, but also how and why he and his colleagues interact and connect with one another.

"He continues to push me," Kate said. "I saw his commitment, his intellect, his curiosity in the words he wrote—and he was National Board Certified, and that told me a lot about his ability to analyze his practice."

Kate, a teacherpreneur in her own right, has deep and thoughtful insights about her teaching colleague Stephen. She quickly saw his ability to communicate complex thought in his writing, and then she saw it in his teaching and leadership:

> When we met I could see readily that for Stephen, teaching is thinking. He questions his teaching. He has a far-reaching perspective, which is the basis for his creativity. He paints pictures of what teaching and learning must look like for others. In this way Stephen is a quintessential teacherpreneur.

RENEE'S COMMITMENT TO THE PROFESSION

"I am not afraid to make my teaching visible; I am not afraid to make views on teaching heard," Renee told us one afternoon as we talked about her two-plus-decade career in teaching.

Renee's career is rooted not just in educating young people but also in serving her faith, family, and community, and making sure the ideas of those who teach are heard in the small towns of the Delta, in her state capital, and across the nation. Over just a few months in 2012, Renee made the two-hour drive to the Memphis airport to be part of several policy meetings as a director for the National Board for Professional Teaching Standards in Washington DC; to speak at a national "teacher voice" convening of the Bill & Melinda Gates Foundation in Arizona; to lead the deliberations of Mississippi's Commission on Teacher and Administrator Education, Certification, and Licensure in Jackson; and to return to Washington DC to finalize the classroom teacher–led report on the transformation of teaching for the National Education Association (NEA). In fact, Renee played a major role with the Commission on Effective Teaching and Teachers, an effort supported by the National Education Association, so that some of the nation's best teachers could challenge the NEA to think and act differently about the future of the profession. Renee was one of fifteen practicing teachers on the commission, whose deep understanding of student learning would challenge not just policymakers but also the union itself.

Over the years Renee has continued to exert leadership across the nation, with little local recognition for it back home, where many administrators of her past had expected her to teach, but not lead, even when she was a fellow at the Carnegie Foundation for the Advancement of Teaching. Throughout years of teaching at several Delta high schools, she routinely taught 150 students each year, with only fifty minutes provided (officially) each day to develop the highly personalized curriculum she insists on delivering to her students.

"Like many of my colleagues," she told us, "I stole precious time from my own family—nights, weekends, holidays throughout the school year—to get everything done, and that was just for what needed to be done for the classroom."

During the school year, Renee's workdays stretch up to twelve hours long—and longer.

She said:

> All my nonteaching educational activities I do—working on policy committees, advocating, writing, speaking—happen after I take care of my first obligation, which is always my students. And I've been a public school teacher in Mississippi for twenty-two years, with all these accomplishments, and I still earn less than $50,000 per year.

Now that I am full-time teaching at Mississippi Delta Community College (MDCC) [including part-time teaching of high school students], I have a more flexible schedule, but it is every bit as full. This year, in addition to my teaching duties at MDCC, I am also the coordinator of our Quality Enhancement Plan—a student-focused, faculty-developed five-year plan that is critical to the school's reaccreditation.

In part, Renee is better able to lead outside the classroom because she now teaches *only* 120 students a semester in a high school–to–postsecondary program at the local community college—and she has slightly more flexibility with her teaching schedule than whenshe taught in a traditional public school setting. She routinely works more than sixty-five hours a week, which fits around her devotional time as well as gatherings with her four adult children and nine grandchildren. (See Appendix B for typical schedule.)

Battling Inequities

Renee's leadership on the macro policy front of the teaching profession often pales in comparison to what she has done locally—not only to advocate for the students of the Delta at local school board meetings but also to minister, with her husband Clernest, to those in need in her community, home to the White Citizens Council, which sought to further the agenda of the Ku Klux Klan with the quiet persona of the Rotary Club.[9] Renee, who is African American, talked a lot about race and its effects on teaching and learning in the Delta. She taught us much, especially on the fifty-four-mile trip we took with her as she rushed to leave her class in Drew to teach another one at the Greenville Higher Education Center. As we drove down Route 49, Renee said, "There was a time, Barnett Berry, when you and I couldn't ride down this road in the same car—and that wasn't that long ago."

"Did you know that we are still under court order to desegregate our schools here?" she quizzed us, in her teacher voice.

The Delta, where Renee has taught for over two decades, still retains a dual system whereby resources, including technology and textbooks, remain inequitably distributed among those schools serving white and black students. Private academies, almost all of them all white, dot the Mississippi landscape. Between 1967 and 1972 Mississippi's private school enrollment tripled. Today, according to a study by Duke University sociologist Charles Clotfelter, in ten of the state's counties, more than 90 percent of the white students are in private schools.[10]

Renee teaches in Sunflower County, which is also home to Mae Beth and Mathew Carter, black sharecroppers who in 1965 fearlessly sent their eight children to formerly all-white schools—seven of whom later graduated from the University of Mississippi. The story of the Carter family, beautifully portrayed by Constance Curry in *Silver Rights*, tells of their courage, faith, and love in their efforts to make a better life for their own children and so many others of future generations.[11] Marian Wright Edelman, who penned the book's introduction, speaks proudly of Mae Beth's convictions—and it was as if she were also writing about Renee, who has since taught a number of members of the extended Carter family:

> Throughout all the personal and family ordeals and dangers, she prayed and believed in her "protective covering," God's blessing and protection. Her willingness to take enormous risks stemmed partly from this unshrinking faith and partly from her determination as a loving mother to do whatever was necessary to give her children the best possible lives.[12]

After giving us a copy of *Silver Rights*, Renee began to tell us more of her own encounters with racism, often in painful detail. And we hope much of her story of teaching for excellence and equity in the rural South, a region ignored by most urban-centric school reform policies of the Obama administration, will be revealed in later publications.

But Renee, who told us she "still needs to be careful," did say this:

> It is a matter of fact that I was forced to leave several of my teaching positions here. I raised too many questions about which children get what resources. I raised too many questions about white administrators who still do not want black children to be educated. But the Lord has opened doors for me each time. I am not afraid.

"Not being afraid, well, that comes from my upbringing—my family and my faith," Renee said without equivocation. "I am a woman of faith; I don't believe in fear, period." Listening to Renee, we began to learn of the importance of risk taking as a criterion not just in selecting teacherpreneurs but also in recruiting future teachers. Considering the dominance of top-down reforms, divorced from classroom realities, we need more teachers—like Renee—who are not afraid to step up and step out.

Renee, at fifty-seven years of age, is the proud daughter of one of Detroit's first black male police officers and an activist nurse, who was born and remains a proud African Canadian citizen.

"When I look back on my path to leadership, I have to say that I was always the first to try new things because of my faith and my family. Standing up and speaking up have never been new to me," Renee said. She continued,

> I knew I was called to teach before I was a public school teacher. I have been involved in education-related service work, first in my journalism and then in church. And then in the 1980s my husband, Clernest, and I decided to move to the Delta late to start Nu Delta Ministries to serve youth and their families.

Renee also talked about her entry into teaching in the Delta:

> When I started teaching I was a thirty-year-old mother of four children. I already had extensive experience working with hardcore gang members. The first day I walked into the classroom I was not a wide-eyed child with a naive notion about teaching and learning. But I had a lot to learn.

"Clernest pastors here at the Living Faith Baptist Church in the Delta," Renee told us in describing her development as an expert teacher. "Our four children all attended public school in this same small town. I became very well known to my students and their families in ways outside my role as a high school teacher."

Figure 4.4

Renee Moore gets to know each of her students and differentiates lesson plans based on their needs.

Photo courtesy of Renee Moore.

Understanding Cultural Context

Renee understands where her students are coming from, literally and figuratively—and she worries about giving too much homework. "They are taking care of their elderly grandparents or their very young child; they have to work several jobs." Renee's work is about her students as learners in their larger life context. She demonstrates the importance of not just having enormous pedagogical skill but also knowing students in their cultural context. "I meet them where they are, and help them go to a place about which they have never known," she said.

"I worked with inner-city youth of Detroit for years, but I had to learn a lot when I moved here to the Delta," Renee said. "And if it had not been for many teachers who came before me, I would not have learned how to teach like I do now." She continued,

> There were many veteran teachers who took time with me: Francis Isaac, Ruth Smith, Ned Tolliver, Maye Martin, and other great teachers I listened to and watched. I learned a lot about teaching and how I think about students from them. They took me to their side. I spent a lot of hours after school talking with them about what worked in the classroom and what did not. I learned to learn about my students' families from them. It was like the old Southern tradition, when the older ladies would sit on the porch and have the younger women around them.
>
> They taught me so much about teaching. But the first thing they taught me was what it meant to be a teacher in the black community; they taught about teachers in the Delta and how we needed to carry ourselves; they taught me the expectations that Delta families would have for me; and then they taught me how to teach English. That was at East Side High School, my foundational years.

"From whom did you learn the most?" we asked.

"One of my strongest influences was Mrs. Grenell," Renee responded quickly. Dorothy Grenell, who taught English for forty years at East Side High School, was the teacher Renee replaced when she was hired for her first teaching position. Mrs. Grenell taught Renee a great deal and also bolstered her confidence in what she could do as a teacher and a leader.

> She lived across the street from the school. I would sometimes go over to her house after school during that first year. I would go there with tears and say that I couldn't do it, and she would say, "You're doing alright, and they're going to be fine." She gave me her lesson plans and teaching notes. I still use some today. But she also taught me how to get along with coworkers and the Delta customs and

why people say the things they say and why they do what they do, and how to deal with the school board that was not used to a stand-up African American woman from Detroit.

We had a chance to meet with Mrs. Grenell, who has meant so much to Renee as a teacher as well as a mentor. When we asked her what advice she would give to new teachers, she said:

> You have to be committed. You have to know your capabilities and your limitations. You need a sincere love for children. Find yourself a mentor. Don't be afraid to ask questions. Be sincere; never give up. But the best advice I can give you is what my English teacher, Mrs. Mineola Thompson, told me:
>
> > There's a destiny that makes us brothers
> > No one goes this way alone.
> > What we send into the lives of others
> > Will come back into our own.

Figure 4.5

Renee Moore, right, poses with her mentor Dorothy Grenell.

Photo courtesy of Renee Moore.

Renee reminded us that there were numerous African American veteran teachers of the desegregation era—like Mrs. Grenell—who "taught with grace and unwavering faith under conditions most of us could not imagine." In reflecting on the typical new recruit to teaching in the Delta, and her own experiences with "older" teachers who nurtured her development, Renee said to us, "A lot of young teachers would not listen to [these veteran teachers], which is their peril. These women were wise. They had forgotten more about how to teach than some of us know to do now."

It was then that Renee expanded our understanding of teacher leadership, and taught us a core principle of teacherpreneurism. In reflecting on how she learned to teach and lead, she told us: "We are not necessarily the best and the brightest; we are the beneficiaries and reflectors of the accumulated accomplishments of our profession."

Illuminating the Complexity of Teaching

But there is more to Renee as an expert teacher and leader. Renee is a writer—and a very good one.

> I have always been practicing my writing. Sitting down next to people and helping them write, that was marvelous training and fairly serendipitous in my preparation for being a teacher. I tutored others when I was in college; I did the National Writing Project the summer before I started teaching, and later I received a DeWitt Wallace Readers Digest Fellowship to complete my Master of Arts in English at the Bread Loaf School at Middlebury College. [But what is most important is that] I have learned so much from other teachers about their teaching and their writing.

In the late 1990s Renee was one of the first teachers to publish virally—via the Web site of the Carnegie Foundation for the Advancement of Teaching—about the "what," "why," and "how" of her "culturally engaged" teaching in Shelby, Mississippi, and her effectiveness in teaching Standard English to rural African American students. In Renee's published videos and commentaries, she shows and explains what it takes to teach effectively (see http://gallery.carnegiefoundation.org /collections/castl_k12/rmoore/).

In examining Renee's Carnegie Foundation Web pages, you see lesson plans, videos of her teaching, and student work and her analysis of it. Thomas Hatch, a professor of education at Teachers College, Columbia University,

Figure 4.6

This page on the Carnegie Foundation for the Advancement of Teaching's Web site is about Renee Moore and her teaching practice.

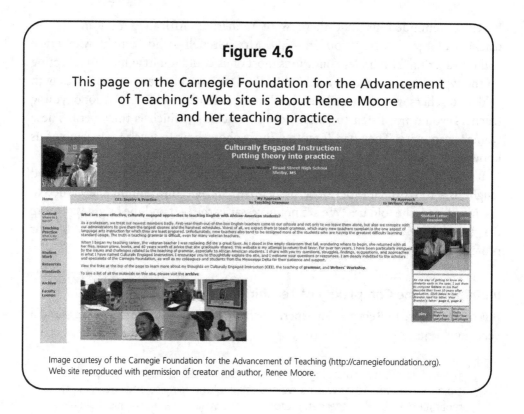

Image courtesy of the Carnegie Foundation for the Advancement of Teaching (http://carnegiefoundation.org). Web site reproduced with permission of creator and author, Renee Moore.

who worked with Renee during her teaching fellowship at the Carnegie Foundation, told us:

> Renee's teaching is akin to the sounds created by expert jazz musicians. She appears to be improvising and making it up as she goes along. But she is highly disciplined and very strategic about what she does from moment to moment as she works with students. It is hard to see her artistry and expertise—much like with the jazz musician—as she pays attention to multiple factors at the same time. She has a plan but adapts it constantly as she reads what her students know and can do.

The Web pages, filled with her analysis of classroom practice, trace how she designs and uses tools like Personal English Plans to help students determine their own strengths and weaknesses relative to curriculum standards and expectations, as well as how she creates classroom cultures so those who successfully "master" a particular skill objective take responsibility for assisting their peers. On the Carnegie Foundation Web site, she writes:

I have found that downplaying competition within the classroom tends to increase students' individual motivation to achieve in order for the entire group to advance together. This cooperative spirit actually flows from the culture of this very rural, very religious African American community. To truly engage students in academic or scholarly work, they must be convinced that work has value for who they are and where they live, not just for some generic future.[13]

It is no wonder Renee has been named her state's Teacher of Year and has been recognized with a $25,000 award by the Milken Family Foundation for excellence in teaching. She is National Board Certified. In 2001, she became the first practicing teacher to sit on the board of directors of the Carnegie Foundation.

Her prolific writing includes work with Thomas Hatch and colleagues, who edited the book *Going Public with Our Teaching*, a result of Renee's (and other teachers') involvement with the Carnegie Foundation.[14] Hatch and colleagues wrote about Renee and other teacher leaders, detailing how they don't take "no" for an answer in terms of their efforts to lead reforms.

In reflecting on how teachers "can influence policy, advance research, and improve [student] performance," Hatch and colleagues make it clear in their book that "there is no single formula or prototype that defines what kinds of teachers have an impact on others."[15] And they are equally clear that the expertise and leadership of these excellent teachers do not just grow out of their "innate abilities and forces of will."[16] "Instead of relying on formal roles and explicit organizational authority," they argue, "building on the power of teachers may depend on recognizing and supporting the informal networks through which ideas and influence can travel."[17] Renee exemplifies how a twenty-five-year teaching veteran translates her pedagogical expertise into policy leadership.

Renee, as described by Hatch and colleagues, is both a "quiet thinker" and "forceful crusader."[18] In a recent interview, Hatch told us:

Whatever she does, she leads. She always learns from what she does, but unlike most people, she then acts on it. It is not just about self-reflection—it is about a constant drive to get better. It is also about her ability to not just record and reflect on her practice but also represent it to a wide variety of audiences. She is expert in using metaphors to explain the complexity of teaching. She is expert in helping others understand the complexity of teaching even when she has left the room. Teachers like Renee can be developed—if they have the platform and the support needed to cultivate representations of their teaching.

We have known Renee since we found her pedagogical expertise on display by the Carnegie Foundation and sought her out to be part of our virtual community of teacher leaders. Renee has been a mover and shaker for several Center for Teaching Quality (CTQ) TeacherSolutions projects,* including ones on pay for performance (2007) and new student assessments and teacher evaluation (2011), and she contributed to the book *Teaching 2030*. And drawing on her 2010 white paper,[19] which she orchestrated and developed with guidance from CTQ Collaboratory members, she has pushed the National Council for the Accreditation of Teacher Education's (NCATE's) Blue Ribbon Panel on Clinical Preparation to invest more in practicing teachers in forging ahead with its recommendations. Despite Renee's growing presence nationally, especially in regard to teacher preparation, her leadership is ignored by local teacher education programs in dire need of expertise. But she recognizes the slow pace of school reform, especially efforts that concentrate on both excellence and equity. She stays steady and focused, influencing where she can.

> Instead of relying on formal roles and explicit organizational authority, building on the power of teachers may depend on recognizing and supporting the informal networks through which ideas and influence can travel.
> —Thomas Hatch,
> Melissa Eiler White,
> & Deborah Faigenbaum

In a 2009 blog, posted appropriately on July 4, Renee wrote:

> For years, I was told that good teachers did not "get involved in politics." The virtuous teacher was the one who just locked herself in the classroom and devoted all her energies to the challenges of teaching. I soon learned, however, that everything about education in America is political, and there were some very uninformed or under-informed people off somewhere making crucial decisions about what I should, could, or must do with the students for whom I am responsible.[20]

Like Stephen and the other teacher leaders we profile, Renee will not just sit back and wait for others who are in control to let teachers have a voice in serious matters of pedagogy and policy. Both Stephen and Renee are very strategic. They make themselves visible. And they will not let anyone else's pedagogy or policy be their "religion." Finally, as they become visible, they are more likely to help elevate the profession in ways that transcend its complicated and rocky past—the focus of our next chapter.

---

* Since 2006, CTQ has developed and refined a systematic TeacherSolutions process to engage and support teacher leaders in dissecting research findings and applying them to their teaching experience as well as crafting and communicating policy solutions.

● Chapter Four Selected Web Sites

Following is a list of online resources that relate to the discussion in this chapter. If you find that any of these links no longer work, please try entering the information in a search engine.

Renee Moore's blog post "Test to the Teach(ing)—Not Vice Versa": http://www.teachingquality.org/content/test-teaching–not-vice-versa

National Center for Fair and Open Testing: http://www.fairtest.org/reports-high-stakes-testing-hurts-education

Institute for Student Achievement: http://www.studentachievement.org/

Stephen Lazar's blog: http://stephenlazar.com/blog/

Gotham Schools: http://gothamschools.org

New York Times article on New York City public school teacher evaluations: http://www.nytimes.com/2012/02/26/nyregion/in-new-york-teacher -ratings-good-test-scores-arent-always-good-enough.html

Center for Civic Education (which sponsors Project Citizen): http://new.civiced .org/

Gotham Schools article highlighting Stephen Lazar's teaching: http://gothamschools.org/2012/03/21/students-look-close-to-home-for -civic-engagement-lessons/

Gotham Schools article on why Stephen Lazar started his own school: http://gothamschools.org/2012/09/25/why-im-starting-a-school-the -particular-answer/

Agnon High School: http://www.agnon.org/

Commission on Effective Teaching and Teachers 2011 report: http://www.nea.org/assets/docs/Transformingteaching2012.pdf

Carnegie Foundation for the Advancement of Teaching, featuring Renee Moore's teaching: http://insideteaching.org/quest/collections/sites/moore_renee/archive.htm

Going Public with Our Teaching book Web site: http://www.goingpublicwithteaching.org/index.html

CTQ TeacherSolutions project on New Student Assessments and Teacher Evaluation: http://bit.ly/YWapwQ

Renee Moore's white paper for NCATE's Blue Ribbon Panel, *Teacher Leaders Advise on Clinical Preparation*: http://www.ncate.org/LinkClick.aspx ?fileticket=h6o66KQ1Vdw%3D&tabid=715

Activity for Chapter Four

Now What?

Trace the Evidence: Linking "Why" to "How"

Goal

After reading Chapter Three, you reflected on the philosophies that guide your pedagogy and practice. From the examples set by Stephen and Renee, we know that teacherpreneurs are able to make these beliefs visible through their words and deeds. We'll now return to the themes you previously identified and trace the evidence that reinforces these values.

Think

Revisit the themes you identified after reading Chapter Three and transfer them to the chart that follows. Then, for each theme, consider evidence from your practice that supports this belief—*how* do you make this value visible through your actions?

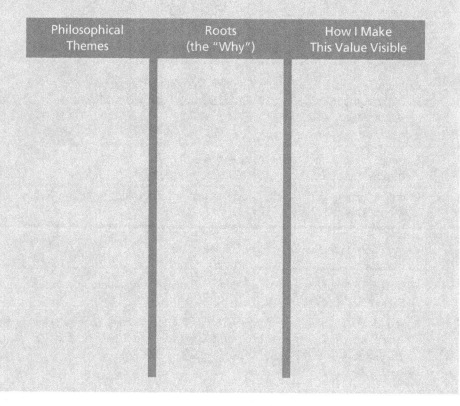

Philosophical Themes	Roots (the "Why")	How I Make This Value Visible

When considering evidence, we encourage you to be as specific as possible and to dig deeply into your practice as a teacher and teacher leader. Possible evidence may include (but certainly is not limited to) ways that you organize and execute

- Classroom design
- Student assessments
- Communication and collaboration strategies
- Lesson structures
- Outreach efforts to parents and the community
- Work and action beyond your classroom or school

Act

Evaluate your updated chart. Which beliefs are most visible within your practice as a teacher leader? Where is there room for additional development and alignment of your beliefs with the practices that represent them to the wider world?

Now, consider areas where this alignment is already firmly in place. What strategies (in and beyond your classroom) might you extend to improve alignment in other areas? You may also want to research new practices and strategies you could implement within your classroom. Choose two approaches to focus on first and create a plan for incorporating them.

Share

Debrief this activity with a colleague within your school or the CTQ Collaboratory (http://www.teachingquality.org). How are your colleague's beliefs represented in his or her words and deeds? Exchange strategies to implement in both of your classrooms.

CHAPTER 5

Transcending Teaching's Past

● *The revolution in teaching is about ready to begin.*

—Shannon C'de Baca

The history of the teaching profession in America is stormy and convoluted—and often framed by the struggle to determine not only who teaches what and how, but also under what conditions they do so and at what cost. Schools are filled with excellent teachers, including the ones we profile here, who can lead the way in transcending teaching's past—an endeavor that is presently complicated by ill-informed policy leaders, rigid-minded reformers, and union leaders who are set in their ways.

The stories of two teacher leaders, Shannon C'de Baca and José Vilson, tell us much about how those who teach can transform their profession. We focus on Shannon and José because of *how* they are leading. In this chapter, we go back and forth between José's and Shannon's stories because together, and in coordination with their colleagues whom they join in *Teacherpreneurs*, they exemplify the transcendence of teaching's past.

SHANNON, AN ONLINE PIONEER

Shannon, a sixty-year-old Latina with thirty-eight years of award-winning teaching experience in science, lives in three locales: Nebraska, New Mexico, and Hawaii. After three decades of teaching in brick-and-mortar schools, she now teaches for

Iowa Learning Online with a teacherpreneurial reach that enhances her work with high school students. "The core of what I do is the same as what I did in the classroom with a technological twist," explains Shannon. "It is doggedly communicating with kids." Her online interaction with one student, Andrew Gibbs, exemplifies her online teaching.

Example of Online Teacher-Student Communication

10:22 Online chat notification: Andrew Gibbs has just beeped you!

10:22 Andrew: question on marble lab what's the group data

10:23 Shannon: hi Andrew

10:23 Shannon: Group data is the data you post and pull off the wiki

10:23 Andrew: ok

10:23 Shannon: The wiki can be found on the homepage in the upper left hand corner. There is a link.

10:24 Andrew: thanks

10:27 Andrew: OK, I see it. That helps. Do we average the group data?

10:28 Shannon: well yes and no. There is a calculation in the lab directions for the group data. But basically all you do is use the compilation of the group data so that you can use the same calculation and have more data to work with.

10:28 Andrew: ok

10:28 Shannon: So, the width of the field and all that stays the same

10:28 Shannon: But the number of trials and the number of hits/misses changes

10:29 Andrew: ok we used a smaller field 34.5cm but I see 12 other groups who used that width should I just use their data?

10:29 Shannon: Yes, that is good. Tell me why you think [you] should only use that data? Want me to look at the group data and help you work through it?

> The core of what I do is the same as what I did in the classroom with a technological twist. It is doggedly communicating with kids.
> —Shannon C'de Baca

The kind of flexible schedule Shannon has carved out for herself allows her also to mentor out-of-field chemistry teachers in rural high-need schools—that is, those teachers assigned to teach chemistry without the preparation or background to do so. After she taught herself "a bit of Arabic," she began to consult and teach colleagues in Bahrain, "who became hungry for online learning and wanted to expand their pedagogical skills." Shannon's teaching has been recognized with honors from the Milken Family Foundation, the National Science Teachers Association, the Iowa Department of Education, Sertoma, and PBS—on the televised series *Using NOVA in the Classroom*. She gives her chemistry students, anytime and anywhere, opportunities to learn such concepts as "pressure" through the study of submarines, secrets, and spies. She has also hosted the Annenberg Foundation–funded television series *The Missing Link in Mathematics*, which to this day she is eager to improve.

Shannon is relentless about maintaining and improving the quality of her work, and in teacherpreneurial fashion she is always the first one to identify how she can improve on what others would think would be a grand success. She is a pioneer in the Wild West of online learning, a domain in which she has accomplished what few have: the development of a vibrant virtual community of learners. She uses Skype and Adobe Connect Pro and two-way audio and video to work with kids—but also understands the importance of "visual cues" in knowing students. Shannon has developed an expansive pedagogical repertoire to adapt to online learning in ways often ignored by today's education entrepreneurs.

JOSÉ, A SEEKER AND POWERFUL SPEAKER

José, a thirty-year-old born in New York City who is immensely proud of his Dominican and Haitian heritage (his parents were born and raised on the island of Hispaniola), has been teaching for seven years. After a brief stint in the world of computer science, he entered teaching to serve "kids just like [him]" in the Washington Heights neighborhood of Manhattan. Even with his deep knowledge of the children of Washington Heights and his tutoring experiences while majoring in computer science at Syracuse University, José was not well prepared for teaching. Entering the profession through the New York Teaching Fellows Program, having gone through only a five-week training program modeled after Teach For America's, José struggled in his "classroom of the most diverse students with widely varied learning needs." But like his colleagues highlighted in this book, José learned to develop a "collaborative spirit" and improve his teaching over time. In many ways, José attributes his "relentless search" for a way of teaching more effectively to his own parochial school teachers whom he watched "sitting down" and "figuring out" problems together. "I think I began my journey as a teacher leader back then," José told us, "because with parochial education the reality is that administrators don't matter when it comes to teaching; teachers run the instructional show."

José's TEDxNYED Talk

José is a committed poet, writer, Web designer, and community organizer. He has consulted for the General Electric Foundation to advance new ideas for educators; created assessment tasks and developed curriculum maps for

http://bit.ly/W2JNaE

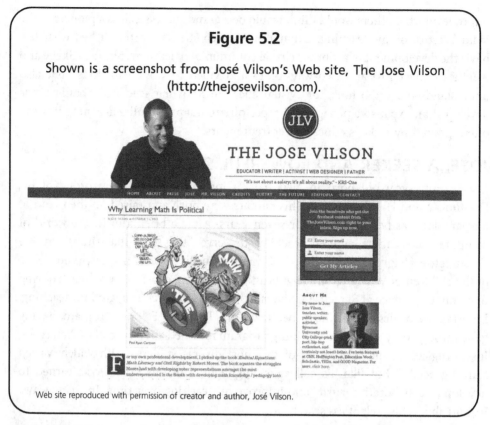

Figure 5.2

Shown is a screenshot from José Vilson's Web site, The Jose Vilson (http://thejosevilson.com).

Web site reproduced with permission of creator and author, José Vilson.

José at SOS

http://bit.ly/XatKa3

his school; and served as a fellow with the Acentos Foundation, a Bronx-based organization dedicated to the development, discussion, and dissemination of poetry and literature by Latino/a writers. His blog posts have won numerous awards, and his writing not only appears on his own Web site, The Jose Vilson, but also has been featured by Black Web 2.0, the *Chicago Sun-Times*, CNN.com, Gotham Schools, *New York Magazine*'s "Daily Intelligencer," and Time Out New York.

His passionate and powerful manner and intelligent humility are beginning to spread virally, and he has gotten recognition for videos of his talk on teacher voice at TEDxNYED (a New York City–based TEDx event focused on education) as well as "This Is Not a Test"—a fiery poem delivered at the Save Our Schools (SOS) march in Washington DC in July 2011.

THE GENDERED HISTORY OF TEACHING

For most of the profession's history, teachers have not been expected by either policymakers or administrators to lead. Initially, America's teachers were hired solely to transmit values and to teach students the basic skills of the day. Historians have documented that teaching has been constrained as a profession because teachers, primarily female, have been expected to perform numerous custodial responsibilities in the service of children and their families.[1] For most of the occupation's past, women not only have worked for much cheaper wages, but also have been seen as more "naturally" inclined to teach children in a job that was thought not to require a great deal of intelligence.

Of course, the women introduced in *Teacherpreneurs*, as well as hundreds of thousands of their colleagues, provide poignant evidence to the contrary. Teachers, both male and female, are often admired by parents for their service, but just as often they bear the brunt of disdain when public education is being criticized. And they are typically appreciated for serving children, but mocked for their assumed lack of intellectual ability and their perceived inability to compete in the larger labor market. Indeed, the younger the student, the less status his or her teachers hold. Even in prestigious professions, like medicine, pediatricians earn less than any number of specialists.[2] In other words, in America, taking care of the young has never generated much prestige for any occupational group.

In explaining the struggle to professionalize teaching, education historian Kate Rousmaniere could not have said it more eloquently:

> The history of teaching in America is a history rife with political dynamics, social drama, and philosophical debate. It is also a history of a class of workers struggling with economic insecurity and social ambiguity while at the same time striving for their own understanding of professional excellence.[3]

Even today, mobilizing teacher leaders to transform their profession is undermined by society's devaluing of women as leaders in organizational life. The documentary film *Miss Representation*[4] draws back the curtain on "how mainstream media contribute to the under-representation of women in positions of power and influence in America"—revealing why policymakers and reformers continue to resist the professionalization of teaching.[5] The film paints a bleak portrait of how, even in twenty-first-century America, our nation ranks ninetieth worldwide in female representation in legislatures, as "a woman's value and power lie in her youth, beauty, and sexuality, and not in her capacity as a leader."[6]

Shannon told us:

> I remember, when I started teaching and coaching volleyball, hearing one of my male peers say within earshot, "How could you pay Shannon as much as 'Bob' who coaches cross-country?" The gender bias was palpable. There is this rich history in education of encouraging men to be administrators and be in more of that powerful sphere of influence. And this history is still with us today, in 2012. In my entire career, I have had only two female administrators. Resistance to teacherpreneurism today comes from policymakers' limited views of teachers versus administrators versus leaders of reform, and who needs to be in charge of whom.

Perhaps it is because of gender bias that very few of today's reforms focus on teachers as an investment to be made. Instead, teachers are treated more as an expense to be lowered. As more females entered teaching beginning in the nineteenth century, they were barred from being married and often taught in exchange for room and board. They were paid considerably less than their male counterparts. The single-salary schedule, a twentieth-century policy invention, was instituted to countermand "overt" gender and later racial discrimination.[7] For many decades now, male and female teachers have been paid the same. But teacher leadership may very well be undermined, we note with serious chagrin, because today the large majority of teachers—76 percent—are women.

TEACHING AS A "SEMI-PROFESSION"

Teaching has been examined closely for a very long time by a wide array of scholars representing varied disciplines. In fact, both Willard Waller's text *The Sociology of Teaching*, which explored teaching before the Great Depression, and Dan Lortie's civil rights–era book *Schoolteacher* address the systematic devaluing of teachers that is still present in American society today. Both speak, with rich empirical evidence, of how school hierarchies isolate and divide teachers and devalue the knowledge and expertise they possess. Waller claimed that in the late 1920s policymakers and administrators sought and demanded teachers with the kind of personality that would allow them to "conform to the necessities of the authority."[8] Waller's illustrative example of a teacher contract depicts teachers' place within the educational hierarchy:

> I promise to remember that I owe a duty to the townspeople who are paying me my wages, that I owe respect to the school board and the superintendent that hired me, and that I shall consider myself at all times the willing servant of the school board and the townspeople.[9]

Like Waller, in *Schoolteacher* Lortie asserts that teachers are trained for conformity rather than creativity. In one chapter, "Divide and Conquer," Lortie discusses the importance of rank and position throughout school systems. He concludes that principals are afraid of central administrators who are afraid of school boards—and that each of the three conspires to keep teachers on the bottom rung of the organizational ladder (above only students). Lortie pointedly addresses egg-crate schools, in which teachers spend most of their work time isolated in their individual classrooms, that stifle both collaboration and leadership.[10]

In 1996 the National Commission on Teaching and America's Future—under the leadership of Linda Darling-Hammond—argued that schools are organized as a "vestige of the Taylor [or factory] model of industrial management from the 1920s, in which jobs are broken up and highly specialized, and some staff are supposed to think, plan, and coordinate work while others are supposed to do it."[11]

In some ways not much has changed since the 1920s, the 1970s, or the 1990s. Teachers are still working in what sociologists like Lortie call a "semi-profession," in which standards of practice are defined by individuals outside of the classroom who know little of what it means to teach effectively in a real-world context.

> Left alone in their classrooms, teachers are not likely to play a major role in defining and improving the core features of their work, another marker of professionalism.
>
> —Elena Silva

Elena Silva, then writing for Education Sector, a Washington DC–based think tank, noted a few years back:

> Studies of the modern work force, across industries, show several markers of professional work. For one, workers are networked in teams—in person or virtually. Teachers, however, typically work alone for most of the roughly 52 hours a week they spend managing, instructing, grading, and planning for hundreds of students with a wide range of needs and skill levels. Even brand-new teachers, nearly a fifth of whom have not had a single hour of classroom training prior to beginning, learn to navigate this complicated world of work by themselves.

Figure 5.3

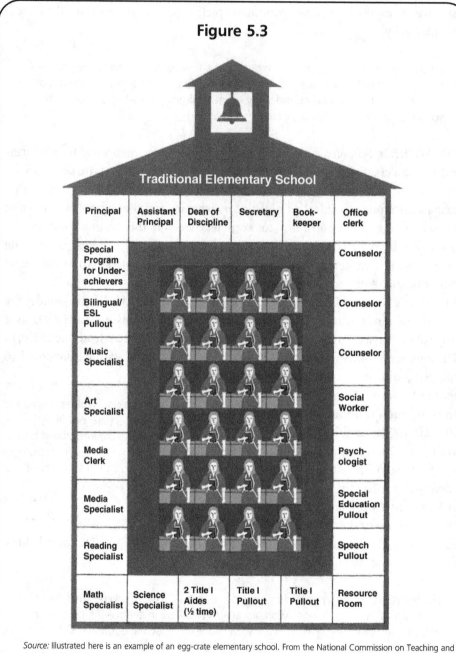

Traditional Elementary School

Principal	Assistant Principal	Dean of Discipline	Secretary	Book-keeper	Office clerk
Special Program for Under-achievers					Counselor
Bilingual/ ESL Pullout					Counselor
Music Specialist					Counselor
Art Specialist					Social Worker
Media Clerk					Psych-ologist
Media Specialist					Special Education Pullout
Reading Specialist					Speech Pullout
Math Specialist	Science Specialist	2 Title I Aides (½ time)	Title I Pullout	Title I Pullout	Resource Room

Source: Illustrated here is an example of an egg-crate elementary school. From the National Commission on Teaching and America's Future report, What Matters Most (1996), p. 106.

Left alone in their classrooms, teachers are not likely to play a major role in defining and improving the core features of their work, another marker of professionalism.[12]

Arthur Wise, former president of the National Council on Accreditation of Teacher Education (and chair of the board of directors of the Center for Teaching Quality [CTQ]), summed up where we are in the teacher leader movement:

I think the frustration of teachers, accomplished teachers—teacher leaders and now teacherpre-neurs—is beginning to really show. They are busting to get out of the cage because they know they have the knowledge and skill to reform the field in ways that allow their expertise to extend not just to the twenty-five or thirty students in front of them but also to hundreds or even thousands more by virtue of their influence on other teachers. This has happened in other fields. Why has that not happened in our field? Why do we not have that level of confidence in teachers? We need a revolution.

Conversation: Arthur Wise and Barnett Berry

http://bit.ly/14EqZm9

A SMALL REVOLUTION BEGINS

José entered teaching thirty years after the publication of *Schoolteacher*, but he found many of the same conditions Lortie documented:

When I began teaching at Inwood Junior High School 52, most teachers were so accustomed to working solo, and they all had so few opportunities to learn new teaching strategies. And they were so beaten down by Department of Education administrators who said "no."

So when I suggested new approaches, they would say, "That's not going to work for me." I then showed them what we could do about it, connecting to social and health services, communicating with parents, divvying up responsibilities. It did not take long for us to learn how to work as a team.

José has led a small revolution in how teachers in his Washington Heights school work with one another—and now he often blogs and speaks about school reform. The Jose Vilson, over four years and the one thousand–plus posts published, also connects readers, including his teaching colleagues, to lesson plans and "bridges to practices" that would not be shared without the Internet. José's writing often chastises both "higher-ups" and his fellow teachers who are "still waiting for manna [or the right program] to drop from the sky."[13] With eloquence, he reveals how policy leaders actually promote the status quo with their accountability schemes; he often disregards what some consider to be union protocols to deliver what he believes kids need; he takes umbrage with teachers who uncritically critique the Common Core State Standards; and, in his "open letter" to New York school commissioner John King, he makes a powerful case that standardized testing is not natural in the realm of teaching and learning.[14] He teaches "no excuses" school reformers about the difference between an excuse and a reason. But unlike pundits on the typical two sides of a policy issue, José has solutions and takes risks: "In other words, just get it done. Ask real questions. And know the ledge before you jump off it."[15]

José takes on reformers like Joel Klein, during whose tenure as the chancellor of the New York City public schools the achievement gap widened between black and Latino/a students and white and Asian students, despite his rhetoric about improving the lives of all students. And he speaks boldly to why we all must do more to attract and retain black and Latino male teachers like himself. Only 2 percent of our nation's teachers are black men.[16]

José's Caribbean roots have something to do with his connectivity with the students he teaches. So does his embrace of pop culture and his skill in using poetry and hip-hop music to communicate with his students. When visiting José's room at Inwood 52, we had a chance to sit down with students from one of his eighth-grade math classes, in which an atmosphere of trust was unmistakable.

We asked students to wait until José left the room, and then, with unbridled enthusiasm, they began to talk at once—with phrases like "he makes us think," he is "very funny," he has "so much patience," and "I am more confident that I can learn when he teaches me." Then Ashley, whom José inspired to engage in community service (and who now wants to be a teacher), got her peers to settle down so she could be heard loud and clear: "I think Mr. Vilson is a really great teacher. In the seventh grade I used to have problems with math, but with his way of teaching I don't. Now it clicks for me. He really knows all of us."

Principals who embrace teacher leaders like José can be catalysts to move the profession forward. Sal Fernandez, who not only taught previously at Inwood 52 but

Figure 5.4

José Vilson is shown with one of his students in his New York City middle school.

Photo courtesy of Alan Wieder.

also spent his junior high school years there, is one such principal. Sal spoke about changing school culture—a process that included José's work as a teacher leader.

> We took that school, which had a lot of challenges. Then we started building this teacher-led mind-set of collaboration. I felt that the teachers really needed to have more input. So I developed an instructional team. I let the assistant principals continue doing their administrative duties, but I know the system and found a

way to build more hybrid roles for teacher leaders like José. We started looking at student work, not just test scores. We did it together. We listened to each other. This is how we have developed our own teacher framework.

José was placed in a hybrid role as math teacher and coach, as well as data analyst and Web developer. His job was to fuel collaboration among teachers inside of Inwood 52, using a new tool he created to examine student performance across the core content areas as well as a Web site he designed to communicate more effectively with the community of Washington Heights.

As we walked down a long hallway in Inwood 52 with a small group of teachers, one of José's colleagues told us:

> José inspires me. He teaches in my room once a week, and I have a chance to see him teach. Right from the beginning, he develops a very strong rapport with his students so there is a very strong level of trust in the class. They aren't afraid to ask him for help. There is mutual respect. Respect is a big thing for our kids. If they feel respected they will follow you.

When we asked about their team meetings, another colleague said:

> He never monopolizes the conversation. He respects us. He knows that all of us are experts. He lets us voice our opinions. He is a good listener, but at the same time he has been very supportive of the math teachers and all teachers in the school. He is our coach. José often visits my class and makes suggestions as to my teaching strategies—but he also wants me to offer suggestions to him.

José told us:

> People want to talk to each other now. They want to see how teachers talk to each other now. The difference is, that is a 180 from when I came in. People don't just work in pockets now, they want to go visit each other's classrooms. [Sal] has really pushed us. At some point, he wants to make it like a peer review, where we conduct Japanese lesson studies [a systematic process in which teachers watch and critique each other in teaching the same lesson] to improve our practice and create more accurate evidence on what our students know or do not know.

The writings of both Waller and Lortie addressed the institutional and societal pulls that have kept teachers from becoming leaders and teacherpreneurs. It is important to emphasize that neither book represented teachers as victims, but rather portrayed them as part of a top-down hierarchy that teachers needed to transcend. For both scholars, it was the co-opting of teaching by higher-ups that lessened the quality of learning and prohibited those who knew the most about teaching and learning—teachers—from being participants in shaping education policy and spreading their pedagogical expertise.

A CLASSROOM WITHOUT WALLS

Shannon's emergence as an online teacher frees her from many of the structural and temporal constraints that undermine her colleagues' teaching in brick-and-mortar buildings. In an Education Week Teacher article, she wrote:

> I walked into my old high school and was comforted by some of the changes I saw in terms of flexible room arrangements and technology. Then a bell rang and I was back in the 1960s. The students still move from teacher to teacher six to seven times each day. We have made many changes, but we have not altered the most powerful variable in the equation: time.
>
> I teach online—and have seen how time can be used differently. Can . . . and must. I have nine students who work more than 40 hours a week on a family farm, eight that handle a significant share of the child care for their working parent(s), six who work two jobs, and many students who have added my class to an already packed daily schedule. I cannot teach from 9 a.m. to 4 p.m. and meet the needs of all of these kids . . . In my classes, we negotiate my day-to-day schedule.[17]

"In face-to-face teaching I can close my door," Shannon told us. "And I have a self-contained curriculum, and I can teach all day long and not see another human being and be very successful—at least in my mind."

Shannon continued:

> In the online world the doors are wide open—my supervisors and parents can see what is going on whenever they want. It is a very open classroom, which is unnerving to some people but very powerful in that it forces me to work differently and I have to collaborate.

She also pointed out that online work requires a new form of collaboration that includes students as well as teachers.

> The content is always available, and my direct instruction is used much more strategically. Students have a regular video meeting with me twice weekly,

Shannon on Classroom Relationships

http://bit.ly/14pwJkz

often on Skype. I can usually gather them into three or four working groups, and those who miss a meeting catch up using the archived video or e-mail.

I teach chemistry, and I can tell you that deep, abstract knowledge requires some think time. Students need to see a concept several times via a variety of lessons and contexts. My goal for my students has always been mastery, and sometimes it takes students more than a day or even a week to reach deep understanding.

Shannon's online work is about *relationships*—about which she speaks eloquently, as evidenced in the video.

Shannon's online teaching is *not* about finding a quicker and less-expensive way of readying students for standardized testing. It leads to serious learning—and is an example of students and their teacher taking control of time, schooling's most critical commodity. In addition, in many ways Shannon's online teaching charts a path to overcome the egg-crate classroom and, in doing so, make teachers more visible.

RESISTING TRADITIONAL HIERARCHIES

What follows is just a sampling of the efforts Shannon has led over the years. Shannon has . . .

- Increased student enrollment in upper-level science courses by 165 percent at Thomas Jefferson High School in Council Bluffs, Iowa

- Served as a district facilitator of the induction of new teachers

- Written a mentoring handbook for new teachers and mentors in the Omaha, Nebraska, metropolitan area

- Chaired a diversity committee at the state level

- Written and implemented the minority parent involvement plan for four school districts
- Designed and implemented six student engagement programs
- Written curriculum standards for the National Center for Education and the Economy
- Conducted equity reviews of student assessment programs
- Led Teacher-to-Teacher training workshops in ten states
- Created *Using NOVA in the Classroom* videos
- Reviewed and analyzed science and mathematics standards documents (for Florida, Illinois, Maryland, Nebraska, Ohio, and Texas as well as the National Research Council)
- Coordinated the hazardous waste cleanup of district science facilities
- Implemented a science outreach program for elementary schools
- Coached basketball and volleyball
- Spearheaded the development of the Iowa Distance Learning Network
- Consulted for Achieve, the Alliance for Restructuring Education, Basic Education, the Council of Chief State School Officers, Iowa Public Television, the Milken Family Foundation, the National Center on Education and the Economy, the National Education Association, the National Science Teacher Foundation, the New Mexico Department of Education, *Using NOVA in the Classroom*, the U.S. Department of Education, the U.S. Department of Energy, and the U.S. Mint

. . . and she never left the classroom.

During her career, Shannon has never looked for high-profile leadership roles. In fact, in spite of her rambunctious sense of humor, she (like *nearly all* of the teachers we profile) is much more of a noiseless leader, described in greater detail by Susan Cain in her popular book *Quiet: The Power of Introverts in a World That Can't Stop Talking*.[18] Cain makes the case that introverts do not always go hand-in-glove with ideas about power and leadership. And perhaps this is why reformers routinely overlook teachers, who may be more introverted than not, as potential leaders outside their school, district, and state. Often it takes just one or two people to see the quiet power of introverts—and to spur them on to lead.

Elizabeth Stage, who is now director of the world-renowned Lawrence Hall of Science at the University of California, Berkeley, and an elected fellow of the

American Association for the Advancement of Science, was "lucky enough" to meet Shannon some twenty years ago when she (Elizabeth) was leading an effort to promote more rigorous science standards nationwide:

> I remember looking for a diverse group of teachers to build consensus around the future of teaching science in America's schools. There was no diversity except from a group selected by the Iowa Department of Education. There was Shannon sitting in the back of the room—and I soon realized how smart she was, how she used humor to diffuse tense situations, and how good she was at driving change from the backseat. She was a problem solver. She was a one-person civil rights commission of sorts.

Elizabeth told us more about how Shannon uses humor, including a bit of sauciness, in leading. She recognized the basis of the teacherpreneurial skills Shannon has and uses:

> The sense of humor that makes Shannon find the preposterousness in many things creates a great deal of creativity as well as takes on an aura of irreverence. I like that, but many people do not like irreverence in teachers.

Elizabeth continued, "Teachers are used to being in a subordinated position where they are not supposed to publicly question authority. It's a gentleman's agreement between the teachers and principals that what happens in the classroom stays in the classroom." But according to Elizabeth, Shannon learned how to "negotiate a different circumstance"—allowing her to find more and more opportunities to lead in provocative ways. Because Elizabeth clearly understood Shannon's untapped potential to make a huge difference beyond the classroom, she searched for a way to work through Shannon's district bureaucracy to buy out her time. Such a negotiation was an "out of the box" model that required the egg crate to be slightly reshaped. Once this new role had been successfully negotiated, Shannon took full advantage of the precious time it afforded her. "I took that contract and stretched it to the limits, giving me a chance to work with other groups," Shannon said. In recalling her early days of working for education reform on the national stage, Shannon noted:

> In the 1990s I was asked by Marc Tucker and Lauren Resnick—who were big fishes in the education reform world—to work with them on new science standards and assessments. I had learned to translate how I connected to students to how I worked with parents, administrators, and school board members. I used those same skills on the national level. I have always had

professional relationships with a vast array of education stakeholders and quite frankly different segments of our society. I can't remember a time I wasn't occupying a role that wasn't just a little outside the classroom—and it has just grown.

Shannon continued,

> When I got significant push back from my administration I began to do most of my work with outside groups out of my contract hours. The work with PBS and Iowa Public Television gave me an audience outside the school system and a large policy voice in the state. I took those contracts because I love the [television] medium and it gave me a chance to bring my kids into the mix. I did get to use my classroom for filming on multiple projects. That made me view how well my day-to-day work could communicate to an outside audience what I found important to focus on and have the students engage with. I loved those jobs because they gave me a wider view but also, like the student work with the New Standards Project, really improved my practice. I was becoming much better at my craft.

But for Shannon, the "crab-bucket" culture of schools—in which teachers try to undermine their teaching colleagues' efforts to differentiate themselves—prevailed.

> Okay, here is where I tell you that the added attention took a toll. There was some lack of understanding with my colleagues in my building about my work and role. That hurt me as a leader in my building, but my leadership in the state was expanding. But this did not stop me.

Shannon wonders, however, how her career might have been different if she had been able to "manage this all through the district without treating it like two separate jobs." One thing she does know is that there are many teachers like her. "My guess is there are at least 20 percent who are ready to lead and capitalize on opportunities like I have," she said. "Online learning is going to enable us to spread our expertise like never before." Shannon continued, "I may have never wanted or needed to lead from the top. However, I became well-connected plankton. Plankton may be at the lower levels of the ocean food chain, but it is everywhere and you can't get rid of it."

If Shannon is correct, over six hundred thousand teachers are ready to lead in bold ways. So what are the key qualities that undergird their leadership?

Dennis Bartels, executive director of the Exploratorium, a world-renowned museum of science, art, and human perception in San Francisco, also met Shannon two decades ago—and almost immediately saw impressive qualities in her. As an international expert in science education, Dennis has had opportunities, since

Figure 5.5

Shannon C'de Baca speaks about the role of the teacherpreneur.

Photo courtesy of TheCTQTube (http://www.youtube.com/profile?user=thectqtube).

1991, to work with Shannon on developing new standards and assessments. He noted:

> Shannon is uniquely bilingual in both policy and pedagogy. By that I mean she has learned to communicate effectively in both worlds. She is deeply curious about how systems work. If an alien from Mars landed on Earth, some people would be threatened by their differences. They might be afraid and either retreat or lash out. Not Shannon. She would want to know how Martians work. Now if only the Internet can help us cultivate more *Shannons* and make them more known to the public—I bet it can.

As Shannon told us:

> Soon teachers will be able to show to the public what they do—and the benefit they provide to students, families, and community. The public needs to know more than the individual teachers who taught them or their children. They need to know more of them as a collective, both in their community as well as in others. Identifying and elevating teachers, most notably in the eyes of the public, will galvanize enormous possibilities of transformative leadership from the classroom to the Capitol—and everywhere in between. And the demand will

follow. Soon teachers, mobilized through the powerful virtual communities like ours as well as others that will be emulating ours, will bring greater clarity to the complexity of teaching and how and why teacherpreneurism drives the kind of twenty-first-century public education system all students deserve.

Some eighty years ago, Waller argued that schools exist within the "despotic political structure."[19] His analysis (and Lortie's that followed) pointed out how a societal and educational *hierarchy isolates and divides teachers, and devalues the knowledge and expertise that teachers possess*—a system that the teacher leaders like Shannon and José challenge, resist, and contradict. And we agree with Dennis that the Internet will not only help make such teachers more visible but will also help a first generation of teacherpreneurs create more opportunities for those that follow them. In doing so, teaching's past—dominated by stark lines of distinction between those who teach and those who lead—will finally become history. More teachers will lead, more administrators will teach, and in doing so they will blur the lines of distinction between teachers and leaders. With that in mind, in the next chapter we turn to Lori Nazareno, and the role of teacher-led schools in reaching toward teaching's future.

● Chapter Five Selected Web Sites

Following is a list of online resources that relate to the discussion in this chapter. If you find that any of these links no longer work, please try entering the information in a search engine.

Classroom activity from Shannon C'de Baca for *Using NOVA in the Classroom,* a PBS series dedicated to integrating science and technology resources into the classroom:
http://www.pbs.org/wgbh/nova/education/ideas/2602_subsecre.html

Example of Shannon C'de Baca's eLearning workshop:
http://www.paec.org/teacher2teacher/scienceandcsi.html

José Vilson's Web site: http://thejosevilson.com

"On the State of Teacher Voice 2011" by José Vilson: http://www.huffingtonpost.com/jose-vilson/on-the-state-of-teacher-v_b_824359.html

"This Is Not a Test" by José Vilson: https://www.facebook.com/notes/jose-vilson/my-remarks-for-the-sos-march-this-is-not-a-test/10150326716415126

More information about the award-winning documentary *Miss Representation*: http://www.missrepresentation.org/the-film/

"The Reason Why the Black Male 'Crisis' Is a Hoax" by José Vilson: http://www
.huffingtonpost.com/jose-vilson/the-reason-why-the-black-_b_783299.html

Links to additional work by José Vilson:

http://thejosevilson.com/2009/07/07/on-the-reason-why-you-may-only-get
-one-black-male-teacher-ever-in-your-life-if-at-all/

http://thejosevilson.com/2010/08/31/poverty-the-difference-between-a
-reason-and-an-excuse/

http://thejosevilson.com/2010/09/29/the-union-said-i-couldnt-wear-my
-favorite-color-and-other-absurd-assertions-in-education-nation/

http://thejosevilson.com/2012/07/23/a-letter-about-my-view-on-the
-common-core-learning-standards-because-shut-up-isnt-clear-enough/

http://thejosevilson.com/2012/05/29/an-open-letter-to-nys-education
-commissioner-john-b-king-testing-isnt-natural/

Inwood Junior High School 52: http://inwood52.org/

Video and article about Susan Cain's book *Quiet: The Power of Introverts in a
World That Can't Stop Talking*:
http://www.thepowerofintroverts.com/about-the-book/

The Lawrence Hall of Science, UC Berkeley's public science center:
http://www.lawrencehallofscience.org/

American Association for the Advancement of Science: http://www.aaas.org/

Exploratorium: http://www.exploratorium.edu/

Activity for Chapter Five

Now What?

Integrate Outside Interests

Goal

Now that you've given thought to your goals, philosophies, and actions as a teacher, it's time to take inventory of your interests and skills beyond the classroom's walls. Both Shannon and José have found ways to connect their "extracurricular" interests and activities to their teaching. From coaching a sport to designing Web sites, taking on leadership roles beyond the classroom is a key characteristic of a teacherpreneur. Not only do you get to spend time doing what you love, but you can also invest energy toward helping your colleagues, students, and school.

Think

What skills, hobbies, or interests do you have that could intersect with your role as a teacher leader? How do these match up with needs you see in your school community or in your district? Do you like to write? Consider starting a blog about a topic in education you care about. Do you like to read? Maybe you could start an education book club at your school. Have a penchant for technology? Host an informal HTML tutorial over lunch. Like photography? Start a photography club after school. (Think about ways you might partner with your colleagues as well. For example, see if the physical education teacher wants to partner in starting a yoga club.)

Act

Once you've pinpointed a few areas you'd like to focus on, develop an action plan to make it happen. Some questions to consider:

1. Do you need any permissions or approvals before starting? If so, which people do you need to contact? (If your idea is self-reliant—for example, starting a Twitter account to share your thoughts on the Common Core State Standards—you might want to reach out to teachers with successful Twitter accounts, who will probably be glad to offer you tips and guidance.)

2. How much time will this require? (See Chapter Eight's activity for more on calendar planning.)

3. What supports and supplies will you need? Identify some ways you could get them, drawing on colleagues and CTQ Collaboratory members to help you.

Share

Join a discussion thread within the CTQ Collaboratory (http://www.teachingquality.org), through which you can brainstorm ideas with colleagues and the teacherpreneurs profiled in this book. Your teaching peers can help you connect to people and resources to get started. And sharing what you've been doing to integrate your interests with your teaching career might just inspire another teacher to do something similar.

Cultivating Teacherpreneurs for Teacher-Led Schools

● *There are lots and lots of teachers who can lead like me.*

—Lori Nazareno

The teaching career of Lori Nazareno captures a great deal about the cultivation of teacherpreneurs for tomorrow's schools, many of which will be led by those who still teach. Her story is not just about her pedagogical skill, carefully developed over decades, or her ongoing quest to find out where and why others teach effectively. Her story is not about her teaching honors and earning advanced certificates of accomplished teaching, or about creating her own nonprofit to support teacher leaders in spite of the intransigence of district administrators and benign neglect by union leaders. Lori's leadership story is also not just about how she came to incubate an idea for a teacher-led school, and then executed it.

Lori is an introvert who exemplifies the types of individuals Susan Cain has described in *Quiet: The Power of Introverts in a World That Can't Stop Talking*—those who know how to focus internally and still create and innovate.[1] She is also a cultivator of teacher leaders. Her leadership is not about her. It is, however, all about collaboration and systems. And in spite of the fact that she is strong and somewhat self-made, as you will see later in the chapter, she clearly credits her National Board Certification and her colleagues in the Center for Teaching

Quality (CTQ) Collaboratory with helping her cultivate her pedagogy and leadership:

> Okay, if you live on an island, you only know the island. The Collaboratory was like I took the boat to the mainland and it was like, wow, there's a whole world out there. There's a whole bunch of other people, and they want to do some of the same things that I want to do, and some have done more, and I can learn from them.

In addition, she cites three teachers as leadership role models—Ann Byrd, Renee Moore, and Kathy Wiebke, all National Board Certified as well. Lori reflected on women and teacher leadership historically:

> You know, in a profession dominated by women there aren't a whole lot of role models in terms of teacher leadership—especially ten to fifteen years ago. Then, administrators didn't know what we were talking about in terms of teachers leading their profession. In the case of Ann and Renee, I looked to them and they provided really good role models of how to be strong and assertive to stand up for your beliefs and values—but to do so in a way that you can be heard, not in a whiny, complaining, bitchy sort of way. Women are subjected to so much criticism, even if they are exhibiting exactly the same behavior as men. Women get labeled as a bitch when they are really just being assertive and standing up for what they believe in.

Specifically speaking about Ann and Kathy, she added:

> They're just really good role models of what a professional woman in education would look like, but also they have created and run pretty influential organizations that have been proactive and solutions oriented. They have taught me a lot.

MATH AND SCIENCE LEADERSHIP ACADEMY (DENVER, COLORADO)

As a cofounder of the teacher-led Math and Science Leadership Academy (MSLA), Lori, with her own brand of low-key leadership, has shown how teachers can transcend the raucous policy debates over evaluation and tenure as well as testing and accountability, and create their own school that teaches the whole child—with twenty-first-century learning in mind, and without sacrificing the basic skills of the past or future.

Nestled in southwest Denver, MSLA is a vibrant school for a community of immigrant families seeking a rich educational experience for its children. Launched in 2009, MSLA offers students a technologically infused, child-centered, inquiry-based approach to teaching and learning. All of the school's 350 students, even the youngest ones, engage in service learning that allows them to connect academics to real-life applications that enhance the local community. Despite the high-stakes accountability system promoted by the Denver Public Schools, students at MSLA do not learn "by the numbers"; they learn by doing—writing books, conducting science experiments, and delivering oral histories. They love learning—just as much as teachers love teaching there.

The drive up West Alameda toward South Tejon (the street that is home to MSLA) includes a view of taquerias, Vietnamese restaurants, small shops, and a number of fast-food chains. A left turn toward the school, which shares space with a KIPP Academy franchise, offers a picture of well-cared-for homes perched across the street from the school itself. The Mexican and Vietnamese eateries, as well as the neighborhood houses, foreshadow the diversity and spirit within MSLA and the pride that students, parents, and teachers have in their community. There is a waiting list of parents who want their children to attend MSLA because many of its teachers "can speak their language." Students are taught in Spanish, in English, and in both languages simultaneously. The students themselves have identified several "passion learning" areas that supplement the core curriculum, including cooking, fly-fishing, Legos, bead making, magic, and knitting.

On one of our many visits to MSLA, a parent sitting in the office waiting to pick up her child told us, "The teachers really know us, and our children love to learn here. They are not going to be at this school just for a year or two."

Maria Elena Aceves, the mother of a first grader, noted that she chose MSLA for her son because of his love of science. Because of the ways the teachers teach, he "feels like a leader," and Maria believes this is because MSLA teachers are leaders themselves.

And MSLA has the results to show how teacher leadership can influence student learning—even on conventional measures. MSLA has been in business for three years, serving some of the district's most academically challenged children (70 percent are second-language learners, and 95 percent live in poverty). But in 2012 the school's third graders (who started at MSLA as first graders) exceeded or matched district averages for four out of five assessments, and that fifth assessment was missed by only one percentage point. During this same period, MSLA students showed enormous growth in test score performance, even as teachers questioned the utility of the standardized assessments themselves.

MSLA Third-Grade Standardized Test Scores: Percentages of Students Proficient

	Reading	Writing	Mathematics	Lectura	Escritura
2011	24%	17%	37%	50%	45%
2012	52%	43%	56%	64%	82%
Change 2011–2012	+28 points +117%	+26 points +152%	+19 points +51%	+14 points +28%	+37 points +82%

Although the idea of teacher-led schools isn't unique, it "has gained [some growing] currency as debates rage over the best ways to ensure that teachers can bring up student achievement."[2] Teacher-led schools, by definition, will not be cookie-cutter institutions. That said, they tend to have common characteristics, including small learning communities of teachers, which offer them more opportunities to collaborate with one another as well as build relationships with students; more teacher influence over who is recruited and hired to teach at what grade level and subject; and more flexibility with instruction, including more "control over designing curriculum and ongoing assessments that can engage and challenge students."[3] Lori, after twenty-two years of teaching, worked with other like-minded teaching colleagues and her union, the Denver Classroom Teachers Association, to promote a different approach to school reform—one that has classroom experts leading with this mantra: "Hold us accountable. But let us do it our way."[4]

Lori and her colleagues recognize, unlike many school reformers across the nation as well as in Colorado, that ethics and grit matter more than how students perform on a standardized test built in the twentieth century. The principles on which MSLA is grounded mirror the empirical findings of researchers, such as labor economist C. Kirabo Jackson.[5] His recent study found that students' noncognitive skills are far more important than test scores in determining a student's later success in getting into college, earning income, and avoiding criminal behavior. Jackson found that the noncognitive skills of students, especially those who are low income (like those at MSLA), are even more important than the cognitive ones.

Lori knows that the skills students must develop for work and citizenship are very different from when she began teaching—and MSLA is built on this belief as well as a growing body of research evidence. Sitting in her small office, Lori pointed to her bookshelf, stacked with the writings of scholars and progressive educators, and told us, "We must build a curriculum for students and their families that begins with trust."

Figure 6.1

Lori Nazareno listens to her students at the Math and Science Leadership Academy in Denver, Colorado.

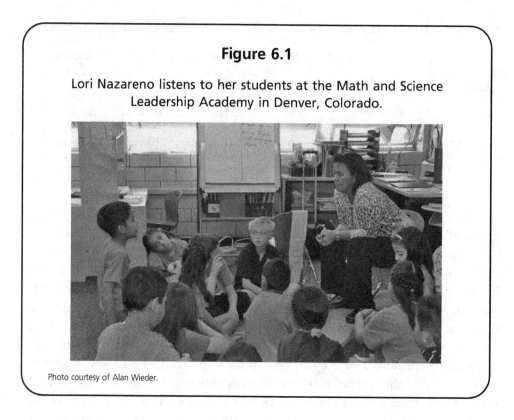

Photo courtesy of Alan Wieder.

Engagement and Trust

Walking into her classroom, we watched Lori easily grab the attention of every one of the twenty-five second graders in her midst. She was teaching them a lesson on the life cycle and food chains. Once she snapped her fingers a few times, the children left their desks and gathered around her, at which point she began to assess what they knew and led them in listening to and learning from one another. The students talked about life and death of both humans and animals. Lori encouraged them to connect their discussion of food chains to how we as humans get our daily sustenance. Throughout the full hour, Lori was in conversation with her students—probing, asking questions, carefully parsing each of their words to help them manage their own learning. The looks on her students' faces reflected their coming to understand how various animals have different structures and behaviors that serve differing functions in growth and survival. Before long she had them engaged in a game—inside the classroom and then on the playground—in which they played out how the dwellers of the Earth sustain life and live and die within the life cycle.

Figure 6.2

Lori Nazareno exudes a quiet but powerful type of leadership among both her students and her colleagues.

Photo courtesy of Alan Wieder.

Throughout our time observing, Lori and her students were connected to each other—the learning for them was deep and joyful. Later she talked about her lesson:

> I guess you could do online games, but given their age, physical level, and depth of content, we need to really engage them. In this class, there are several kids who have ADHD, and even more have serious learning disabilities, but you would never know it. I like to be very intentional about using a physical learning activity first so the students have a context and a frame to hang both concepts and facts.

Cultivating Teacherpreneurs for Teacher-Led Schools **109**

We came to understand how Lori's expert teaching and how she relates so well to children translates into how she works with adults. She listens, shares, adapts, and respects. If anything, Lori is first among equals with the teachers at MSLA. Yet none of her colleagues struggle, as is common in other schools, with her leading and earning recognition for her own accomplishments and those of the school. It is in part her unpretentiousness that leads to high levels of trust.

But there is more.

Teachers Leading Teachers

As Lori has noted on more than one occasion, "We all always watch each other." But MSLA also takes it further, having built a peer review system that is both demanding and supportive. Researchers have shown how peer review not only is far more accurate in assessing teachers, in terms of identifying those who are effective or not, but also ensures that teaching expertise spreads.[6] Good teaching practices, like what we saw in Lori's second-grade class, are well known to all MSLA teachers. And MSLA teachers are expected to emulate each of these practices.

> We are more nimble than most traditional schools. We can act quickly.
> —Lori Nazareno, describing the teacher-led culture of MSLA

Lori has a more specific explanation for their success:

> I have found that our teachers feel a greater sense of ownership and responsibility for student outcomes. If our students are not learning, we cannot "blame" it on anyone else. Nobody is keeping anybody from doing anything that he or she wants to do on behalf of students. Our teachers cannot say, "Well, the principal wouldn't let me." We own whatever results we are getting! That is powerful. We are more nimble than most traditional schools. We can act quickly.

This nimbleness may explain why MSLA is leading the way in the Denver Public Schools in teaching to the internationally benchmarked Common Core State Standards. And this is why NBC television highlighted MSLA in its spring 2012 Education Nation program.[7]

Among the educators on the Education Nation panel in Denver, Lori stood out with her teacherpreneurial skills and her well-traveledness—making the connection missed by many school reformers that if teachers do not have opportunities to be creative in their teaching, then students will not have opportunities to be creative in their learning (and in meeting the Common Core State Standards). Lori noted in the panel discussion:

> We are preparing [students] for a world that doesn't yet exist. What materials are going to be available for teachers, what types of training will we be able to have, what flexibility are teachers going to be able to have? Is there opportunity for us as teachers to embrace the types of thinking and changes that our children are expected to engage in as they get older?[8]

But when it comes to MSLA and its district, there is much more to this story than the school's academic progress and its leadership. Teachers are lining up to teach at MSLA, which is part of an urban school system with a long history of difficulty in attracting and retaining teachers. The district employs 4,250 teachers and loses about 700 per year, even with its highly touted performance pay plan, ProComp, which offers bonus pay for those who teach in a high-need school. As MSLA has staffed up (they have been adding a grade level per year), the school has had fifteen applicants for every position, with several teachers uprooting their family to teach at a teacher-led school. And over the last several years, the only teachers who have left include one who moved because of her family and another who was not teaching as the MSLA peers expected.

MSLA second-grade teacher Bernadette Lopez's journey in and out of teaching adds powerful insight into how important the MSLA model is for the future of the profession. Bernadette had successfully taught in Denver previously, but after growing frustrated by work under administrators who seemed more focused on procedures and test scores than on the best interests of students, she moved away and worked in the private sector, where she could also earn considerably more money. She told us:

> I returned to teaching because of MSLA. I certainly didn't want to put myself in a situation where I didn't think I'd be successful if the administration was anti-teacher or if they really didn't want us to stand up and speak for the children and say what we felt was best for them. I really wanted to work with Lori. She really knows how to lead.

Lori's career in teaching has spanned elementary and high schools in some of the highest-poverty communities in both the Miami-Dade and Denver public schools. She began teaching in 1987, but "definitely had to muddle" her way through her first years in the classroom; she confesses that she has "never done anything the traditional way."

> I had graduated from Occidental College with a degree in exercise science, with lots of knowledge about human anatomy, exercise physiology, nutrition, and motor learning. But I was not ready to teach when I got my first job at North

Miami Beach High School. I thought they wanted me to coach volleyball, not teach biology to all the ninth graders that no other teacher wanted to teach. I had to enter teaching on an emergency license, and my "mentor" didn't get selected or identified to me until the end of October. It was a classic first-year "eat our young teacher alive" situation. But I survived.

> I have found that our teachers [at a teacher-led school] feel a greater sense of ownership and responsibility for student outcomes . . . Nobody is keeping anybody from doing anything that he or she wants to do on behalf of students.
> —Lori Nazareno

Most everything I have learned through trial and error or going out on my own. I've read a lot [pointing to her bookcase], and there are three times more books in my home library. It was like, "Oh, I'm having an issue with boys," so I'd go read about gender issues.

THE VALUE OF NATIONAL BOARD CERTIFICATION

Later in the day during our visit, when we asked Lori to tell us more about how she learned to teach and lead, she responded, "Twenty-five years of practice." Then she said:

Actually, the National Board Certification [work] really, really helped a lot. In that process, prior to that, nobody had asked the question you asked me after watching me teach today: "Why did you do it that way?" I mean, it's so embedded in the National Board process so you have to really be able to answer that specifically. Why did you do it that way, that day, and for those kids? That process really changed all of my teaching. So then for every lesson I can answer that question, and I didn't used to be able to do that.

And then achieving National Board Certification placed a "seal of approval" on my teaching practice. It gave me the confidence to be able to step up and know that my practice is accomplished and that I have credibility when speaking about instructional issues. It helped me begin looking for leadership opportunities. The National Board process does not identify teacher leaders, but it can serve as a launching pad for folks to go, "Oh, I really do know what I am talking about."

After earning her first National Board Certificate in science in 2002, Lori created her own nonprofit, the National Board Certified Teachers (NBCTs) of Miami-Dade, to organize growing numbers of accomplished teachers in an effort to support new and struggling teachers because "neither the district nor the union was doing its job." She recalled:

We had that whole thing with the superintendent and the union, neither liked that I launched the NBCTs of Miami-Dade. They were saying we're going to crush you and you can't do this and make your own organization. We were like, "Okay, we are just going to move ahead like you didn't say that," and then we got some support from a local funder and the door opened. We were prepared to take advantage of a state policy that paid NBCTs for mentoring.

Then she joined the CTQ Collaboratory and soon found more "kindred spirits":

I often say 90 to 95 percent of my teacher leadership learnings came from what was then Teacher Leaders Network [now the CTQ Collaboratory]—just reading what other people were doing, how they approached things, how they prepared for meetings, what they made sure they did or didn't do when they talked to people.

After teaching in one of the district's alternative high schools, Lori and three other NBCTs—Michele Ivy, Donna Laffitte, and Mickey Weiner—all moved to Myrtle Grove Elementary, one of Miami-Dade's most underperforming schools, as part of the district's three-year, $100 million Zone Initiative. The brainchild of then-superintendent Rudy Crew, the Zone created more student learning time and more time for teachers to participate in meaningful professional development. Students would attend school for an extra hour each day, and teachers would engage in fifty-six additional hours of professional development each year as well as work ten more days. The Zone was designed on the principles of decentralized authority and a "lightning-fast ramp-up, coupled with differential treatment for a target group of schools."[9]

In moving to Myrtle Grove, Lori and crew believed they would be able to "work with like-minded colleagues" to design and lead their own professional development and use their own professional judgment—not a scripted curriculum—in teaching their students.

But centralized authority prevailed when it came to curriculum, assessment, and professional development. Within a few years, the Zone was deemed a failure as chronicled by *Education Week* and researchers who found "no consistent positive impact" on student achievement; administrators and teachers were "fatigued and burn[ed] out."[10] In an evaluation of the program, less than one-half of Zone teachers reported that their principal was supportive of them (41 percent) or respected them (47 percent)—far less than the control group in both instances.[11] Granted, this was *not* the case for Lori and her NBCT colleagues, whose principal at Myrtle Grove, Barbara Johnson, wanted to find new ways to improve student learning and use teacher leaders. But she did not necessarily know how to do so.

As Lori noted:

> From my own experience, Barbara really wanted to make it work for us to lead, but it is challenging to figure out, from a [school] logistical and cultural perspective, how to effectively utilize teacher leaders. Unfortunately, at Myrtle Grove there were no structures in place for any of the NBCTs (or other teacher leaders for that matter) to be able to spread our expertise. Our role was never defined, and no schedules or protocols were put in place to support the spreading of our expertise. It was unfortunate because I believe that Barbara would have been supportive of all of these things . . . She just didn't do them.

Barbara, as reported in an *Education Week* article, later made it clear that most administrators, including her, "have no idea what [National Board Certified Teachers] can do."[12]

Lori continued:

> Right now most principals are like, "I'm a leader and everyone is supposed to do it my way." Then if there is a teacher leader, they are like, "Okay," as long as the administrators get to tell you what they want. It is like we are told as teachers, "This is how I want instruction to happen, and no way will I want you to be my proxy; it's my responsibility to hold you accountable, not for you to lead."
>
> I have seen this issue in all three of the schools that I have been in since I began describing myself as a teacher leader. I honestly believe that principals who are halfway sane (which most are) want to have teacher leaders help them . . . They just don't know what that might look like. In part I left Miami-Dade because of my frustration with the lack of opportunities for teachers to lead in meaningful ways.

A QUIET KIND OF LEADERSHIP

In reflecting on her experience in Miami-Dade as well as in the Denver Public Schools, Lori asserted that reformers believe they are focused on major changes that will lead to better results for students, but that their plans and proposals tend to tinker around the edges. "It's the typical, 'We keep the same damn system with the same structures and try to do something different.' We created a system that is used to making phonographs, and we are shocked we aren't spitting out iPods."

Like the *quiet* leaders Cain describes in her book, Lori has many qualities of the thoughtful and introspective introvert.[13] She is very comfortable with who she is and how she has come to view and be viewed in her role as teacher leader. Gordon Lawrence, in his 1979 book *People Types and Tiger Stripes*,[14] suggests that teaching attracts introverts who quietly fit inside of top-down school hierarchies in which teachers are expected to embrace egalitarianism among the ranks—and everyone is supposed to be alike. Lori knows how to communicate effectively with teachers and administrators inside of this culture of egalitarianism and control while working deliberately to transform it.

And after a few years of very successful teaching (and mentoring a number of underprepared alternative certification recruits) at Barnum Elementary School in Denver, Lori was ready to join forces with other teachers to create their own school:

> We thought we should go the opposite way of current school reform with its scripted curriculum and rigid approaches to teacher evaluation. We were going to empower teachers—they're going to make the decisions. We would engage in peer review, like other professions do. Teachers will decide how we spend our public money, how we structure the schedule, what programs and activities we bring in . . . And we [would] make all the decisions based on what's best for the kids—not what the district wants, not what adults want, not what anybody else is saying. That's the environment that will attract highly accomplished teachers.

And MSLA has attracted topflight teachers, among whom many, like Lori, increasingly are learning to lead outside the school and district. Walking down the hall to watch Lori teach, we ran into Paty Gonzalez Holt, a young teacher with seven years of experience (three of them at MSLA), who had this to say about the school's lead teacher:

> I think the fact that Lori is teaching every day makes a huge difference because she understands what we're going through. She's teaching. She's planning. She knows the kids. She teaches the service learning projects as well. So she knows every single kid just as intimately as we do. She leads with such quiet confidence and calm.

Leadership from the ranks means that Lori has earned her influence, but she does not force it on others. She told us:

> Obviously, I know I can have a lot of influence. If it is something I feel really strongly about, I can sit down any of our teams. There are times when the staff has made decisions when it wouldn't necessarily be the decision I would make, but I go with it. I trust them; they are responsible. We would not be a teacher-led school if I did not trust them and they were not responsible for their decisions.

Then Lori told us more about her quiet leadership—which rests on trust and responsibility—and how it has developed over time:

> I live in a space where everybody has unique gifts to share and develop. This is kind of a spiritual thing as well. I have a sense that this is the path I came here to take . . . I have been very fortunate because I've had opportunities that others haven't had. To some degree though, as Deepak Chopra says, there is no such thing as luck. It is preparation plus opportunity.[15] I have prepared to act even when the opportunity was not there. I was prepared when it came time to create the NBCTs of Miami-Dade. I already had the elevator speech down pat. I was prepared to move as a team to Myrtle Grove, even though the district, school, and principal were not ready for our brand of teacher leadership. I have learned a great deal from so many colleagues in the Collaboratory—and now, of late, I have had so many opportunities to learn in so many different contexts. All of this has helped me come to be the leader that I am and build the kind of teacher leadership we have at MSLA.

In fact, over the last several years, Lori has been appointed to the National Education Association Commission for Effective Teachers and Teaching and to a Bill & Melinda Gates Foundation advisory board on "innovative professional development." She is the cochair of the Denver Public Schools' Teacher Effectiveness Design Team, whose goal is to redesign the district's teacher evaluation system. She continues to expand her leadership outside of her school district, and in doing so, with teacherpreneurial spirit and intention, she brings back more opportunities for her teaching colleagues to develop as leaders themselves.

Lori continued:

> I really, really, honestly truly believe that part of my role in this life is to shape what education looks like and influence other people. I know I have the ability to see things and how they can be different. One of my strengths is leading teachers, many of whom have been socialized to work in isolation, to move in the same direction. Again, I've been fortunate that these opportunities popped up that I had prepared for, so I was able to step through those doors when they were cracked open.

THE POTENTIAL FOR GREATER IMPACT

Our observations of and conversations with Lori, along with each of the other teacher leaders we profile in this book, led us to conclude that the cultivation of teachers involves not just the skills of quiet leadership but also intelligent humility, reciprocal mentoring, well-traveledness, and calculated risk taking. And we wondered what proportion of American teachers, among the estimated 3.2 million, could lead like Lori.

"There are lots and lots of teachers who can lead like me," Lori said. "I would say the ballpark figure would be about *one-third*. But they would have to receive preparation and support as well as a much different work structure so they can develop and lead." Lori's estimate suggests that—under the right conditions—one million teachers could create networks, develop and execute a business plan for a teacher-led school, and advocate for their profession. But, as Lori reminded us, there is a lot of work to do to overcome both teaching's past and current school reforms that may be stifling the spread of teacher leadership.

> I regularly have to remind folks here that, "You can make that decision." It takes a lot of training and support for folks to even understand that. You don't have to check in with me on that; you can do that yourself.

So we asked Lori about the likelihood that the ideas behind MSLA will spread across Denver. She answered:

> That's really a good question. The district administration talks more about teacher leadership than ever before. And we have this new schools office and this whole innovation thing. But then you look at what is really going on, and you ask what the heck are people doing that is actually different? Waiving the contract so teachers can teach a longer day, well that's not so different. We did that in Miami-Dade. How about using your time differently? The district is not doing much to rethink who teaches and when. In these new schools, the curriculum may push a different scope and sequence of topics. But these schools are not really promoting a curriculum that encourages curiosity, persistence, and risk taking.
>
> The district administration, which was very supportive of us getting started, creates and reinforces so many roadblocks in hiring, communication, and professional development. Trying to spread anything that does not fit how their "factory" is set up is almost impossible.

Lori reminded us again, "I will tell you there are lots and lots of teachers who can lead the way I do, but not if we don't create a system to do so." For the 2012–2013 school year, Lori is working with CTQ as a teacher in residence, taking a break from the classroom to work more closely with policymakers and administrators as well as her teaching colleagues on advancing new school designs based on her work at MSLA. As part of her residency with CTQ, Lori is developing teacher leadership curricula for colleagues nationwide; working as a mentor for other teachers in our virtual network; leading alternative, classroom reality–based efforts to implement teacher evaluation reforms in her home state of Colorado; and incubating a strategy to mobilize more teacher leaders to create their own school. However, like the other teacherpreneurs we describe along with countless others with the same skills and characteristics, Lori, in spite of her enthusiasm for this role, struggled to leave her school and the students she served:

> I must say that the transition out of MSLA was absolutely, hands-down, the hardest thing I have ever had to do in my career—and possibly in my entire life. It caught me very much by surprise. A basic tenet of Buddhism, and a belief that I hold to, is that attachment is the root of all suffering. I have to admit that this notion played itself out in many ways as I worked to extract myself from MSLA. I really had to test and check myself about not only my professional beliefs but my personal ones as well. It is easy to say that I trust the judgment of highly accomplished teacher professionals with whom I have worked. I do. I found myself very attached to both the students I taught every day as well as the efforts I wanted to lead in the next evolution of MSLA.
>
> I hold a deep and abiding belief that everything always works out as it is supposed to, but there were lots of moments where my belief in that was also severely tested. I cannot tell you how many times throughout the last four years this idea has proven to be true, and yet I found myself doubting as I tried to pretend that I wasn't struggling with giving up control of the school. I have been profoundly challenged with the idea that I would no longer be seeing students every day—after twenty-five years!
>
> Even on my most challenging days as lead teacher at MSLA, it was always easy to get myself back on track by walking through classes or, better yet, sitting in one for a while. And so, on the very last day I was in the school, I had intended to go and speak to the third-, fourth-, and fifth-grade classes, but I only made it through two classes. As hard as I tried, I couldn't hold myself together enough to tell them goodbye and wish them well in a way that could support them in the transition. Even in this moment, I am struggling with the idea that I couldn't tell them good-bye. And so, the idea that I may not return to working directly with kids full-time is a challenge if that is part of everything working out how it's supposed to.

Aspiring teacher leaders should not be forced to choose between teaching and leading. School reform, which is filled with a cacophony of voices but is most owned by those who do not teach students, needs to be led by Lori and the many teachers like her who can become the teacherpreneurs of tomorrow. However, there are numerous barriers—cultural, organizational, and political—that must be recognized, addressed, and overcome. Our work in the Collaboratory with many classroom experts helped us surface a number of lessons about meeting resistance and crossing borders, which we share in the next chapter.

● Chapter Six Selected Web Sites

Following is a list of online resources that relate to the discussion in this chapter. If you find that any of these links no longer work, please try entering the information in a search engine.

Common Core State Standards: http://www.corestandards.org

Education Nation special featuring Lori Nazareno: http://www.9news.com/rss/story.aspx?storyid=263226

NBCTs of Miami-Dade: http://www.nbctofmiami-dade.org/index.html

Education Week article on the failure of the Zone Initiative: http://blogs.edweek.org/edweek/high-school-connections/2009/05/miamis_zone_not_so_much_improv.html

Activity for Chapter Six

Now What?

Find Models of Teacher Leadership

Goal

In the past five chapters, you've been thinking carefully about your own beliefs, experiences, skills, and goals. However, effective teacherpreneurs must learn from one another and share their experiences, their successes, and their failures. For Lori, having models of female teacher leaders was especially powerful and inspirational in pursuing her own career trajectory. Having mentors or other people you respect and admire is important as you navigate the relatively new territory of teacherpreneurism. Likewise, maybe without even realizing it, you yourself may be a model of teacher leadership for someone else. These relationships are integral to effecting lasting and large-scale change of the teaching profession.

Think

As you consider the questions that follow, you may find yourself thinking of a particular person who inspires you, as the framing of the questions suggests. However, if several people (or a group) come to mind for you, that is fine as well.

- Who inspires you as a leader? (This person may not necessarily be a teacher, and you don't necessarily have to know him or her personally. Think about someone whom you respect as a leader and influencer.)
- Why does this person inspire you? What values do you share?
- Which of this person's specific accomplishments and achievements can you seek to emulate in your own career?

Act

If it's possible, try reaching out to the person or people who inspire you. Introduce yourself, and share your position, your reason for writing, and why you respect them and their experience. If you're lucky enough to already have a relationship with a role model or mentor, ask that person if you could regularly meet with him or her to discuss challenges, goals, and general day-to-day experiences.

And because mentorship goes both ways, think about whether there are any teachers who look to you for advice or guidance. Remember that even a more accomplished professional may be able to learn from your unique strengths and experiences. Consider reaching out to your mentor or perhaps another teacher, especially a novice, to provide a listening ear and to offer guidance and support.

CHAPTER 7

Meeting Resistance—and Crossing Borders

● *I found myself in this weird place of a teacher who knows too much.*

—Jessica Keigan

During her year (2011–2012) as a Center for Teaching Quality (CTQ)–supported teacherpreneur, Jessica Keigan had terrific support from many people, including a number of principals and district administrators in Colorado's Adams 12 Five Star Schools, as she developed her teaching expertise and her leadership skills. "I would not be able to do what I have done without so many of my colleagues as well as many, many administrators," she said.

But over the course of her year as a teacherpreneur, based part-time at Horizon High School, Jessica's leadership became more prominent, and she began to feel a coolness when she met with some administrators, both in her district and statewide. It did not take long for Jessica's knowledge of the Common Core State Standards and teacher evaluation—which she demonstrated, for example, in testifying before the state board of education, writing for EdNews Colorado and her blog on CTQ's Web site, speaking at national conferences, and appearing on television talk shows—to get the attention of many educators in and out of her district. Jessica soon created a name for herself as both a teacher and a reformer. As she told us, "There are leaders who want to know things first, and all of a sudden I found myself in this weird place of a teacher who knows too much" and "with administrators who began to feel uncomfortable if I knew more about policy than they did."

Many district administrators, who themselves must serve the early-twentieth-century principles of bureaucracy that undergird their school district, are not in the habit of communicating effectively to the many teachers who teach twenty-five to thirty-five students at a time in an isolated classroom. District officials face many demands themselves, as they fit right in the middle of the organizational pyramid of public education. When they consider the needs of classroom teachers, they are buffeted by any number of conflicting top-down mandates from state and federal policymakers while responding to local exigencies driven by the diverse takes on public education by school boards, union leaders, mayors, advocacy groups, community leaders, and parents.

Jessica attributes the resistance she felt from others to her crossing those lines between her teacher role and what emerged in her role as a leader:

> I don't think a number of administrators really got what my role would be. I don't think they realized that I was going to have an audience that was a much broader audience than just district or building leadership. I kind of felt some of them pulling back a little bit and being more guarded about information. The fact that I knew a lot about things only administrators are supposed to know appeared to be a bit unnerving for them. It is a subtle thing that I began to sense. At first I was seen as a resource, but it seemed, as the year progressed, I was seen more as competition.

Jessica's experience with her administrators reflects one of a number of cultural as well as organizational and political barriers to cultivating and mobilizing teacher leaders to transform teaching and learning. The historical hierarchies in American education that we portrayed in Chapter Five correspond to borders representing lines of authority and influence that teachers are not supposed to cross. Presently our school systems—and their teaching development apparatus—sustain their own borders, often with stark divides between administrators who supervise teachers and a range of educators in the private and public sectors who work on behalf of their profession.

As defined by Israeli activist and writer Michael Warschawski, borders are based on "power and prohibitions."[1] Granted, teachers often have solidified the borders between themselves, on the one hand, and administrators and policymakers, on the other. Dan Lortie documented how teachers, wedded to teaching's long-standing culture of individualism, have shunned opportunities to drive change outside of their own egg-crate classrooms—content to teach children but not to lead adults. Historically, teachers have done so, in large part, because others have belittled their special schooling and because they themselves have questioned whether they really

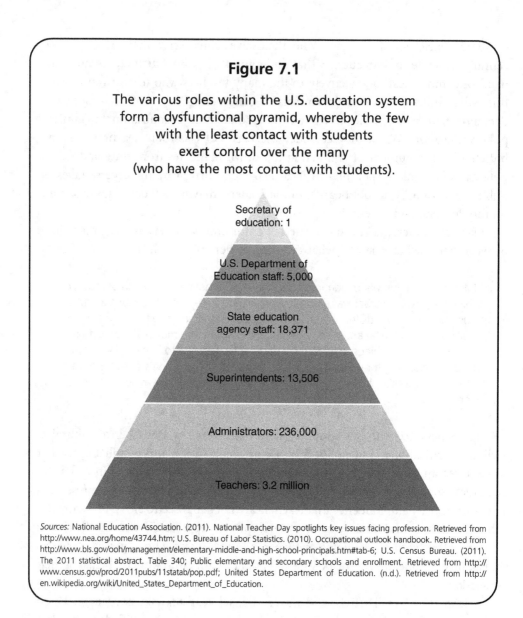

Figure 7.1

The various roles within the U.S. education system form a dysfunctional pyramid, whereby the few with the least contact with students exert control over the many (who have the most contact with students).

Secretary of education: 1

U.S. Department of Education staff: 5,000

State education agency staff: 18,371

Superintendents: 13,506

Administrators: 236,000

Teachers: 3.2 million

Sources: National Education Association. (2011). National Teacher Day spotlights key issues facing profession. Retrieved from http://www.nea.org/home/43744.htm; U.S. Bureau of Labor Statistics. (2010). Occupational outlook handbook. Retrieved from http://www.bls.gov/ooh/management/elementary-middle-and-high-school-principals.htm#tab-6; U.S. Census Bureau. (2011). The 2011 statistical abstract. Table 340; Public elementary and secondary schools and enrollment. Retrieved from http://www.census.gov/prod/2011pubs/11statab/pop.pdf; United States Department of Education. (n.d.). Retrieved from http://en.wikipedia.org/wiki/United_States_Department_of_Education.

possess a specialized body of knowledge.[2] Teachers, like those in New York City, who still use time cards and punch clocks, continue to work in early-twentieth-century, assembly-line factory fashion.

But Jessica's story and several more that we will tell here also reflect a set of additional obstacles defined by school bureaucracy and education politics. Teacher

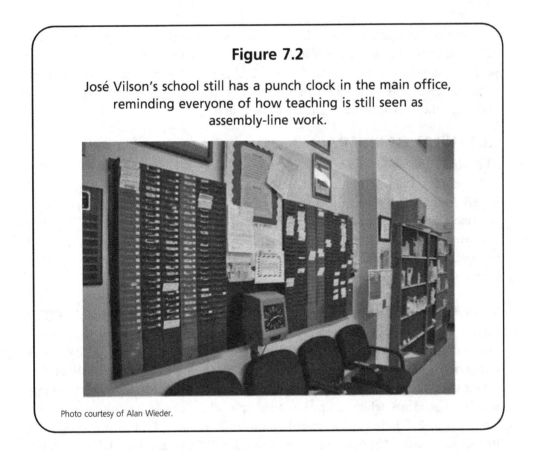

Figure 7.2

José Vilson's school still has a punch clock in the main office, reminding everyone of how teaching is still seen as assembly-line work.

Photo courtesy of Alan Wieder.

leaders, especially teacherpreneurs whose time is not defined solely by administrators, can easily unsettle school district managers who seek uniformity among their employees. What is more, teacher leaders who have more time to study research findings and engage with diverse policy ideas can present "an inconvenient truth" to reformers who seek to control the $600 billion public school enterprise as well as to some old-guard union leaders who use labor-management conflict to maintain the status quo.

We tell the following six stories to make more public what often undermines the good intentions of many policymakers, reformers, administrators, and union leaders who do indeed seek to transcend teaching's past and create a more hopeful future for public education.

> Our experience suggests that this sentiment—that teachers are to be managed and controlled—is commonplace. As a result, when it comes to leading school reform, teachers are an afterthought.

According to Warschawski, a border is not merely a place of "separation where differences are asserted; it can also be a place of exchange and enrichment where pluralist identities can flourish."[3] We tell these stories—revealing the cultural, organizational, and political barriers to teacher leadership—to find that place of exchange and enrichment. It is there to be found.

CULTURAL BARRIERS

The stories that follow have been documented over the last several years (2007–2012), during which CTQ has been deepening its efforts to elevate the bold ideas of expert teachers and to help them spread their pedagogical and policy expertise to reformers, union leaders, administrators, and their teaching colleagues. We offer anonymity to those in all the stories, to focus on the policy issues (not the personalities) that must be confronted if teaching is to become the profession that students deserve.

Story #1: Weird Looks for Mentioning "Teaching" Alongside "Leading"

Julio was a terrific physics teacher. He should still be teaching. Julio grew up in a town near downtown Denver, but now works with kids who are (he said with a laugh) "just like myself, from the wrong side of the tracks." Julio was and still is a great athlete (he runs a 4.4 forty-yard dash). His interest in sports early in life connected him to a large number of students, which is why he ended up working as a high school teacher and track coach. But Julio was no stereotypical teacher-coach; he is much more of a Renaissance man. Although recently married with a young son, Julio mustered considerable energy to teach five classes of high school science and create an after-school enrichment program for his students while tending to two divergent interests in graduate school. Julio was, by his own account, a "physicist in the making," working closely on a patent with a small research team figuring out a new technique to purify salt water. But he was also equally interested in research in education, particularly how to use longitudinal designs and sophisticated statistical techniques to uncover what motivates minority males to remain in school and achieve academically beyond what is measured on narrowly focused multiple-choice tests.

Julio still found time to join CTQ-Colorado. He was particularly engrossed with the principles of our book *Teaching 2030*—and the role that teacher leaders like himself could play (if given the time) in leading school reform, particularly as they related to his local union. Julio was frustrated by how his school administrators as well as union leaders were always at odds over the wrong issues and rarely took the advice of those who taught students every day.

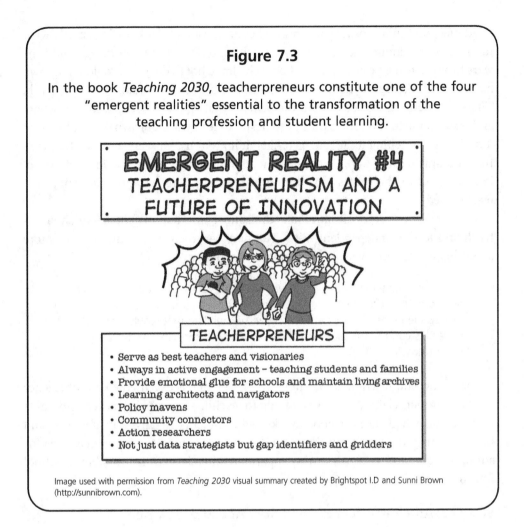

Figure 7.3

In the book *Teaching 2030*, teacherpreneurs constitute one of the four "emergent realities" essential to the transformation of the teaching profession and student learning.

Image used with permission from *Teaching 2030* visual summary created by Brightspot I.D and Sunni Brown (http://sunnibrown.com).

When Julio approached his principal about serving as a CTQ-supported teacherpreneur, which would allow him to explore issues around research on student engagement as well as the transformation of unions as local guilds focused more on quality control than on salaries and benefits, he received a look that was quizzical at best. "It was like I was speaking a foreign language," Julio pointed out. "It was like, 'What are you talking about?' and I got really weird looks. One administrator told me, 'You should leave teaching and become an administrator.'"

Julio met with his principal at least four times—and sent him countless e-mails with brief hybrid job descriptions. "The message he sent back was that 'I was trying to get out of his building' and that 'I was selfishly furthering my own career.'"

At one point Julio's principal expressed concerns about not knowing exactly what Julio would be doing when he was not teaching physics in the morning. And if he were to approve the position, which he was inclined not to do, Julio would on his own have to find his replacement for the afternoon classes he would no longer teach. There was never any discussion of the benefits that could be accrued for the school and district, much less Julio's own deep desire to lead without leaving what he loved doing most—teaching disadvantaged kids. Julio told us, "It seemed to me that they [my administrators] weren't connecting it immediately with the idea of school improvement or the professionalization of teaching. This was not something that teachers led."

Julio's administrators did not make the connection that one could—or should—teach and lead in independent ways. Teachers had their place. Julio told us more about his interactions with his principal in particular:

> He did not view me as a team player or believe that I wanted to be a teacher anymore. Nothing could be further from the truth. If I took on this hybrid role, all of a sudden there would be a teacher in his building that would not be totally under his control. I think that was uncomfortable for him. Then it turned into instant hostility.

Julio soon quit teaching altogether, even though he is exactly the kind of teacher school reformers claim they seek to recruit to teaching—a scholar-teacher who wants to teach in a high-need school, works with students in any way possible, and improves his profession from the ground up. But he raised too many questions for administrators and reformers, who apparently already had the answers to school improvement.

Story #2: Administrators Have to Stay Ahead of Teachers

(This story is as noted in Chapter One.) In spring 2012 we attended a Washington DC meeting of varied education interest groups to discuss how they learn from and work with one another in the implementation of the Common Core State Standards. There were about one hundred school reformers and educators of sorts in attendance, sitting around tables at a local hotel just off Dupont Circle—a part of town where many education trade associations are headquartered. Those who attended the convening were primarily school administrators or representatives of think tanks that routinely produced white papers on education reform, on topics including teacher quality and the Common Core State Standards. CTQ was one of the few organizations that "lived outside the Beltway," and it was the only one that brought a practicing teacher to the meeting.

Involving teachers in deliberations like this one is often a postscript at best. As a representative from one Washington DC–based trade association said in an opening session, "School leaders have to stay ahead of the teachers or else the work never gets done."

Our experience suggests that this sentiment—that teachers are to be managed and controlled—is commonplace. It is historical, as we revealed in Chapter Four, and it is still with us. As a result, when it comes to leading school reform, teachers are an afterthought. A federal official, who taught many years ago and likes to proclaim that he now works for the "dark side of school reform," stood up and made the case that the organizations represented at the meeting "had to make sure teachers know how to teach to the Common Core." Another reformer made this argument: "Teachers, and the way they are trained in universities, are in the trees. [Principals] need to manage the forest." Yet another participant complained that administrator associations and their work were not given preference over the nation's teachers' unions and their efforts to organize classroom teachers to lead Common Core State Standards reforms. We felt that no one had any sense that a large group of expert teachers, with both intense pedagogical skill and leadership acumen, could lead the way. The classroom expert, who is National Board Certified, was invisible to many of the school reformers who sat around the tables.

Mary, on behalf of CTQ, began to speak out just like any other policy maven, but she drew on her classroom experience to identify gaps in strategy and practice, reforms du jour, and the realities of classrooms. Several of the policy officials and trade association leaders tuned out; however, slowly but surely a few of them started to listen as Mary's ability to speak "policy tightly woven in practice" began to resonate.

As discussion turned to the staff development days that would be needed to implement the Common Core State Standards, Mary pointedly spoke to the lack of cohesion and consistency in professional development that frustrates so many teachers who are deeply committed to improving their craft. Rattling off the names of several popular professional development series that her school and district had haphazardly strung together over her teaching career, Mary described the growing library of books and binders (*Whale Done! The Power of Positive Relationships*, *Six Thinking Hats*, and others) that have accumulated on the shelves of her classroom and in the trunk of her car. She made a powerful point:

> I found myself energized after each new strategy was introduced over the course of an entire staff development day, but there was never any follow-through to see how they were being implemented and what challenges teachers encountered. No sooner had I worked through the kinks of one "focus for the year" than it was replaced by another that came with its own staff development day. As the targets shift from one professional development day to the next without any

input from classroom practitioners, there is rarely an opportunity to truly develop and enhance the instructional strategies, engagement activities, collaborative groupings, differentiated instruction, and higher-order thinking skills that we know from research will lead to positive outcomes for students.

A foundation official, sitting in the back of the room and observing the deliberations, came up to Mary after the meeting and thanked her for being present. He also shared that her insights and the involvement of teachers are critical to these types of meetings, and told her, "You really held your own" with the group. But we wondered how much Mary could be heard and embraced. There was only one of her.

Administrators and reformers reinforce many of the cultural barriers that get in the way of teacher leadership and teacherpreneurism. But they are not the only ones. Teachers themselves also do this. The next story illustrates that disheartening reality.

Story #3: A Division Between Teaching and Leading

Andrea had been part of the CTQ virtual community for some time, showing a lot of promise as a teacher leader and a teacherpreneur. She had taught for five years—very successfully according to a number of administrators in her district. And she had a lot of enthusiasm for leading. Andrea was, according to her most recent principal, "a go-getter" who "likes to jump in and do something new." Granted, she had left her teaching post recently to become a literacy coach for her fellow teachers in her district, but the respect that both administrators and teachers showed her was a good sign. And she was absolutely enthralled with the idea of getting involved with policy reform while remaining closely connected with her district and teaching colleagues. Her role with CTQ was to work locally with a state-level nonprofit to advance reform initiatives in teacher evaluation and school redesign while remaining as a literacy coach in the other half of her job. Although we did not have a chance to assemble firsthand evidence of her teaching, she definitely had a "good way," as one administrator told us, with her fellow teachers.

Andrea was outgoing and could communicate well. Unlike other teachers who are often uncomfortable presenting in front of adults, she had no problem doing so. She actually embraced the opportunities, and we watched her in action. Andrea was effective, and we saw her perform especially well in one potentially contentious meeting with union officials concerning teacher evaluation.

But early in the year there were signs that Andrea was not the best fit for being a teacher leader and teacherpreneur, as we have envisioned these roles. She told us that she had "become a conduit" between the state education system and her district, and she was very proud of the role and the knowledge she had that others did not have. Soon we heard her referring to the teaching colleagues whom she was coaching as "my teachers." Andrea's hybrid role seemed to be a way for her to distinguish herself from her classroom colleagues. One told us, "She is not a teacher; she is an administrator for all practical matters."

It was not long before Andrea started having a difficult time, overly compartmentalizing her coaching role, which took her into schools at regularly scheduled times to observe, assess, and support teachers, in relation to her CTQ-supported teacherpreneurial role, which demanded a great deal of flexibility in managing school reform efforts that are anything but routine. Soon she could not handle any "CTQ work" on the days she was in schools coaching teachers, and she struggled mightily with moving from the micro tasks associated with public schooling to the macro ones linked to school reform. Although we suspect she worked hard as a teacher and coach, she struggled with writing—both for public audiences as well as in conversations in the virtual network to which she belonged. But most important, over time it seemed that Andrea was more comfortable out of the classroom, serving in a distinctive leadership role, detached from her teaching colleagues. In the end, Andrea was not a good fit as a teacherpreneur, despite her meaningful efforts and ours.

ORGANIZATIONAL BARRIERS

Recently the Broad Center for the Management of School Systems pointed to seventy-five examples of "how bureaucracy stands in the way of America's students and teachers."[4] But its list of barriers reflects an approach to reform that will only modestly improve our twentieth-century system of teaching and learning (e.g., districts' and states' not getting standardized test results to teachers more quickly and superintendents' having to adhere to collective bargaining agreements). There is nothing on the Broad list of reform obstacles that speaks to how school district administrators get in the way of teacher leadership. Of the seventy-five barriers, the closest that the Broad policy analysts came to recognizing this school reform fact of life was: "Teachers don't have access to instructional pacing guides" (from barrier #18); "Teachers lack access to mentors, master teachers, [and] collaborative planning time" (from barrier #20); and "Teachers don't feel that principals or central office personnel meet their needs" (from barrier #22).[5]

Story #4: There Is No HR Form for This Type of Teacher

There is nothing on the Broad list about how school district administrators just do not want any type of teacher leadership that diverges from how they do business. Madeline, a highly accomplished middle school science teacher, offers another example of how organizational barriers get in the way of teacher leadership. This midcareer, alternative route recruit, who entered teaching after a career in health care (which included serious management responsibilities), seems to fit the profile of a teacher whom reformers would want to see enter and remain in teaching. One would never know it.

Madeline is a National Board Certified Teacher (NBCT) and self-made technology expert who created Internet-based venues for her students to analyze developments in various scientific fields and learn with their peers in classrooms around the globe. She sought her own professional development to make sure she was "ahead of the game" when it came to Common Core State Standards student assessments. We wanted her to serve as a teacherpreneur to lead our virtual community of NBCTs.

Madeline's principal was not totally opposed to her getting more involved in a hybrid role in which she would teach three days a week and then lead a Common Core State Standards professional learning community (PLC) for fellow teachers nationwide during the rest of the week. We had designed a system with Madeline so that our virtual PLC on the Common Core State Standards could easily include big numbers of teachers from her own school district. But her principal was not all that committed to making things happen—and Madeline's district administration, particularly the HR director, wanted no part of it.

"My principal is very well educated and smart," Madeline told us, "but she has an attention span of about ten seconds. Nothing gets on her radar until it becomes a crisis."

Madeline had developed a great plan for how she would work with another teacher to cover the time she would not be in the classroom, but this still did not inspire her principal. "She is not a possibility thinker," Madeline told us with a shrug. "I was persistent," she continued, "and finally got her on board when she could see how much assessment knowledge I could bring back to our school."

But Madeline, as she expected, had to go through proper channels. Her principal thought the next stop would be the HR department. But that was not the case—and Madeline received a reprimand from the district office when she contacted HR without first going to the supervisor of instruction. The supervisor of instruction, while intrigued with the idea, was not encouraging. He told us that he didn't think the district would be all that interested because its test scores were good enough.

Madeline took her case to the HR director and drew on a wide range of examples of teacher leadership from CTQ's virtual network. She could not get the HR director interested; and then the bureaucratic reasons for not pursuing Madeline's idea began to roll off his lips. First Madeline was told that, despite the check that CTQ would send the district for 50 percent of her salary and benefits, the district would have to label her as a part-time teacher, and thus she would lose her health insurance and her seniority ranking, thereby preventing her from earning regularly scheduled salary increases. Madeline was stunned and asked us to assist in communicating to the HR director how the teacherpreneurial role was being implemented in other districts. He said he would not reconsider, telling us, "There is not a form in HR for this type of teacher."

Story #5: I Just Cannot Do These Two Jobs

Kelsey, a twenty-eight-year-old elementary school music teacher, loved being part of our virtual community of teacher leaders, and as she did more work online with her colleagues, she discovered how much more influence she could—and should—have in education policy. She taught in the same metropolitan area with Andrea (from Story #3), and worked well with her in advancing teacher evaluation and school redesign reforms. Kelsey was concerned that her state's high-stakes accountability laws would divert attention from a much-needed focus on the arts for cultivating and elevating creativity among young children. She readily grasped the intricacies of policy development and was not intimidated by research studies laden with abstract statistical analysis. She was an ideal teacherpreneurial candidate, and our CTQ team worked hard at convincing her to serve in the 2011–2012 school year.

"I am still really passionate and excited about teaching, and I think that CTQ has played a huge role in stoking my enthusiasm for remaining in the classroom," she said. "I have had three close friends drop out of the profession, and all did so because they got burnt out."

"One was being micromanaged by her principal," she continued, "another one was getting no support, and the third was bored by the scripted curriculum so many teachers were forced to use."

No doubt, Kelsey is a terrific teacher. Watching her teach, we could see how she integrated core content (particularly mathematics) in her music lessons while offering all kinds of ways for thirty-two diverse students to engage in small- and large-group activities. Walking into her classroom, one sees students experiencing the joy of learning.

We were anxious to find a teacherpreneurial role for Kelsey to fill. How often do policymakers get a chance to learn from those who teach music to six- to ten-year-olds? We had watched her steal the show (so to speak) at a community forum in which local union leaders and several school reformers debated the policy merits of a popular movie promoting the primacy of performance pay for teachers based on test scores. Her knowledge of child development and how teachers teach effectively transcended the movie's reform message and offered a fresh perspective that was different from the ones articulated by the other panelists.

And Kelsey's principal and superintendent really loved the idea of her becoming a teacherpreneur. Her principal told us, "Kelsey is so smart, and I know she will learn a lot about redesign of elementary schools, from which I am certain we will all benefit." How often do you find a principal, like Kelsey's, who thought it was a great opportunity for a young teacher to lead outside the school, district, and even state?

But Kelsey fell prey to several major organizational realities—and turned down the offer of a hybrid role. First, many schools are organized so that only one teacher is responsible for teaching a restricted group of students. "I really wanted to take on the hybrid role, but I could not get comfortable with who would be teaching my students when I was not there," she told us. "I was worried about the continuity of learning and the lack of time I would have to connect with students outside of class." Ironically, in her teacherpreneurial role, Kelsey could have learned more about and taken back to her school strategies and approaches pertaining to how elementary schools could be redesigned.

Second, Kelsey was concerned that if she took on a half-time teaching assignment her district might lose interest in the kind of music teaching she offers. "Not many districts invest in music or art anymore," she noted. "I wondered if I took on the teacherpreneurial role, maybe my district would end up doing away with the position entirely."

Finally, she was worried about the workload associated with the "full-timeness" of both teaching and policy work. Kelsey said, "Teaching is a full-time job even if you teach a reduced load. You have to plan as much for three classes as you do for six." She continued, "There is a reason why you are either a policy reformer or a teacher. They both have their stresses and time commitments, but are built on very different rhythms." One reason Kelsey is so good at teaching music is that she is still a musician. "I worried about finding time to create my own songs and play with my band; this is very important to me."

Kelsey is still involved with CTQ's virtual network and blogs regularly about pedagogy and policy, but we could not convince her to become a teacherpreneur. In the end, she told us, "I just cannot do these two jobs." The guilt and pressure of "leaving her students" for part of the day created too much doubt for Kelsey to gamble on her own career. We were disappointed, but we understood.

> We see the teacher leaders featured in this book as border runners whose refrain is not the condemnation of administrators or reformers, but rather the creation of a "fourth way" of leadership that transcends the debate over having individual teachers teach whatever they wish versus prescriptive curricula and overzealous approaches to high-stakes testing.

POLITICAL BARRIERS

Teachers' efforts to lead in bold ways are often undermined by not just cultural and organizational barriers but also political ones. We could tell hundreds of stories, encountered by CTQ staff and members of the Collaboratory, but the one that follows captures best why authentic teacher leadership is routinely resisted.

Story #6: What Happens When Teachers Deliver an Inconvenient Truth?

In late 2012 we had just walked out of another Washington DC–based convening—this time hosted by a think tank that had been very influential in passing the 2002 No Child Left Behind Act. The organization was still advocating for high-stakes accountability, drawing on limited measures of student achievement. Toward the end of the session, someone had brought up how in Finland—home to some of the world's top-performing students (even when accounting for socioeconomic status)[6]—they do not use any high-stakes achievement tests, nor do they even have a systematic approach to teacher evaluation because of the rigor and uniformity of their high-quality approaches to preparing new recruits to teaching. As we left the Dupont Circle building, we had a chance to continue the conversation with Ralph, one of the think tank's leaders. We thought now was the time to see if his organization (which had begun to express a need for bold approaches to Common Core State Standards implementation and teacher reforms) would be willing to consider lessons not just from top-performing nations but also from classroom experts who could inform the think tank's efforts and vice versa. So we invited him for a cup of coffee.

At the local Starbucks, we soon discovered that his organization was working in two of the same school districts in which we were supporting teacher leaders with the Common Core State Standards and teacher evaluation reforms. The difference: his organization was focused on school boards and administrators, whereas we were working with those who teach students each day. We had a virtual network, and the think tank was conducting all of its deliberations in face-to-face venues.

Without question, our organizations had some different approaches to closing the achievement gap. Theirs focused more on top-down policies and leadership development of those who currently control the decision making in public education. Ours focused on connecting, readying, and mobilizing expert teachers so they can lead the transformation of their profession and student learning. We thought "different" would be good—combining varied perspectives in the creation of new ideas that might not be cultivated otherwise. We were hopeful in forging an exchange on how advocacy organizations and think tanks as well as superintendents of high-need schools and union leaders could begin to find some common ground on teaching and learning. We thought this could really work.

We were wrong.

As we told Ralph more of the "what" and "how" of our approach to teacher leadership, he sat expressionless. We then mentioned how we were using new technologies and supporting more teachers as virtual community organizers, and highlighted our Web platform's potential to electronically connect more teachers with one another and administrators, making for more authentic conversations aimed toward identifying problems and seeking effective solutions.

Ralph remained hard to read and continued not to say a word.

Finally he spoke. "We are working with superintendents and chief academic officers and do not have the bandwidth to also work with teacher leaders."

After explaining that working with teacher leaders is what *we* do, Ralph sat quietly, again expressionless. We reminded him of teaching's complexity and the challenges of implementing the Common Core State Standards, including the organizational structures that impede the spread of teachers' technical expertise, especially that related to building local curriculum, selecting resources, and using formative assessments. We also shared that teachers in our network have some interesting solutions and want to learn more with policymakers and administrators.

Ralph nodded politely, and then began talking about teachers' unions and how they typically get in the way of progress. Although we had not considered bringing up unions, we shared that our own efforts did not favor administrators or unions. And we explained how our work aims to transcend the usual divide between those who lead and those who teach.

Then Ralph replied, "Godspeed in what you are trying to do." Later, his organization released its own report on teacher leaders. Message received: no interest here in working with you and your brand of teacher leaders.

We later told this story to a Washington insider, who knew Ralph and his organization well. She said bluntly, "Teachers, especially expert ones like the ones in your network, can provide a powerful but inconvenient truth to his reform agenda." And then she asked us a question: "What if these teacher leaders, who know and care for students, families, and communities deeply, had 'a larger say' in the future of the $600 billion public school enterprise?"

We think of these cultural, organizational, and political barriers as borders—lines that teachers can cross, with the right knowledge and support.

We see the teacher leaders featured in this book as border runners whose refrain is not the condemnation of administrators or reformers, but rather the creation of a "fourth way" of leadership that transcends the debate over having individual teachers teach whatever they wish versus prescriptive curricula and overzealous approaches to high-stakes testing. The fourth way, with teachers initiating transformative changes in pedagogy and policy, challenges the status quo and traditional boundaries.[7] Again, Warschawski's insights are relevant:

> In fighting for democracy, one cannot limit oneself to that which is explicitly authorized. It is imperative to test the law, to occupy all the free space not explicitly forbidden, and sometimes to challenge the law in order to establish new freedoms.[8]

The same is true for a bold new brand of teacher leadership. We are certain that resistance—as defined by stories shared here—will continue. And we have some ideas about how to begin to select, support, and sustain teacherpreneurs in ways that will encourage them to continue to cross borders. In the next chapter we begin to describe and specify how school districts, associations, community-based organizations, and nonprofits can select, support, and sustain teacherpreneurs.

Activity for Chapter Seven[*]

Now What?

Seek "Anti-Barrier" Solutions

Goal

Throughout this chapter, we shared six stories that reflect the cultural, organizational, and political barriers many teachers face as they explore new leadership roles in their school and district. Whether you receive "weird" looks when you talk about leading, encounter controlling administrators, deliver an inconvenient truth, or experience obstacles not listed here, you must be prepared to address these barriers head-on. In doing so, you can begin to pursue your own teacherpreneurial role and transform teaching and learning in your community.

Think

Reflect on the stories of barriers to teacherpreneurism presented in this chapter. Which might you be most likely to encounter in your own exploration of a teacherpreneurial role?

Now flip that scenario around to formulate the "anti-barrier," or the exact opposite of what you may face. (For example, if your barrier is an administrator who is too controlling of your time and work as a teacher leader, the anti-barrier might be an administrator who controls very little or who is actively supportive.) Be as specific as possible about what this looks like. In this anti-barrier scenario, what might you feel, experience, hear from others, and see yourself and others do?

Next, brainstorm strategies to achieve your anti-barrier by writing one possible strategy on each of a number of sticky notes. Spend about ten to fifteen uninterrupted minutes developing as many ideas as possible. You should have a pile of solutions from which to choose when you finish.

[*]This activity is based on the Anti-Barrier Activity from the book *Gamestorming: A Playbook for Innovators, Rulebreakers, and Changemakers* (Gray, D., Brown, S., & Macanufo, J. [2010]. Sebastopol, CA: O'Reilly Media).

Act

Find a teaching colleague who understands the barriers you might face in developing a teacherpreneurial role. Share the anti-barrier and sort through the potential solutions you generated. What might work, and how do you know? Reflect as a pair on how this activity has helped you evaluate your original barrier differently. In what ways have you broken out of existing patterns in your thinking? What new understandings have you gained—about yourself and your barrier?

Share

Log into CTQ's virtual network (http://www.teachingquality.org) to share your barriers and potential solutions for overcoming them. Be sure to check out how other teachers have addressed the obstacles in their school and district.

CHAPTER 8

Creating What We Have Imagined

● *Be [your] own advocate . . . Get connected with other teachers . . . Once you're doing the work you're passionate about, find the people who can advocate with [you] and on your behalf.*

—Ryan Kinser, offering advice to future teacherpreneurs

In *Teaching 2030*, we set the tone for our expanded vision of the teaching profession's future by titling our prologue "We Cannot Create What We Cannot Imagine." Since its publication in 2011, we have been working toward realizing that vision as a nonprofit focused on connecting, readying, and mobilizing teacher leaders so they can transform their profession.

With support from several philanthropies, including the Bill & Melinda Gates Foundation, MetLife Foundation, the Rose Community Foundation, and the Stuart Foundation, we launched a *test run* of teacherpreneurs as policy reformers. Our experiment, which included the successful efforts of Jessica Keigan (2011–2012) and Noah Zeichner (2011–2013), took us from the theoretical and aspirational vision of a bold idea to the pragmatic and diligent reality of public school life.

Being a teacherpreneur is not just about being at the table, speaking up, taking a stand, or putting students first—these are givens. In the policy reform landscape, the usual suspects at the table often have the voice but rarely have ever taught. And if they did teach, it was so long ago that they no longer know the intricacies of teaching and learning.

Teacherpreneurs assess and analyze policy issues and implications through the classroom lens of their pedagogical practice in and out of school—a perspective that is more important that any other when deliberating what will be in the best interests of students. Teacherpreneurs *teach*. Daily. They have credibility with the vast majority of their teaching colleagues. And despite the resistance from some administrators, we believe that many, many superintendents and principals have deep respect for teachers.

Jessica's and Noah's success and impact, although they are still in the nascent stages of their efforts, extend beyond the teacher voice movement of today to one that Ariel Sacks wrote about boldly in an Education Week Teacher essay:

> Several years ago, shortly after President Obama was elected, I took a day away from teaching to attend a meeting at a prominent policy organization. The group was convened to generate recommendations on education for the new administration. I was one of two teachers in attendance . . . Strangely, though, the final recommendations included nothing that was even remotely connected to anything my teacher colleague or I had said.
>
> I can deal with disappointment—but I couldn't shake the questions, "What was the purpose of my being there? Why was I given time to speak and then ignored?" Though I'll never know for sure, my conclusion was that my colleague and I were there as "token" teachers—so someone could say that teachers were involved in these decisions. More than anything, I was upset that I had missed a day with my students—only to fill a seat, not make a difference.[1]

So far, we have surfaced the stories of Noah and Jessica, whom we supported in official roles as teacherpreneurs to advance teaching policies locally and nationally, as well as the teacherpreneurial thinking and actions of Ariel, Shannon C'de Baca, Stephen Lazar, Renee Moore, Lori Nazareno, and José Vilson.

They all have taught us much about what it takes to be a teacherpreneur, including their knowledge and skills as well as characteristics. We have learned much about the importance of well-traveledness, intelligent humility, and reciprocal mentoring as well as the power and potential of ambitious introverts who can drive an agenda while also listening carefully to all around them.

We did not know enough about selecting and supporting teacherpreneurs before we began to do so. But these eight teacherpreneurial leaders, as well as many with whom we have been working in our virtual community, have taught us a great deal about how we should create more of what we have imagined. They've provided us with lessons in *knowing by doing*—much like those learned through the scholarly experiments of John Dewey and in popular movies featuring such teachers as Sean Maguire (played by Robin Williams) in *Good Will Hunting* and Richard Dreyfuss's title character in *Mr. Holland's Opus*.

In this chapter, we will discuss how school districts and associations as well as a host of community-based organizations and nonprofits can select, support, and sustain teacherpreneurs. So here is how to make the bold idea of teacherpreneurism work, beginning with teachers' considering if they *want* to be teacherpreneurs.

ARE YOU READY TO BE A TEACHERPRENEUR?

Despite the rhetoric of site-based decision making and autonomy in the classroom, much of the locus of control in education is still higher up in the educational hierarchy. Not surprisingly, the role of the teacherpreneur creates tension between the top-down approach of today's reforms and the closed classroom door of the isolated teacher of the past. Somewhere between these two extremes lies the opportunity to fully tap the potential of teacherpreneurs' expertise and leadership capacity so that they can help lead the way. As Roland Barth suggested a few years ago in a panel discussion at Harvard, our public schools need to "unlock the tremendous overabundance of underutilized talent that gets left in the parking lot every day."[2]

Following is a list of questions for aspiring teacherpreneurs to ask when considering entering into a relationship with a sponsoring or supporting organization:

- Are there supports in place, and do they support the areas in which I need to grow? (This assumes you have a high enough level of consciousness to know where you need and want to grow.)

- Is the role designed to total no more than 1.0 full-time equivalent (FTE) position? (Teachers should bear in mind that 1.0 FTE for a teacher at the top of his or her game is not necessarily only an eight-hour day.)

- Do I have the ability to cocreate the role to meet my own goals as a teacher leader, with the caveat that the supporting organization will probably have goals of its own to fulfill? (If the values align, then aligning the goals may already be done for you to some extent.)

- Do the district and sponsoring organization have the ability to step back once we agree on goals? (There has to be space to plan and do without someone looking over your shoulder. That's how growth and learning happen. If there's no space to fail, the teacherpreneur will also not have space to truly succeed and lead. Teacherpreneurs should be advised, collaborated with, and coached, not directed or managed. If a sponsoring organization finds it needs to direct or manage a teacherpreneur, this suggests a poor fit for the role.)

- Am I able to make space in my life to have this transition as my central challenge, at least during the first year of my role? (Naturally, big personal changes and big professional changes of this magnitude happening simultaneously can be a recipe for confusion, burnout, and ineffectiveness.)

- Am I ready for this type of role professionally? Do I have the knowledge and skills? What more do I need to learn—and how can I learn it? (The characteristics of teacherpreneurs described in this chapter should help with reflecting on this decision.)

What may be most important is for teachers to identify teacherpreneurism in themselves. Ryan Kinser, a 2012–2013 Center for Teaching Quality (CTQ) teacherpreneur, offers this advice in his interview published by EdSurge:

> Be [your] own advocate. Do the work and make sure it's needed by someone else . . . Get connected with other teachers. With social media it's impossible not to connect [to] someone that knows someone else. Once you're doing the work you're passionate about, find the people who can advocate with [you] and on your behalf.[3]

SELECTING TEACHERPRENEURS

At the beginning of 2011, as we set out on a three- to six-month journey to find a few teacherpreneurs from among our growing network of classroom experts, we examined the somewhat limited body of research on teacher leadership. Twenty-five years ago, J. F. Rogus claimed that teacher leaders needed to be selected from those who were skilled teachers and possessed an inquiry-based orientation toward teaching as well as had experiences in creating community, leading curriculum reviews, fostering ownership among peers, communicating a vision (and developing political support) for change, and demonstrating patience and persistence.[4] We knew from Mark Smylie and Jack Denny's thoughtful research that teacher leadership involves more than revising roles and developing the work skills needed to execute them.[5] Teacher leadership also takes into account how the teacher leaders and those around them respond to and "mediate" these new roles and how organizational structures get in the way—or not.[6]

> Solving ambiguous and complicated problems requires far more than a short list of technical leadership skills combined with measurable teaching expertise.

We at CTQ faced our own challenges in nurturing these new teacherpreneurial roles. CTQ is a nonprofit that is rapidly shifting from a think tank approach, with a focus on conducting research, producing papers, and hosting policy briefings, to a teacher leader Collaboratory, funded almost solely by philanthropy. Our ability to fund the teacherpreneurial roles hinged on the good graces of foundations and their funding cycles, which were not always in sync with school district calendars and schools' HR protocols. In addition, we had to find teacherpreneurs who not only had the "right stuff" in general but also would not be beset by the cultural, organizational, and political barriers we had faced in our preliminary efforts to engage other teacher leaders like Julio, Andrea, Madeline, and Kelsey (highlighted in Chapter Seven).

We initially based our decisions about the traits we would seek in teacherpreneurial recruits on five primary areas: (1) teacher effectiveness; (2) respect and credibility among their peers and administrators; (3) a solutions-focused approach to problems and issues; (4) active participation and involvement as team members in CTQ projects; and (5) potential to have an impact beyond their own classroom, particularly at the district and state levels.

We asked for each of the applicants to submit evidence of his or her teaching and student learning, but also looked for well-crafted lessons, engaged students, responsive teaching strategies, tools for monitoring learning, and clear and strong classroom communication and questioning strategies.

In assessing their leadership skills, we drew on a range of evidence (such as interviews, artifacts, and observations) to first and foremost determine how well they could talk about their effectiveness as teachers as well as communicate the need for their teacherpreneurial roles to varied stakeholders and constituents of the public education system. Because all of them would have to serve as boundary spanners, we sought to learn about our applicants from how they each spoke about their role as a teaching professional and school district employee as well as their role as a leader inside of CTQ's nonprofit world of policy and research. Also, because our new teacherpreneurs would focus on both policy and pedagogical reforms, we were most interested in how they could synthesize and use evidence as well as balance diverse perspectives.

We developed our own scoring rubric to combine all of the data assembled, honing in on not only content knowledge and the ability to connect the worlds of policy and practice, but also skills and primary traits—like efficacy, flexibility, craftsmanship, consciousness, and interdependence. These are all states of mind that the Center for

Cognitive Coaching notes can help leaders use internal and external resources effectively.[7] In assessing their teacherpreneurial readiness, we always looked for a solutions-focused stance; that was a nonnegotiable. Teacherpreneurs are not stuck on "either-or," but rather default to "both-and" when receiving or generating ideas. This flexibility ideally is complemented by persistence and resourcefulness in getting work accomplished and advancing individual as well as team goals.

The degree to which teacherpreneurial candidates were able to form these habits of mind and practice, along with their balance of oral and written communication fluency, were of paramount importance to us. But there was no highly precise way to identify the essential teacherpreneurial skills and traits. And remember, teacherpreneurs must deal with complex problems that often do not present easy solutions and that remain difficult to overcome without systemic change.[8] Solving ambiguous and complicated problems requires far more than a short list of technical leadership skills combined with measurable teaching expertise.

According to British policy expert Paul Williams, difficult problems require boundary spanners who have interorganizational experience, transdisciplinary knowledge, and strong cognitive capabilities.[9] In many cases, teachers who step out of their classroom, which is an isolated and contained environment, often have not had the experiences of working in different organizations and across disciplinary boundaries. Teacherpreneurs will find themselves highly accountable to at least two very different worlds—and they have to be skilled and relatively comfortable in navigating both. We sought and found many of these qualities in our teacherpreneurs. But we also discovered that these qualities can be readily developed, especially if teachers have the private space to test out their skills in bridging the ideas, languages, and processes of teaching students and building coalitions among adults. Being able to maintain a high level of flexibility in balancing the diverse and often clashing perspectives of these worlds is critical.

As we continue to learn more from our current cohort of four teacherpreneurs, we recognize that our list falls far short of what should be taken into consideration when looking for the goodness of fit that will set a teacherpreneur up for success. As described in Chapter Seven, many barriers must be overcome, and often the degree to which the teacher leader is armed with the skills and experience to meet these challenges can be critical to his or her teacherpreneurial success. But we have also learned how important it is for teacherpreneurs to be well traveled and possess the kind of intelligent humility that engages their colleagues as well as those who have typically stood "above" them in the policy world. All eight of the teachers profiled in this book hold these characteristics, as do the teacherpreneurs and teachers in residence selected for 2012–2013.

CTQ TEACHERPRENEURS AND TEACHERS IN RESIDENCE, 2012–2013

With backing from four different philanthropies, in 2012–2013 CTQ supported four teacherpreneurs and two teachers in residence—both financially and programmatically. Many of the lessons described herein framed the selection and current work of these six teacher leaders. For sure, we learn something new weekly from their experiences and their continued reflection with us on their work and its impact. What follows are brief descriptions of each of these six phenomenal educators and a glimpse of some of their impact beyond their respective classrooms.

Noah Zeichner (Seattle, Washington)

We were thrilled when Noah applied for a second year of teacherpreneurial thinking and action. In year one (2011–2012), Noah's role focused heavily on leadership that was structurally and substantively "outside" his role as a teacher within his school. He concentrated primarily on growing and sustaining a community of teacher leaders in the Puget Sound area who studied and worked at district and regional levels to advance teacher evaluation policies—policies that supported as well as measured teaching mastery that mattered for student achievement. In his first year as a teacherpreneur, Noah helped launch a district-level teacher advisory board, and his leadership was lauded by both district and union officials. But he didn't necessarily draw on his specific knowledge of and skills in regard to global education in driving teacher evaluation reforms in his school.

Noah wanted his teacherpreneurial role to be more directly connected to his Chief Sealth International High School teaching colleagues—and used his time in year one to define more of what would be his ideal leadership focus in year two. His future thinking and actions inspired us to generate support for an international community of teacher leaders, connected to his district's involvement with the Asia Society's Global Cities Education Network and the work that he does daily with his fellow teachers at Chief Sealth and about five hundred of his colleagues in the Seattle Public Schools. Both administrators and union leaders had always had deep respect for Noah's leadership in the classroom and beyond, but after a year they were beginning to see the huge benefit of his hybrid role.

Jessica Cuthbertson (Aurora, Colorado)

In contrast to our yearlong relationship with Noah prior to his becoming a teacherpreneur, Jessica Cuthbertson was a member of our network for only a few months before submitting her application for the teacherpreneurial role in early

Figure 8.1

Lori Nazareno, left, and Jessica Cuthbertson plan their goals for the year at the Summer 2012 teacherpreneur and teacher in residence retreat in North Carolina.

Photo courtesy of CTQ.

2012. She was just completing her work toward National Board Certification at the time and serving as a coach in the Aurora Public Schools outside of Denver—but she was eager to return to a classroom of her own at Vista Peak Exploratory and its innovative pre-K through postsecondary approach.

With nine years of teaching and coaching experience, Jessica, in 2012–2013, is applying her deep pedagogical expertise and policy knowledge to her work with the Colorado Department of Education's Curriculum Development Project, helping build the capacity of a growing number of CTQ-Colorado members to align their instruction and assessment practices to the Common Core State Standards. In addition, she serves as an association representative for her building, helping the local affiliate transform as a "new union" organization that focuses more of its time and resources on teacher learning (rather than just salary and benefits issues). Jessica taught for six years before serving as an instructional coach for three. She returned to teaching and her teacherpreneurial role because, as Jessica told us: "I had learned so much that I had to get into the classroom to implement what I had learned." But early

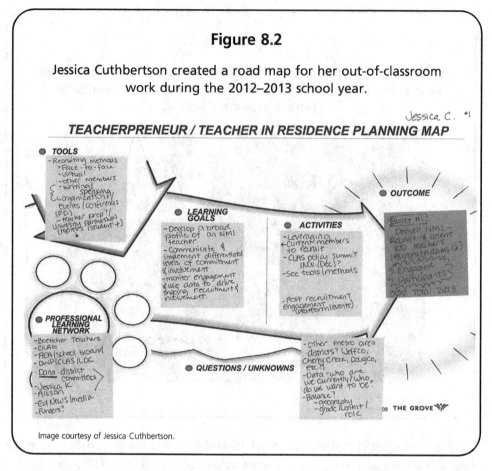

Figure 8.2

Jessica Cuthbertson created a road map for her out-of-classroom work during the 2012–2013 school year.

Image courtesy of Jessica Cuthbertson.

in fall 2012, Jessica struggled, like so many other highly committed career teachers, in finding the balance between time with her students and time to spread her expertise to colleagues and policymakers. Jessica said, "At the end of the day I want to look at my seventy sixth graders and say, 'You are first.'" Jessica's writing, particularly her CTQ blog, copublished with EdNews Colorado, deepened quickly, and she began to use her position as a teacherpreneur to elevate the voices of her students.[10]

Ryan Kinser and Megan Allen (Hillsborough County, Florida)

We are fortunate, as we write this, to have two teacherpreneurs—Ryan Kinser and Megan Allen—in Hillsborough County, Florida. Their district is one of the epicenters of American education reform, as it has started Common Core State Standards implementation and designed and put in place a new teacher evaluation system in just a few years' time.

Ryan's "Blow the Doors"

http://bit.ly/12gi51b

Ryan's teacherpreneurial work seeks to help teachers make practical, integrated sense of these reforms. He launched an online professional learning community in his school (Walker Middle Magnet School for International Studies) early in the 2012–2013 school year, which he is now growing to include hundreds of other teachers across the district—merging technology tools, his teaching know-how, and his expertise in virtual communities gained through work with CTQ. In doing so, Ryan has emerged as a kind of policy and practice

Figure 8.3

Ryan Kinser talks to his sixth-grade students in his Florida classroom.

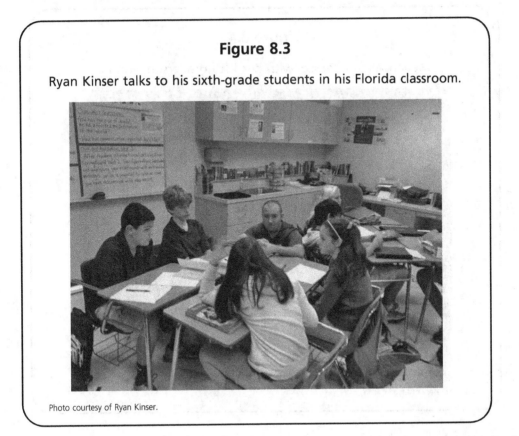

Photo courtesy of Ryan Kinser.

connector, and he is developing strategic plans to "sell" his approach to other districts and states. He has created an animated video (http://www.youtube.com/watch?v= NQd_QVjmuBA&feature=youtu.be) that makes the case that teachers should "blow the doors off" their classroom and learn from one another in an online community—and offers practical tips for how to do so.

Megan, who teaches at Shaw Elementary School (one of her district's highest-need schools), has focused more of her teacherpreneurial work on policy. With a wealth of contacts statewide thanks to her being the 2010 Florida Teacher of the Year, she is connecting the work of the Hillsborough County Public Schools (HCPS) team of teacher leaders with that of counterparts in other districts this year—including Escambia County School District and Pinellas County Schools. And together, Megan and Ryan are working with HCPS officials as part of a work group designing formal hybrid teacher leader roles: fifteen teachers will be selected to serve in these roles in 2013–2014, and thirty will be chosen the school year after. In addition, Megan is focused on building demand for teacher leadership inside of her district and others

Figure 8.4

Megan Allen interacts with her fifth graders in Florida.

Photo courtesy of Megan Allen.

across Florida, developing a variety of tools and resources to engage policymakers and the public as well as administrators.

Her visibility and effectiveness in speaking on behalf of her students led to her testifying on Capitol Hill early in winter 2013 on how the federal sequester would negatively affect her thirty-six students (ten of whom have special needs, with disabilities ranging from emotional and behavioral disorders to schizophrenia). Her words were captured both by the *Washington Post*[11] and C-SPAN.[12] Megan's powerful statements, and presence, put the faces of children on the then-looming issue of federal budget cuts.

Megan has found a sweet spot in her career. Her work teaching students every day, as she says, "grounds, inspires, and teaches her." But she also wants to lead, and help many other teachers do so. No organization in Florida—including the state education agency—has organized the state's former teachers of the year and its 6,300 National Board Certified Teachers (NBCTs) to advance pedagogical reforms. By early spring 2013, Megan had begun to do so with her NBCT colleagues. Her efforts have contributed to the creation of a teacher leader framework to allow HCPS to use its 534 NBCTs, and it is already spreading to other school districts in the state.

Lori Nazareno (Denver, Colorado)

Lori, whose teacherpreneurial story was told in Chapter Six, is taking a leave of absence from coleading the Math and Science Leadership Academy in 2012–2013 to serve as a teacher in residence with CTQ. In her time away from students and families as well as teaching colleagues of the Athmar Park neighborhood in West Denver, Lori is leading a number of initiatives. She is building and codifying a curriculum for other teachers to learn how to lead Common Core State Standards and teacher evaluation reforms as well as design their own schools. She is working closely with Jessica C. in advancing the work of CTQ-Colorado, which will include the production of policy podcasts and conversation guides to aid in the implementation of their state's teacher evaluation law. Lori and Jessica have also been integral in launching a teacher cabinet for state senator Mike Johnston to advise him on education policy matters—even when his policy proposals, like the one allowing a teacher to earn a teaching license without any preparation whatsoever, run counter to both the research evidence[13] and the recommendations from expert teachers like them.[14]

Sarah Henchey (Carrboro, North Carolina)

And finally, Sarah Henchey of Carrboro, North Carolina—like Lori—is released from teaching full-time this year to work with CTQ as a teacher in residence. Sarah's story is especially meaningful to us because she has been connected with our network for each of the eight years of her career. As she likes to say, "CTQ raised me professionally," and she credits the formal and informal mentoring she has received from others with aiding in the rapid development of her capacity as a teacher leader. Her school is just minutes away from our office, and she is still engaged with colleagues there and at two other local middle schools to help them align their teaching with the coming Common Core State Standards—an extension of the work that she leads nationally with other teachers in a growing number of states.

Sarah's expertise—in terms of leading CTQ's virtual community organizer training as well as developing strategies to use NBCTs as curriculum experts—quickly translated into funding for a network of forty Kentucky NBCTs. Her work also led to

Figure 8.5

Sarah Henchey is a current teacher in residence
in Carrboro, North Carolina.

Photo courtesy of CTQ.

the selection and support of a teacherpreneur, to drive Common Core State Standards reforms for hundreds, and later thousands, of the state's classroom teachers. Most of the ideas, as well as the strategies for the initiative, supported by the Kentucky Department of Education, came from Sarah.

SUPPORTING TEACHERPRENEURS

Selecting teacher leaders who have the right stuff of teacherpreneurism (or the qualifications to be teachers in residence) is paramount, but so is supporting them. Support must come from a variety of stakeholders and advocates, including administrators at the school and district levels, colleagues, union leaders, sponsoring organizations, and community and family members. Of course, mandating the provision of such support is counterproductive; there must be mutual agreement to do so among the teacher, the sponsor, and the district. Support must start with authentic conversations among all parties involved, followed by a formal agreement.

For both Noah and Jessica K., as well as for each of our new teacherpreneurs, we forged a memorandum of understanding (MOU) that covers the general parameters of what both CTQ and the district that employs the teacherpreneur will do. The MOU lays out the scope of the teacherpreneur's work, what communication and publicity will look like, and the workspace the teacherpreneur will have, and it guarantees the transfer of funds from CTQ to the district to cover one-half (in these two cases, although the percentage can be more or less) of the teacherpreneur's total annual compensation (see Appendix C for a sample MOU). Most important, the MOU is a sound understanding among district and union leaders, the sponsoring organization, and the teacherpreneur in regard to the purpose and focus of the teacherpreneurial role. The same basic MOU agreements were also created for teachers in residence with full-time release.

In our first years of piloting the teacherpreneurial role, we found extraordinary educators and stakeholders who embraced the promise and possibility of this bold idea. Among administrators, we found no greater supporter of teacherpreneurs than Dan Rubenstein, cofounder and executive director of Brooklyn Prospect Charter School, who had a great deal to say about Ariel and her leadership, and the potential for many more teachers to lead. Dan told us:

> Ariel is brilliant and was so well prepared for her teaching in a school with so many different types of learners, but I suspect there are hundreds of thousands of teachers who can lead like she does. They are out there. It's just a question of getting them to a place where they are in an environment that doesn't just allow it but also fosters interesting leadership ideas and getting in a place where there is no "okay plateau."

Dan was an excellent classroom teacher, and continues to see himself as a teacher and a "third-pillar advocate" for the teaching profession who transcends the reform "screamers" (pillar one) and the unions that seem to resist almost any change (pillar two). Dan told us, "The key to supporting teacher leaders is to ensure that they have opportunities to deepen their pedagogical practice over time, not just a year or two before they move on." He went on to say:

> We are trying to create an institution here at Brooklyn Prospect that has lots of success but is also sustainable, which is not an easy thing to do. That is one of the things we talk about. I think that schools, not teachers or principals, have become the unit of reform. We've really lionized the leaders and the principal as the way that this is getting done, but it is really about the master teacher. We're not going to get to that place of success for students without that large group of teacher leaders—and teacherpreneurs.

Anthony Jones, principal of Walker Middle Magnet in Hillsborough County, Florida, works with Ryan and embraces teacherpreneurs with gusto. "It is a very neat concept, and I know Ryan will connect with a lot of awesome teachers. This will help us here at our school," Anthony said.

Anthony is deeply appreciative of the complexities of his district's efforts to implement a new teacher evaluation system that draws on a range of evidence, including controversial (and often unstable) measures that statistically link student achievement test scores to those who teach them. "Ryan is infinitely creative, willing to try new things, and interested in learning ideas," Anthony said. "He is very good at spreading his knowledge and ideas to his teammates." Most important, this administrator realizes that he cannot lead the teacher evaluation reforms by himself or with an assistant principal or two. "Some principals are about total control, but not me," he continued. Anthony believes that teachers must view themselves as leaders, and that Ryan will help in "making the transition."

Lisa Maltezos, principal of Shaw Elementary, also in Hillsborough County, is very supportive of Megan's leadership, in and out of the district. "Megan is so important to us," Lisa noted. "She brings much knowledge and skill to our building, and she has impacted so many other teachers here." In particular, she mentioned how the fifth-grade team of which Megan is a part, in just a few short months, has evolved from being the most insular to the most collaborative.

> Our fifth-grade team has taken to Megan, and has learned so much about teaching and the big picture behind what she does in the classroom. She also has infected the team with the grand way she respects our students here at Shaw.

Lisa made it clear that Megan's experience in her leadership role this year has been valuable. "I sure hope we can afford to keep her in this teacherpreneurial role next year," she said.

Garrett Rosa, then the director at Vista Peaks, was thrilled to support Jessica C.'s teacherpreneurial role. Garrett, a big fan of Dan Pink and his popular theories of how the "old carrot-and-stick notion of motivation is failing" our businesses and schools,[15] told us no one was better suited for a teacherpreneurial role than Jessica because of the way she was trained to "do things differently with time, space, walls, and clocks as well as the harsh hand of accountability." Unlike many other administrators, Garrett embraced the idea that Jessica would be involved in conversations with researchers and reformers from across the nation—and was looking forward to learning from and with her.

But teacherpreneurs need direct support from others outside of their school as well.

In 2011–2012 we worked closely with Noah and Jessica K. to support their teacherpreneurism. Having a support system in place to facilitate their venture into this uncharted territory was critical to their success, but perhaps even more important was what it taught us at CTQ. We approached our method of supporting them as an exercise in effective teaching: we were responsive to their needs, had a "curriculum" aligned to their progression of development, and used mediated questioning (an approach to facilitate self-reflection). Writing seemed to discipline our thinking and action, and we asked both our teacherpreneurs and our staff who supported them to engage in formal monthly reflections (see Appendix D for a sample teacherpreneur reflection report). Noah's and Jessica's communications (online, via phone, and in person) about their roles and impact were consistently reviewed, and approaches for supporting their growth were recalibrated by CTQ staff, as circumstances required.

With CTQ based in North Carolina, Jessica K. in Colorado, and Noah in Washington, our eight years of experience in building deeply engaged online learning proved to be invaluable. Although we did visit Jessica and Noah at their school and community sites an average of four times during the school year, we also maintained individual formal check-ins with them via phone (at least weekly), with others in their local cohort (at least every other week), and online (monthly). Many other informal connections were also maintained, primarily through ongoing online conversations and occasional impromptu phone calls. Our conversations, both verbal and virtual as well as synchronous and asynchronous, produced a tome of rich

> Teacherpreneurs should be advised, collaborated with, and coached, not directed or managed.

documentation that allowed us to begin thinking through implications for CTQ's work in the short term and for our vision that we hope will be realized of six hundred thousand U.S. teacherpreneurs by 2030. Looking back on our first year of support in 2011–2012, one area of complexity was the practical challenge of how to structure time and scheduling for the teacherpreneurial role.

PLANNING FOR THE TEACHERPRENEURIAL ROLE

Not surprisingly, learning how to effectively plan for this role was an immediate need. The schedule of a teacherpreneur involves a drastic switch from being "controlled to the minute" (the "teacher" half of the day) to having a dauntingly unfamiliar blank block of time (the "preneur" half of the day). Planning for the teacherpreneurial role is a process that must involve not only the teacherpreneur and the sponsoring organization (in this case, CTQ) but also a number of key supporters (administrators at the building and district levels, anchor community organizations, and so on).

In the first year of working with Noah and Jessica K. as teacherpreneurs, none of us involved fully knew enough about what to expect from this hybrid role. But we did learn to expect the unexpected—and built in protocols to make sure we could manage the inherent ambiguity in forging ahead with teacher leaders who had to work in two different worlds.

In terms of the individual teacherpreneur's plans for effectively executing work, detailed work plans are key. A guiding document that delineates goals, how those goals will be reached, a timeline, and a plan for balancing teaching with "preneuring" responsibilities is critical (see Appendix E for a sample teacherpreneur work plan). Although all work plans, just like effective lesson plans, need not follow a strictly prescriptive format, such plans do help in identifying questions to be resolved in defining roles and trigger good conversations among teacherpreneurs and those who support them.

As with support for practitioners in any new role, frequent check-ins between the teacherpreneurs and the sponsoring organization as well as among the teacherpreneurs themselves are vital to overcoming isolation and to the mutual advancement of professional growth and learning. These check-ins, which typically occur weekly, include exchanging updates, offering strategic counsel, and troubleshooting with the sponsoring organization. Structuring an ongoing parallel conversation with a key point of contact at the school building level is a strategy we have employed in year two, keeping all the pieces of the teacherpreneur's role unified and preventing too much separation between the "teacher" half and the "preneur" half of the teacherpreneur's schedule. In addition to the weekly check-ins concerning day-to-day challenges and successes, monthly opportunities to step back and look at the big picture are also important to informing the role. These meetings are set aside to revisit the work plan; reflect on big-picture goals; and consider what might need shifting, what is working well, and what new supports are helping. Both individually and as a group, teacherpreneurs and their key supporters explore what might need to become part of the evolving system of support. Teacherpreneurs, in general, agree that the simple moral support from sharing their common experiences is a lifeline, reducing the sense of isolation in the role.

Planning matters, but teacherpreneurial positions cannot be planned for in uniform ways. For instance, the nature of teaching in self-contained K–5 classrooms means that schools can't simply divide a teacherpreneur's course load in half to make time for leadership. Instead, elementary-level teacherpreneurs like Megan require a teaching partner who can effectively job-share. This partner must be able to teach at the same mastery level as the teacherpreneur, communicate seamlessly about their common students, and remain flexible to accommodate the teacherpreneur's sometimes-shifting schedule.

Megan began the 2012–2013 school year with such a teaching partner, but the stresses of teaching in a very high-need school with an extended-day schedule resulted in her coteacher's departure in October. These same challenges, in combination with the uniqueness of the role, made it difficult to find a replacement. However, when this ideal plan failed, Megan's principal and assistant principal stepped forward, as Megan put it, "to proactively create plans B through F." They worked *with* Megan to redesign her schedule from three days teaching and two days released to mornings in the classroom, with students going to enrichment classes like art, music, and physical education or receiving supplemental instruction from specialists or interventionists in the afternoon. This was not ideal, but they brought in long-term subs to provide class coverage where needed during the interim. Megan's administrators believed that much in what she was trying to create for her students, school, and profession.

And most important, Megan's principal and assistant principal remained in direct contact with her—staying available to her in on-the-fly meetings or via late-night texts—to offer support during the transition and elicit her input in ongoing attempts to hire a new coteacher. In sum, even the best plans sometimes have to be re-laid. When that becomes necessary, it's critical to have supportive administrators like Megan's to step in, working alongside the sponsoring organization and the teacherpreneur, to make the right decisions to support this teacher leader and the students he or she serves.

SUSTAINING TEACHERPRENEURS

Almost twenty years ago, Richard Elmore published a stunningly insightful piece, "Getting to Scale with Good Educational Practice." Reviewing evidence from two attempts at large-scale school reform in the past—the progressive movement and the National Science Foundation's curriculum reform projects of the 1950s and 1960s—Elmore pointed out that the problem of scale in spreading good educational practice is not due to schools' failure to change.[16] In 1996 he made the case that schools change all the time by adopting new curricula and tests, grouping students differently, and creating new mechanisms for teachers to participate in decision making.

Now, in the early part of 2013, we have seen school reform focus on charter schools that are freed from typical labor-management contracts, extended-day and extended-year calendars to add more instruction time, and new teacher evaluation and tenure rules to judge teachers more on student test scores than has been the case in the past and to remove ineffective teachers more readily. But as Elmore noted back in the mid-1990s, "within this vortex of change" the rudimentary roles that teachers and students play in constructing knowledge as well as the classroom, school, and district structures in facilitating learning "remain relatively static."[17]

Reflecting on what we have learned after eighteen months of working with teacherpreneurs, and on how to scale up the concept of teacherpreneurism, we have begun to consider how universities and their tightly defined bureaucracies have readily embraced joint appointments and hybrid roles for their faculty. If it is okay for university teachers to be teacherpreneurial, can't it one day be okay for classroom experts from the world of K–12 public education to take on a teacherpreneurial role?

Elmore makes it clear that the "problems of scale are deeply rooted in the incentives and cultural norms of the institutions, and cannot be fixed with simple policy shifts or exhortations from people with money."[18] But he does point to how to tackle, at least initially, the problem of scale, including the development of "strong external normative structures for practice" so the reforms can be made more public as well as "creat[ing] intentional processes for the reproduction of successes."[19] Here are three takeaways, built from Elmore's framework, for sustaining teacherpreneurs.

1. Make Teacherpreneurs More Public

Shannon expressed concern that too much of today's leadership from the classroom is made intentionally invisible by administrators and teachers alike, and offered a clear suggestion in regard to how to make teacherpreneurs more public:

To make teacherpreneurs more visible they have to be part of the social fabric of the school—and recognized as an important part. We have to be very explicit about making more visible what teacherpreneurs *actually do*—like serving as community connectors or policy mavens.

Ariel believes that all teachers must be expected to publicly "sort out issues of practice"—but that they will need help in doing so. Teacherpreneurs could play this role—making them essential for administrators building a case to the public for the kinds of school designs, curriculum and assessment tools, and teaching strategies essential for twenty-first-century student learning. Dan Rubenstein and LaNolia Omowanile, as administrators who know teaching intimately and respect teacher leadership, have done much to help Ariel sort out her pedagogical practices inside of Brooklyn Prospect and have encouraged her to make her policy ideas public. They could serve as role models for how those who don't teach can support the leadership of those who do. Lori told us there are many, many teachers who can lead like she has over the last twenty-five years, and who have done so. Dan told us that there are many, many administrators who could and would support teacher leaders in the way he and LaNolia have. Making teacherpreneurs more public will require tapping into their own networks—and elevating the visibility of administrators who seek to blur the lines of distinction between those who teach in schools and those who lead them.

2. Use Teacher Evaluation and Pay Systems to Elevate Teacherpreneurism

We wondered if teacher evaluation systems could be transformed to assess teacherpreneurial skills, as do those in Singapore, where mastery of teaching demands the ability to "address long-term fundamental issues . . . influencing the school's relation to the external world" as well as "highlight and resolve issues that affect teacher effectiveness." Teacher evaluation in Singapore is designed for public collaboration and professional participation, both simultaneously essential for building trust between schools and communities.[20] Even the most advanced teacher evaluation systems in the United States expect far too little of classroom practitioners when it comes to the publicness of their teaching.

For teacher leaders to receive the highest ratings within an improved teacher evaluation system, they would have to make their teaching visible to the public and make sense of their practice relative to the needs of students, both in and out of their classroom. We also wondered if pay for performance systems could be revolutionized to encourage teachers to spread their teaching expertise publicly in the interest of improving both pedagogical practice and parent engagement. Ariel drew on a current corporate example to suggest another way to restructure schools and roles around the critical issue of time, so the most accomplished teachers can spread their teaching expertise. Ariel pointed to Internet search giant Google's practice of setting aside a portion of its engineers' time to work on projects of their own invention and interest—a policy that produced, among other innovations, AdSense and Google Mail. Ariel noted:

> To break away from the hierarchical structures that keep losing us great teachers and moving at a snail's pace, we'll need to carve out significant time, like Google's 20 percent, or even up to 50 percent for some, to expand teachers' roles as leaders and innovators who are able to respond better and faster to the needs of students . . . Teachers do this kind of real-time problem solving constantly on a micro scale—like finding a new way to reach a struggling student—but we rarely have the time to do it on a large scale and share out what we learn.

3. Prepare New Teachers Early in Their Training to Teach, Lead, and Not Leave

As we probed Elmore's framework further, Stephen shared with us a paper he was writing about the "shifting structural landscape of American urban schools and the necessity of both in- and out-of-school education stakeholders' leveraging their activities to maximize the contribution of classroom teachers to the educational field." He identified several factors necessary to transform teachers from isolated individual practitioners to actualized teacher leaders—and eventually teacherpreneurs. Although Stephen talked about schools' creating space for teacher leaders to practice and develop their new identity, he also identified the need for novice teachers to be formally trained, socialized, and recognized as potential teacher leaders. Too few novices today are prepared to teach and lead as teacherpreneurs—and all too often they are expected to leave well before they develop deep pedagogical expertise.

In examining the possibilities of sustaining teacherpreneurs, we turned to the efforts of the Stanford Graduate School of Education, in partnership with the American Association of Colleges of Teacher Education, to create a Teacher Performance Assessment (TPA) for novices. Instead of new teachers' having to prove themselves with what have been pedantic and thin paper-and-pencil tests to be licensed, they will soon be required to prove themselves by explaining their lesson plans and analyzing digital recordings of their "practice" teaching. In spring 2012 over 7,200 candidates at 165 universities and colleges across twenty-two states participated in a field test—and for the first time a large group of new recruits across different contexts and communities engaged in the same teaching assessment.

We thought back on teaching's past and the root causes of the historical isolation of teachers. Then we mused on the fact that this was the first time that core expectations for what novice teachers need to know and do were set and demanded on a national level. And then we considered the power and potential of the TPA, with candidates mentored and supported by NBCTs, to serve as the bedrock for building collective responsibility and making teachers' practice more public. And how is this possible? Through the TPA and National Board processes, both the new recruits and the seasoned veterans use video to better understand the impact of their teaching on student learning and show it to others. Now is the time for them to do so together, drawing on both the video images of teaching and their commentaries to demonstrate what teachers of the twenty-first century must know and do. And it is time for them to share that knowledge and expertise inside and outside of the profession.

We reflected on our own growing online community of pedagogical power-houses—who have extensive experience in using digital recordings of their teaching practice to document their accomplishments—and the role such a partnership between novice and veteran teachers could play in advancing teacherpreneurism.

We acknowledge that teacherpreneurism in 2013 is still a nascent concept, but as Lori reminded us:

> I am wondering if there is something to be learned from other scenarios in other contexts. What comes to mind first is ATMs and debit cards. We didn't know we needed them until we had them. Now I can't even imagine how we managed without them. Certainly, making the work of current teacherpreneurs publicly known, particularly their impact on student learning and school improvement, is crucial to creating demand. What if we started with new recruits to teaching?

In closing, Elmore makes the case that any reform is about learning, and for humans to learn they must have "encouragement and support, access to special knowledge, time to focus on the requirements of the new task, [and] time to observe others doing it."[21] He makes the case quite eloquently that these conditions rarely are in place when schools and districts or teachers and administrators take on any new complicated practice (like the teaching of Man: A Course of Study in the 1960s or the Common Core State Standards in the 2010s). And as we have documented, it takes those who already have teacherpreneurial know-how to drive transformations in education leadership and to support increasing numbers of teachers who lead without leaving the classroom.

We wonder if universities, with new structures and incentives, can jettison their long-standing efforts to prepare as many teachers as possible—irrespective of labor market supply and demand. Instead of preparing two hundred thousand or so new teachers a year, what if universities prepared only one hundred thousand, as well as about twenty thousand teacherpreneurs? That said, neither universities nor any other teacher training provider will recruit and train teacherpreneurs one by one in isolation. The viral power of the Internet will begin to unleash teachers like Ariel, Jessica K., José, Lori, Noah, Renee, Shannon, and Stephen, as well as Jessica C., Megan, Ryan, and Sarah. Such teachers will start to document and spread their expertise, particularly for members of the American public, the vast majority of whom have deep trust and confidence in teachers.[22] They also will begin to connect with teacher leaders from top-performing nations who will assist them in making more visible the power of investing in those who both teach and lead. We point to these possibilities in the next chapter.

Activity for Chapter Eight

Now What?

Create Your Calendar

Goal

The supplemental activities thus far have required you to reflect on your own development and influences as a teacher leader, analyze your teaching philosophy, identify evidence of effectiveness, and address potential barriers. Chapter Eight provides practical ideas about and recommendations for how to create and sustain a hybrid role as a teacherpreneur. This activity takes your planning a step further by having you map out your ideal schedule, dividing your time between teaching and leading throughout a sample workweek.

Think

Take some time to review the purpose and goals of the teacherpreneurial role you've envisioned. Using the calendar on the next page, outline how you'd spend your time during an ideal workweek. Your hybrid role may allow for teaching half days throughout the week, or alternating days in the classroom (for instance, teaching Mondays, Wednesdays, and half days on Fridays, with Tuesdays, Thursdays, and half days on Fridays spent on leadership work beyond the classroom).

We encourage you to review Renee's teacherpreneur schedule in Appendix B to learn more about how one teacher leader from our network has allocated her time. Be realistic and consider your schoolwide duties outside of the classroom as well as personal obligations and needs, as Renee does.

Act

Set up a time to meet with a building (or district) administrator. Explore the idea of creating a teacherpreneurial role. Discuss the hybrid schedule you outlined on the weekly calendar. What concerns do you—and your administrator—have about the division of time between teaching and leading? What practical issues would need to be addressed? How realistic is your proposed schedule?

Share

Upload your sample calendar to CTQ's virtual network (http://www.teaching quality.org) along with your questions and concerns raised in your reflections on and conversations about how best to make this schedule work well for you, your students, and others whom your work will touch. Seek out the advice of online colleagues for improving the hybrid division of labor.

	Monday	Tuesday	Wednesday	Thursday	Friday
7:00 a.m.					
7:30 a.m.					
8:00 a.m.					
8:30 a.m.					
9:00 a.m.					
9:30 a.m.					
10:00 a.m.					
10:30 a.m.					
11:00 a.m.					
11:30 a.m.					
12:00 p.m.					
12:30 p.m.					
1:00 p.m.					
1:30 p.m.					
2:00 p.m.					
2:30 p.m.					
3:00 p.m.					
3:30 p.m.					
4:00 p.m.					
4:30 p.m.					

CHAPTER 9

Finnish(ing) Lessons for Teacherpreneurism

 *All teachers [in Finland] see themselves as leaders, in one way or another.*
—Leena Semi

Shortly after first meeting Marianna Sydanmaanlakka and Leena Semi, both veterans of classroom teaching, they explained a great deal to us about Finland's rapid rise as the world's top-performing nation.

"It is about well-prepared teachers and the way we can lead in so many ways," Marianna said.

Much has been written over the last several years about Finland. In 2008 even the *Wall Street Journal* (which has shown little past reverence for teachers in America) praised Finland's success in raising student achievement and pointed to the role its investments in teaching played in doing so.[1] In the 1970s the Finns used government inspectors to make sure teachers, who had to record their teaching practices in special diaries, were following the national curriculum in lock-step fashion.

No more.

As *New York Times* columnist Thomas Friedman recently noted, in Finland the curriculum emphasizes creativity, not facts, and students have a choice of many electives—all with a shorter school day, little homework, and almost no standardized testing. Quoting Tony Wagner of Harvard University, he made the claim that

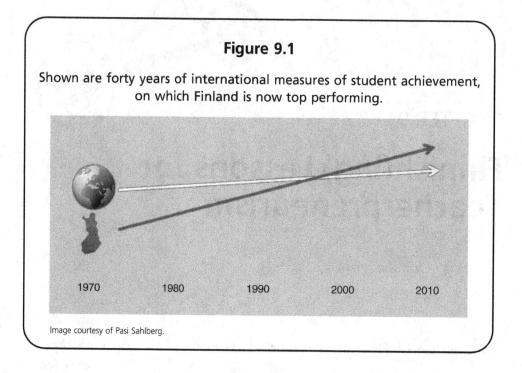

Figure 9.1

Shown are forty years of international measures of student achievement, on which Finland is now top performing.

1970   1980   1990   2000   2010

Image courtesy of Pasi Sahlberg.

"Finland is one of the most innovative economies in the world . . . and it is the only country where students leave high school 'innovation-ready.'"[2]

And in Finland, it is about the nation's systematic investment in teachers as leaders.

TEACHERS LEAD, AND LEADERS TEACH

Finnish teachers are trusted, and the teaching profession is the cornerstone of the Finns' rapid rise over the last decade to the top of the heap on the world's most respected measures of academic achievement, the Program for International Student Assessment (PISA). As late as the 1980s and early 1990s, Finnish students performed at best at the average level on international assessments. Since 2000, however, Finland has had a rapid rise to the top in the PISA rankings in math, reading, and science—all while the United States has floundered in the middle of the pack of the forty-plus nations whose students take the authoritative and rigorous achievement tests. In a recent *Atlantic Monthly* essay, journalist Anu Partanen let us know that "one of the hottest trends in education reform lately is looking at the stunning success of the West's reigning education superpower, Finland."[3]

Marianna and Leena were in the United States in 2012 on a Fulbright teaching fellowship. Marianna is a guidance counselor who helps students learn a number of subjects on the virtual islands of Second Life. Leena speaks three languages (and is proudly qualified to teach two of them to middle and high school–age students) while also writing English textbooks, working with teachers from around the world in an online community, and serving as a teacher education professor.

They packed a lot of insight into our forty-five-minute conversation and pushed us to think a bit differently about teacher leadership and teacherpreneurism. We realized quickly that in Finland there would be no need for a Center for Teaching Quality (CTQ), primarily because there is very little distinction in Finland between teachers and administrators.

"All teachers see themselves as leaders, in one way or another," Leena noted.

"The principal does not really have the highest status in the school," Marianna added. "When teachers challenge a principal's ideas, and this happens a lot, he or she will rethink the decision."

We asked Marianna why this was the case.

"As you may know, they teach as well. They are teachers, too," she said.

And then Marianna summed it all up for us: "In America, we have heard principals refer to 'my school' and 'my teachers'; but in Finland, you will never hear them use those words. They always say 'our school' and 'my colleagues.'"

In Finland, policymakers as well as practitioners do not struggle *at all* with the notion of *blurring the lines of distinction* between those who teach in schools and those who lead them. There just are not any lines to blur.

We had read a great deal about Finland, including Pasi Sahlberg's best seller, *Finnish Lessons*, which explains education reform in his country.[4] But we were fortunate, as part of a U.S. delegation to Helsinki, to learn a lot more about Finland's system of early childhood care, its comprehensive and vocational schools, its teacher training institutes, and the history and culture behind all of it. The weeklong study was led in part by Pasi—who is the director general for the Centre for International Mobility and Cooperation in Finland's Ministry of Education—and he taught us much. We walked away with a multilayered view of Finland's investments in young people as well as teachers and the respect members of the Eduskunta (Finland's parliament) have for the teaching profession.

Marianna and Leena's words of wisdom did not just confirm but rather intensified our understanding of what we had read and observed about Finland.

"What I get from teachers in the United States," Leena noted, "is that they are in a hurry all the time—and they are frustrated with what they *have* to do."

"But teacher leadership is built into our day in Finland," Marianna said, "and we are educated to lead and have influence outside of our schools."

Both Marianna and Leena readily made connections between the teaching profession and what students learn—or don't learn. Leena said:

> I have seen U.S. teachers, because of the accountability pressures, teach to the test. They have to meet all these standards and have to keep students in their place to reach the goals. They have no time to plan with their colleagues, at least not in meaningful ways. This translates into not giving their students a lot of responsibility. American students are not given as much freedom and responsibility as in Finland.

And Marianna, drawing on a recent experience of her own child who was temporarily enrolled in a U.S. middle school while she was here on her Fulbright, shared:

> For example, my fourteen-year-old told me that in his American school there is a lot of talk about students taking responsibility for their work, but his teachers don't give him much responsibility like we do in Finland. In the United States it seems that students have to learn in quite a linear fashion, and they must learn a list of topics given to teachers to teach.

In contrast, Finnish teachers are instrumental in creating evidence of their effectiveness, drawing on assessments that *they develop* (but that are all tied to the national curriculum). Nearly all educators belong to the nation's one teachers' union, which is part of a larger confederation of other organized professionals, including doctors. But teachers also belong to their respective subject-specific associations, and together they develop "a lot of jointly produced teaching and learning materials as well as optional models for assessing student learning outcomes."[5]

Teachers in Finland lead to benefit students. And they can do so because every teacher is well prepared before beginning to practice independently.

INVESTMENT IN TEACHER PREPARATION

Finnish teachers are expected to teach students of mixed abilities, all together, and to take care of different learners in increasing not just their academic prowess but also their love of learning. This type of teaching cannot be scripted. Finnish students are taught for fewer hours by their teachers when compared to their peers around the world and in the United States; but they learn more.[6]

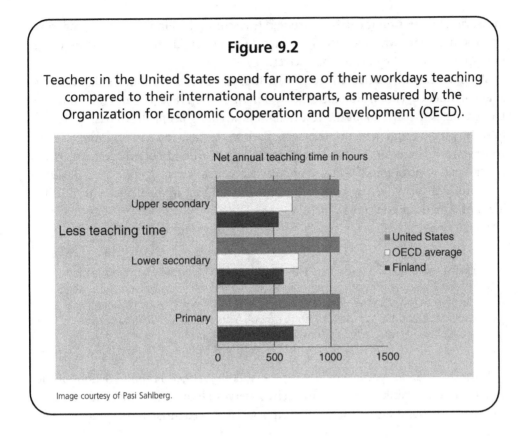

Figure 9.2

Teachers in the United States spend far more of their workdays teaching compared to their international counterparts, as measured by the Organization for Economic Cooperation and Development (OECD).

Net annual teaching time in hours

Less teaching time

Upper secondary

Lower secondary

Primary

■ United States
□ OECD average
■ Finland

0   500   1000   1500

Image courtesy of Pasi Sahlberg.

In America, leading policymakers often call for more respect for teachers and the complexity of their work, yet promote policies that work against professionalizing teaching. Well-prepared teachers given time and trust to use their professional judgment constitute the centerpiece of Finnish school reform. Linda Darling-Hammond, who is one of America's foremost experts on teachers and teaching, and who has led, with Pasi, several policy tours of the Finnish education system, told us that "preparing teachers for a research-based profession has been the central idea of teacher education developments in Finland."

Partanen, in critiquing U.S. education policy promoted of late by both the Bush and Obama administrations, makes it clear that Finland does not use any standardized test of students for teacher accountability.* She notes that instead of focusing on

---

* The purpose of Finland's National Matriculation Exam is not to promote high-stakes accountability for teachers, but to help educators and parents determine whether fifteen-year-olds should focus on more of a college or vocational approach to the end of the voluntary upper secondary schooling.

measuring teachers on the basis of student test scores, the Finns invest in preparing classroom experts who are "[well] trained to assess children in classrooms using independent tests they create themselves."[7]

We have learned, particularly from Pasi, that part of Finland's success has been its study of other education systems. And beginning in the 1980s, Finland turned to the United States to learn about the research on how young people learn best as well as how to prepare and support teachers. Pasi wrote in a recent *Education Week* commentary, "I am one of the domestic messengers who imported great American educational innovations"[8]—including teacher education programs like those at Stanford University, led by Linda. But it is Finland that implements, with fidelity, ideas of American educators.

Linda writes:

> Unlike the U.S., where teachers either go into debt to prepare for a profession that will pay them poorly or enter with little or no training, Finland made the decision to invest in a uniformly well-prepared teaching force by recruiting top candidates and paying them to go to school. Slots in teacher training programs are highly coveted and shortages are virtually unheard of.[9]

With the U.S. delegation, we visited the Viikki Teacher Training School of the University of Helsinki. The training school serves almost one thousand students and has 102 teachers who have been specially credentialed to prepare new teachers.

Jyrki Loima, both a principal of the school and a professor at the university, explained the "what," "why," and "how" of the preparation of new recruits in his school. In his one-hour talk, he used the words *judgment* and *trust* a combined total of thirty-eight times—such qualities are the basis of how teacher candidates are selected (in addition to performance on a hundred-item test that measures their ability to analyze research articles). Judgment and trust are also the foundation of how preservice teachers are trained and evaluated in tightly sequenced basic, applied, and advanced training programs.

The university prepares two hundred "student teachers" a year, which means it ensures that the training school is filled with new recruits who are supervised and supported strategically to escalate their teaching skills and enhance the learning opportunities for the one thousand children and teenagers in the building. The student teachers take pedagogical courses at Viikki, and record and analyze videos of lessons. A team of school and university faculty assesses the student teachers.

Perhaps most important, the teaching faculty at Viikki engage in a variety of research projects in collaboration with their university colleagues. Together, they study such topics as the effects of the acquisition of multiple languages and the impact of various approaches to teacher education. And the student teachers—like those in the other seven teacher training institutes across Finland—learn how to conduct research themselves, preparing to assemble evidence, develop and analyze formative assessments, and collaborate with colleagues. Each new recruit to teaching must demonstrate that he or she knows how to design, conduct, and present original research on a practical or theoretical aspect of teaching and learning. During our visit, Leena Krokfors, professor at the University of Helsinki, told us, "Teachers have to make lots of decisions, and what they decide to do needs to be based on evidence of what works." And we heard clearly from Pertti Kansanen, Emeritus Professor of Teacher Education, that "all of our graduates can justify their decisions."

We wanted to learn more—and met with Marianna at the Finnish Lessons conference in Seattle, Washington, at which school reformers and educators (including teachers) could learn directly from Pasi and delve into Finland's success.

What It Means to Be a Finnish Teacher Leader

Noah Zeichner and Lori Nazareno were at the Finnish Lessons conference in Seattle as well, and we all had a school reform conversation with Marianna that pushed our thinking about the prospects for teacher leadership and teacherpreneurism in the United States. As a former communication expert who now has taught for eight years, Marianna drew on her experiences both as a media consultant and a public school teacher in defining her vision for the teaching profession. "We are all leaders," she told us in the conversation with Noah and Lori. "Granted, some teachers lead more than others, but we do not expect those who do not teach to tell us how to teach."

As Marianna described the work of teachers in Finland, we thought of how university professors in the United States are expected to perform their roles of teaching, scholarship, and service. Finnish teachers, first and foremost, focus on their work with students, and all are expected to care about not just the students they teach but all children in the school. Similarly, principals are expected to care about all children in their municipality. What is more, principals and teachers are expected to work together to benefit all students, "rather than concentrating on giving a competitive edge to the children in their own school."[10] And just like one would find in an American university, some Finnish teachers focus primarily on teaching and service to their local school and community, whereas others find a variety of

Figure 9.3

Marianna Sydanmaanlakka talks with teachers in Seattle, Washington, about Finnish schools.

Photo courtesy of Noah Zeichner.

venues to lead outside the school. We learned that many classroom practitioners in Finland also serve as teacher educators, educational game developers, online mentors, curriculum and assessment designers, and textbook authors. Many work in local politics to support public education. Others are active bloggers, as is the case with Marianna, who scoops Finnish education news for teachers world-wide. But perhaps most of all, Finnish teachers, as leaders, are expected to help one another teach more effectively.

We asked Marianna how Finnish teachers learn to lead. "It is the way teachers are prepared as researchers," she said, "but it is also the working conditions. Because of the collaborative atmosphere, teachers are encouraged to be the leaders of their profession."

Noah hypothesized that some of the things that administrators do in U.S. schools, teachers do in Finnish schools. "That is true," Marianna agreed. "We have teachers

Lori Talks About Teacher Education

http://bit.ly/WR7otp

leading a lot of what goes on in our school, like with curriculum and assessment as well as student and teacher well-being that deals with equality and fairness." In most Finnish schools, Marianna emphasized again, all of the administrators teach as well.

> Judgment and trust are also the foundation of how preservice teachers [in Finland] are trained and evaluated in tightly sequenced basic, applied, and advanced training programs.

"This seems a lot like the structure we have, too," Noah said, "but in Finland it seems you do not get too hung up on [contractual] time."

Marianna nodded in agreement. "Once you teach your lessons in school, there is flexibility for teachers to determine when they do their work," she noted.

A typical Finnish teacher teaches just under 600 hours a year, whereas the average American teacher teaches students over 1,600 hours annually. And according to a recent Bill & Melinda Gates Foundation–sponsored study of the teaching profession, U.S. teachers habitually work an average of about ten hours and forty minutes a day, with a great deal of this time spent teaching and supervising students.[11]

Marianna said,

> Our teachers who teach languages for which many essays have to be graded often have fewer lessons. And they can decide on their own where they get that work done. They may teach two lessons one day and then go home or to the gym around noon—and then correct papers or work online with students later in the evening.

Lori noted, "In America, it is seen by administrators and policymakers that if you are not in front of students, you are not working." Then Noah added, "We have high schools here where teachers have to sign in by a certain time; otherwise they may or may not get their paycheck."

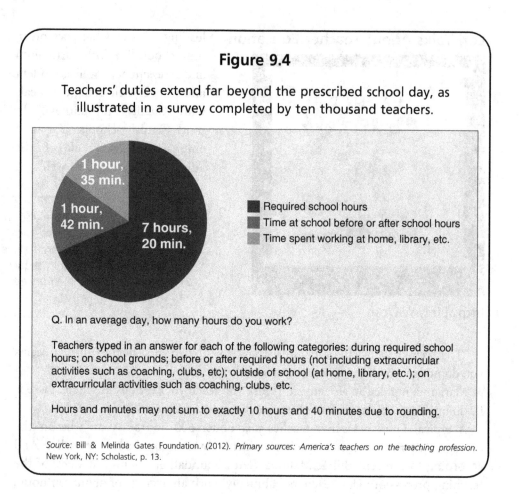

Figure 9.4

Teachers' duties extend far beyond the prescribed school day, as illustrated in a survey completed by ten thousand teachers.

1 hour, 35 min.

1 hour, 42 min.

7 hours, 20 min.

■ Required school hours
■ Time at school before or after school hours
■ Time spent working at home, library, etc.

Q. In an average day, how many hours do you work?

Teachers typed in an answer for each of the following categories: during required school hours; on school grounds; before or after required hours (not including extracurricular activities such as coaching, clubs, etc); outside of school (at home, library, etc.); on extracurricular activities such as coaching, clubs, etc.

Hours and minutes may not sum to exactly 10 hours and 40 minutes due to rounding.

Source: Bill & Melinda Gates Foundation. (2012). *Primary sources: America's teachers on the teaching profession.* New York, NY: Scholastic, p. 13.

Conditions That Foster Collaboration

And then we learned a bit more about what leverages leadership among teachers, particularly how the structure of a teacher's school day and week fuels innovation from those who teach.

"The school day varies for teachers," Marianna told us. "Some teachers teach more or fewer courses inside of our six-week periods. Sometimes you may teach three or four seventy-five-minute lessons a day—some days you may only have one."

Noah noted, "The teaching schedule is staggered in Finland; here it is very rigid, with most teachers teaching the same schedule day after day for 180 days."

"And what goes on inside of a teacher's planning time is very different in Finland and in America," Lori added.

Noah said, "Our teachers in Seattle meet about two hours a week for common planning, like you do in Finland, but the big difference is that in our two hours we are supposed to receive professional development, but teachers in your country get to create their own professional development to further their school."

Then we began discussing the concept of reciprocal mentoring and its importance in cultivating teacher leaders and teacherpreneurism. "I believe in my country," Marianna added, "we would call it benchmarking."

"It is typical that a group of teachers would meet with and observe those who teach their same subjects in other schools to have a reflective observation," Marianna continued.

Lori's eyes lit up a bit when she asked, "You actually know other teachers who teach in other schools? Who sets this up?"

"We do know teachers in our cities. We are supposed to," Marianna quickly responded. "And our principals are supposed to encourage us to do this; it is their job."

And then we asked Lori if, in her twenty-five years of teaching in two inner-city school districts, in a wide variety of elementary, secondary, and alternative schools, she was ever asked to go observe another teacher in another building.

Not surprisingly, the answer was, "No."

Noah then speculated on the "untapped" reciprocal mentorship that could be created in our nation's preservice teacher education programs (both traditional and alternative), in which new recruits into teaching are expected to learn solely from a mentor teacher, university professor, or consultant hired by a nonprofit or district. "It is all one-way," he noted. "There is nothing reciprocal in the mentoring that goes on among student teachers and those who teach them."

Marianna told us, "It is the flexibility that leads to trust, and this is where teacher leaders are developed; we do not feel we are controlled by outside forces."

We then reflected on the fact that in America this is how university professors are developed as leaders. They are afforded flexibility in their schedule, with staggered times to teach, and often additional rewards for scholarship that is carved into their routine professional work. We wondered how the trust American policymakers have in university professors could be established for America's public school teachers. We wondered how the trust Finnish policymakers have in Finnish public school teachers could be embraced by their American counterparts. We know of the importance of making teacherpreneurs more public; using teacher evaluation and pay systems to elevate teacherpreneurism; and preparing new teachers—early in their training—to teach, lead, and not leave. We wondered what it would take to communicate to policymakers and administrators as well as the public both the evidence and the emotion of trusting teachers—and teacherpreneurs like those profiled in this book. We would start with foreseeing what public education might look like in 2030, and how we would get there. We do so in the next, our final, chapter.

● **Chapter Nine Selected Web Sites**

Following is a list of online resources that relate to the discussion in this chapter. If you find that either of these links no longer works, please try entering the information in a search engine.

Pasi Sahlberg's Web site for his book *Finnish Lessons*:
   http://www.finnishlessons.com

Marianna Sydanmaanlakka's blog for teachers, *Education in Finland*:
   http://www.scoop.it/t/education-in-finland

Activity for Chapter Nine

Now What?

Learn to Practice Futurespection

Goal

Linda Darling-Hammond has written that the teaching profession today is where the medical profession was in 1910.[12] Through the concerted efforts of professional associations, practitioners, medical schools, and state-regulating agencies, the quality and effectiveness of doctors increased dramatically as barriers to entering the profession were raised, extensive preparation was required, and research grounded practice.

Now that you have read about an education system in Finland that is built on the expertise of practicing teachers, it is time to synthesize your own planning to answer this question: How do we get there from here? Where are the tipping points that teacherpreneurs can leverage toward an education system driven by teacher leaders?

Think

Our discussion of the stark divide between the teaching profession experienced by Marianna and Leena and the one in which Lori and Noah work has touched on a number of factors: teacher preparation, working conditions, education policy, and school leadership structures. As you reflect on the distinctions between the American and Finnish systems that you learned about in this chapter, which of these factors resonates most with your understanding of what matters most for teaching and learning? Make time to map out the current state of that particular structural difference between the American and Finnish systems by considering how it is designed, implemented, and refined.

Now consider how a system informed by teacherpreneurs would transform that structure. What is the future state of teacher preparation, school working conditions, leadership opportunities, or policy when teacherpreneurs are developing, executing, and improving existing models? What will you do to get from here to there? You may want to detail your ideas in a series of bullets; a fully written text; or a drawn "map," chart, or timeline. The important thing is to capture your ideas in some way so that you can reflect on and share them.

Act

Write a letter to a graduating class of teaching candidates in the year 2030. Use the ideas you sketched in the preceding part of this exercise to describe how teacherpreneurs transformed the antiquated American teaching profession at the turn of the twenty-first century into the one recognized as an international leader in supporting pedagogical expertise, research, and practice. What legacy of those efforts should the teachers of 2030 carry forward?

Share

Now, actually "send" the letter! You may want to share it at an upcoming meeting with your professional learning community at school (if you have one), or with a student teacher or the teacher who supervised your own student teaching. You can also publish the letter via social media networks or on a blog, or submit it as a commentary to your local newspaper. Listen to feedback and revise your letter. What new ideas or understandings are you developing as you share the letter with different audiences?

Upload your letter to CTQ's virtual network (http://www.teachingquality .org), including information about to whom you sent the letter, where you had it published as a blog post or commentary, and what kind of feedback you received when sharing it with your social or professional learning networks.

CHAPTER 10

Foreseeing 2030

● *The term* teacherpreneur *will have outworn its utility by 2030—as the current teacherpreneurs and many thousands who have joined them will continue to reshape the profession and its image so that we no longer need a special label to send a signal about the importance of those who teach and lead, but do not leave the classroom.*

—Ann Byrd

We began this book inside of Renee Moore's classroom in Drew, Mississippi, with the story of how she developed her pedagogical and policy expertise in the face of a grossly inequitable school system, recalcitrant administrators, and rigid reform agendas. We had known Renee for many years, ever since her expertise in "culturally engaged" teaching of English was recognized on the Carnegie Foundation for the Advancement of Teaching's Web site. She had long since emerged as a leader of teacher leaders among the thousands of classroom experts who work with and learn from one another through the Center for Teaching Quality (CTQ) Collaboratory. But the Prologue's account was of our first visit to Renee's classroom, and we saw up close and personal how school segregation and grossly unjust funding of schools in America still persist. We observed, with greater clarity, how important it is for more teachers like Renee to lead in bold ways.

The rhetoric of reformers, in and outside of Washington DC, often ignores the reality that in many school communities today power, control, and ideology trump excellence and equality in education for students of color. Modest changes in teacher evaluation and pay as well as stricter accountability measures and school choice will not ensure that all students have access to twenty-first-century teaching and learning opportunities.

> It is so important for all children across America to be taught by innovative teachers who lead but do not leave.

The visit to Renee's classroom and community was profound for us—because she helped remind us in crystal-clear ways of public education's unfulfilled promise and why it is so important for all children across America to be taught by *innovative teachers who lead but do not leave*. The visit was weighty and wondrous, as were our visits with Shannon C'de Baca, Jessica Keigan, Stephen Lazar, Lori Nazareno, Ariel Sacks, José Vilson, and Noah Zeichner—during which we came to better understand the contexts in which they teach and lead.

Then we had the opportunity to get to know more deeply Megan Allen, Jessica Cuthbertson, Sarah Henchey, and Ryan Kinser, and we were able to support them as teacherpreneurs and teachers in residence. We began to do what we could only see needed doing before. Lori reminded us that there are numerous other teachers who can lead the way she does. We knew then that their stories must be told if our nation's education policies are ever to focus less on blaming teachers and more on building demand for the many, many classroom experts like those profiled in this book. We knew the journey ahead to cultivating and connecting teacherpreneurs—innovative teachers who lead but do not leave—would not be easy, but the road for us was now clearly marked. And we hope by now that the *road maps* we have defined and surfaced can inspire and inform the paths many teachers will take to transform their profession in the years ahead.

PROMISING DEVELOPMENTS

In our previous book (*Teaching 2030*) we pointed out that empirical evidence and high-profile think tank reports alone would not transform the teaching profession, in which the policies and perspectives of those in charge are deeply rooted in social customs and their need to maintain control over the $600 billion–a-year public education enterprise. We recognized a few years ago that it was too early to tell whether the current reforms put forth by the federal government and major philanthropies would actually expand beyond narrow definitions of effective teaching, past and present, and embrace and truly cultivate teacher leaders as drivers of the transformation of their own profession.

Since we penned *Teaching 2030* we have felt some shifts, even if they cannot be described as seismic. The Internet continues to create opportunities whereby mass collaboration makes it more possible for anybody, anywhere, to connect, prepare, and mobilize around any set of ideas and ideals. The Internet, as described by Ori

Brafman and Rod Beckstrom, has already "unleashed" a new form of decentralized "starfish" organizations that rely on the power of peer relationships—"knocking down traditional businesses, altering entire industries, affecting how we relate to each other, and influencing world politics."[1] And we project that soon the Internet will unbridle hundreds of thousands of individual teachers who will collectively unleash their powerful ideas and disrupt the "spider" organization of public schooling, with its rigid hierarchies and top-down leadership. As explained by Brafman and Beckstrom, adopting the starfish approach is key to the future of an organization that wants to change the "traditional leadership" framework:

> Starfish have a miraculous quality to them. Cut off the leg of a spider, and you have a seven-legged creature on your hands; cut off its head and you have a dead spider. But cut off the arm of a starfish and it will grow a new one. Not only that, but the severed arm can grow an entirely new body. Starfish can achieve this feat because, unlike spiders, they are decentralized; every major organ is replicated across each arm.[2]

Lori turned us on to Brafman and Beckstrom's book and took the lead in helping us think about the future of the CTQ Collaboratory by sharing her vision for the future of her profession. Lori told us, "Effective leadership in schools often means leading from the middle, not the front" and "listening more than telling." No wonder Lori helped us think about where CTQ is today and where it needs to be tomorrow.

Beckstrom, in talking about his book, speaks of how Toyota is no longer a highly centralized organization, unlike its spider-like rivals GM and Ford; Toyota's professional employees can stop the assembly line anytime. In one of many conversations, Lori asked, "What if teachers as a group stopped bad policy, like the inappropriate standardized testing of young children?" Then, in a later exchange with her teaching colleagues in the Collaboratory, she noted:

> Right now for most policymakers standardized tests are hammers, and policymakers are using them as weapons. We could use them as tools. In a decentralized system, teachers will know how and when to use the "hammer." More and more of these teachers will be well known, and soon.

As mentioned earlier, a starfish is decentralized because each arm can live alone—and its head cannot be cut off because it does not have one. Highly effective organizations in the twenty-first-century—in publishing, manufacturing, and retail—are becoming more decentralized; values are the core of their work, and knowledge is spread throughout. In Brafman and Beckstrom's book, they point to the power of decentralized organizations—like the Apaches, who escaped the powerful Spanish army for two hundred years, and Alcoholics Anonymous, which has reached well over two million members and more than one hundred thousand groups worldwide, both of which operated with only a set of shared principles and without a "leader." As Brafman and Beckstrom note, "At Alcoholics Anonymous, no one's in charge. And yet, at the same time, everyone's in charge."[3] Leadership is by example, not coercion.

Lori is making sure more of her colleagues in the Collaboratory are reading and discussing *The Starfish and the Spider*. She e-mailed us to explain why the starfish metaphor represents both what CTQ is and what it still needs to become:

> Since 2003 when the Teacher Leaders Network [now the CTQ Collaboratory] was first formed, we have had a leg or two removed and grown other starfish. And, now that I think about it, even those teacher leaders who have left the network have also grown into their own starfish. In many ways, education in the United States has gone through a number of stages, from decentralized schoolhouses across the country, to very centralized school districts and now even rigid charter management organizations. We are just starting to head back toward real decentralization—think teacher-led schools, charter schools, and high-quality alternative licensure—to call for teachers to own their profession. I see CTQ helping us create our unions and school districts as "hybrids" in the way Brafman and Beckstrom discuss. Think of teacherpreneurs, working in Wikipedia-, Craigslist-, and eBay-like organizations—leading communities of teachers, parents, and students that control, operate, oversee, and regulate a lot of what goes on with teaching and learning, with centralized leadership providing support and guidance while brokering people and resources.

Make no mistake: we are not futurists like Ray Kurzweil, with special insight into how intelligent machines and nanotechnology might create a boon for teaching and learning. We cannot predict the future. But we do work closely with teachers, and have collaborated with them in a virtual community that has blown off their classroom doors and allowed them to exponentially spread their pedagogical and policy knowledge in ways unimaginable just a few years ago.

Consider this: Kurzweil suggests that by 2030 a $1,000 personal computer will be a thousand times more powerful than the human brain, and that computers will be capable of learning and creating new knowledge entirely without the assistance of people.[4] We see these potential developments as powerful tools for teaching as well as a source of teacherpreneurism: *relationships* between teacher and student as well as school and community will become even more critical while computers continue to enhance the cognitive potential of humans. Teachers will use these technologies not only to know students better but also to find time they currently do not have to lead in bold ways we have yet to imagine. Technological advances of 2013, not to mention the ones forecast by Kurzweil for 2030, will soon free teachers of the bureaucratic obstacles and siloed classrooms that have gotten in the way of teacherpreneurial thinking and action. Our Collaboratory bloggers today reach hundreds of thousands of teachers, parents, and policymakers. And as this book is being published, Marianna Sydanmaanlakka and Leena Semi of Finland have become the first of what will be many international teachers to join our virtual community of teacher leaders to create the global teaching profession that students everywhere deserve.

Kurzweil has been remarkably accurate in his technological forecasts so far. And we are hopeful that we are accurate in anticipating that growing numbers of philanthropies, like the few who support CTQ now, will recognize the need to incubate a bold brand of teacher leadership. Likewise, we are optimistic that progressive school district administrators and union leaders, like those in today's Hillsborough County Public Schools, are moving toward transcending the stark divides of the past and opening new doors so more classroom experts, including teacherpreneurs, can lead without leaving. We are proud to be working with more of them each every day (http://www.teachingquality.org/about/funders).

In 2013 we are just beginning to figure out how to build demand for teacher-preneurs by creating a small supply of them. We are humbled by the challenges of doing so, but we are not daunted. No one was demanding the iPad—"the poster child of the post-PC world"—before it was created and marketed a few years ago.[5] By early October 2012 Apple had sold one hundred million of them. Granted, there is a definitive difference between creating demand for iPads and creating demand for teacherpreneurs. The former requires capitalizing primarily on the desire for convenience, whimsy, and information among individual consumers, whereas the latter entails transforming beliefs and shifting power relationships in entrenched bureaucracies among influential policymakers, interest groups, and educators.

But teachers, who are, as individuals, deeply trusted by the American people, will soon have their pedagogical and policy insights understood more clearly. The long-standing top-down structure of public schooling, with 3.2 million teachers at the bottom of the organizational chart, will be overwhelmed by the kind of mass collaboration embraced in the private sector, in which companies are moving away from "pushing their own ideas and products" and more toward "using the wisdom of crowds to form new and better products and offerings."[6]

Imagining the progress that will be made by 2030 and how our nation will have gotten there, we turned to our eight teaching colleagues profiled in this book—Ariel, Jessica K., José, Noah, Lori, Renee, Shannon, and Stephen—and asked them to speculate on where they will be in seventeen years.

WHERE WE'LL BE IN 2030

Ariel will be forty-eight.

In 2030, I am probably getting a little *verklempt* [Yiddish for "emotional"] in thinking about where I am and what I've done. The truth is, when I started teaching (in 2030 I will have been teaching for twenty-six years), I had no idea I'd be where I am today.

I remember that when I was a student in the public schools I had always thought it was my teachers who didn't know what they were doing. After several years of teaching I began to see that it was a system that didn't know what it was doing, making it harder to teach than I had even thought. No wonder my favorite teachers were always the outsiders. Sometimes they'd let you see their struggle a little bit. Not everyone pushed against the problems, though.

In 2030 I am still teaching—energized by my own ways of exploring and learning. I am working to remove the barriers to good teaching. We have not eliminated them all. But I am working to make our profession sustainable—made possible by many of us serving in hybrid roles that allow us to spread our expertise while teaching half-time.

Jessica K. will be forty-nine.

I have been puzzling over this question for many reasons. First, if someone told me I would have had the experiences and opportunities that I have had in my first ten years of teaching, I would have told them they were crazy, so it is hard to imagine what the next seventeen years will hold. Second, I feel like I am in a time of great transition in my professional life and am eager to see how this next year goes being back in the classroom full-time before I make a call as to what I want to do when I grow up.

That said, by 2030 I will have

- Taught abroad for a year or more—because I am eager to immerse myself in other systems so that I can learn from and share with teachers from all over the world

- Composed my thoughts in a cohesive way so that I have written a book—which is more likely to be a work of fiction than anything else but will share what I have learned as a teacher and teacherpreneur

- Given to young, early-career teachers what my mentors have given to me—working in a hybrid role with universities that have renewed their commitment to preparing teachers for the public schools

- Continued to be part of the CTQ Collaboratory, in which I will still look to support and learn from amazing peers

And I will still be teaching.

José will be forty-eight.

In 2030 I will continue to promote equity for our most disadvantaged students in our public schools. I will be forty-eight, still full of vim and vigor. The Internet will help teacher leaders make the case for creating a better environment for all students and parents and the educators who serve them. Teachers will be able to earn at least as much as school administrators—being paid not in accordance with unstable standardized test scores but based on their skill and expertise. I will still be pitching my ideas online, lending my voice in places where educators don't often get to speak. But my focus will be pushing my pedagogy even further every chance I get—and working with Lori in developing teacher-led schools.

Noah will be fifty-three.

My daughter will be twenty-two, and my son will be seventeen. I anticipate that having my own children in school will have a strong impact on my thinking about public education. In 2030 my daughter will be pursuing a career that perhaps does not yet exist today. Or maybe she will follow me into a transformed profession of teaching. If she chooses to teach, she will be nearing graduation at a teacher training school, structured much like teacher preparation programs in Finland today. She will be working with experienced teachers among the six hundred thousand teachers nationwide serving in hybrid roles, teaching part of the day and, if she's like me, mentoring beginning teachers as well.

> [In 2030 my daughter may] follow me into a transformed profession of teaching . . . She will be working with experienced teachers among the six hundred thousand teachers nationwide serving in hybrid roles, teaching part of the day and . . . mentoring beginning teachers as well.
>
> — Noah Zeichner

At fifty-three, I will still be teaching in a classroom part of the day. During the rest of the day, I might be mentoring preservice or beginning teachers. I'll be writing about action research that I conduct during my classes. And for part of the year I'll be spending the nonteaching half of my day facilitating action research projects with classroom teachers in several countries around the world through an online platform. In any case, I will be teaching K–12 students until I retire.

Lori will be sixty-six.

In 2030 I am retired, though I will still be teaching in some way. I will have long since helped other classroom experts to create their own teacher-led schools. I will have long since been part of an even larger virtual network of this special brand of teacherpreneurs. Perhaps I will become a paraprofessional in a class, quietly urging the teachers with whom I am working to be bolder. In 2030 I may be spending more time on my deck in Conifer, Colorado, reading books and knowing that once upon a time we had a new vision of what schools could look like and become. And they did.

Renee will be seventy-four.

I'll just be catching my second wind (women in my family tend to live to be over a hundred). I might be retired from brick-and-mortar teaching, but maybe not. Lord willing, I'll still be teaching virtually, mentoring (my grandchildren will be working with me in education by then), and writing. What will get me there from here? The same things that got me this far: trusting God. Believing that there is more to learn and more to be done. Expecting new opportunities. Loving those I teach and loving what I do.

Shannon will be seventy-eight.

By then I will have had a hand in building more teacherpreneurs. By then I would have helped lots of teachers carve a new path. And at almost eighty, I will be even more irascible. It will be hard to "shush" a feisty old lady. But as I have throughout my career, I will select battles small enough to win and important enough to matter. That means I will have even more freedom to speak out and help transform teaching and learning and push American public education to be a learning and adaptive system, not the incoherent and hierarchical one that it was in 2013.

In 2013 every excellent teacher knew at least five other excellent teachers—and had opportunities to influence five new recruits to the profession. By 2030 the Internet—well beyond the Web 3.0 stage—will allow us to use these ratios and turn a few hundred teacherpreneurs in 2015 into over six hundred thousand in less than two decades.

Stephen will be forty-nine.

I will still be teaching at Harvest Collegiate High School then—which will be eighteen years of age in 2030. In fact, I'll still be teaching because we will develop and nurture a culture of teacher leadership (and leading of teacher leadership) that replenishes itself over the years. This means being intentional not just with how Harvest develops teachers and systems but also in developing the capabilities of the teachers who come to us. I expect to be someone who has stepped back to create the space for a new generation of teacher leaders to learn and develop in the road I made by walking.

But my path to 2030 will not be a straight line. I expect to have lots of different "teacherpreneurial" experiences between now and then that satisfy my various interests. I will continue to help teachers learn and develop in person and through my writing. I will have written at least one book by 2030. I will continue to play a role in developing assessments that are used in New York City that reflect the fact that the majority of our students will be second-language learners. I will have a seat at the table where major pedagogical and policy decisions are made in NYC as a teacher, rather than as part of the union or the central Department of Education, because the majority of educators at that table must be current teachers. Our parents will have demanded this by 2020, and well before 2030 it will be part of the natural fabric of policymaking in education in NYC as well as nationwide.

> These teacherpreneurs—whose purpose is for the collective good—will join their students and many parents in defining a public education system worthy of America's democratic ideals.
>
> — Alan Wieder

And the three of us who have worked to tell the stories of the eight teacher leaders just mentioned also have thoughts about what 2030 holds.

Alan will be eighty.

I will be living in the Mexican mountains, reading novels, and not reading world news accounts of war, famine, and children suffering because of class disparities and the lack of a twenty-first-century education. I will see schools in the United States and throughout the world that will motivate and empower kids because they will be taught and led by teacherpreneurs who themselves are excited and energized by what they teach, what their students learn, and the world around them. These teacherpreneurs—whose purpose is for the collective good—will join their students and many parents in defining a public education system worthy of America's democratic ideals. And schools and students, catalyzed by technologically connected teacherpreneurs—like those in this book—will have made a difference in changing the face of public education.

Ann will be sixty-nine.

I will not be working full-time in 2030, but I will be working, always. Much of my time will be spent staying plugged into how the critical mass of teacherpreneurs has not just reshaped but rather essentially revolutionized the work world of education. Their promise and power lie not only in how they connect to one another but also in how they imprint their expertise and leadership on growing numbers of teaching colleagues who are no longer confined to four-wall learning spaces of brick and mortar. I will witness before my seventieth birthday (the "new fifty" for sure by then) the blurring of the lines of distinction between those who teach in schools and those who lead them. The term *teacherpreneur* will have outworn its utility by 2030—as the current teacherpreneurs and many thousands who have joined them will continue to reshape the profession and its image so that we no longer need a special label to send a signal about the importance of those who teach and lead, but do not leave the classroom. And I will delight in thinking back on the short "history" of teacherpreneurs that sparked from a discussion among twelve teachers in a conference room in the small CTQ office in North Carolina two decades ago. I am certain I will be delivering an online, highly engaging and interactive experience on the history of the teacherpreneurial role in America's education system and its indirect influence on the United States' being a world leader in education (like Finland is today). I already have lined up the first eight guest experts on my list!

And Barnett will be seventy-four.

I will still be working, but spending much more time with my wife, Meredith (an exceptional teacher of thirty-five years who retired in 2012), as we approach our fifty-fourth wedding anniversary and spend more time with Joseph, forty-seven, and Evan, forty-two, and their respective spouses and children. I will still travel to be with teaching colleagues and partners as well, even though our evolving virtual world of CTQ allows far more opportunities to be present without being someplace other than home. We have always believed that trust grows through people spending time together. And, in 2030, we will still be advancing this ideal.

In 2030 we will have grown in numbers reaching thousands of teacherpreneurs, but as Ann has told us, many will not be using this word that we began using two decades ago to define experts who boldly blur the lines of distinction between those who teach students regularly and those who lead the transformation of teaching and learning. We will be intimately connected to a wide variety of school district consortia, universities, nonprofits, and community-based organizations as well as transformed teachers' unions that have asked us (and other like-minded nonprofits) to help them virtually connect and ready classroom practitioners to lead their profession.

I will be relishing the reality of the last seventeen years as my teaching colleagues far exceeded expectations in leading but not leaving. Many others will have begun their own teacherpreneurial journey after reading this book about exceptional teachers who are not the exception. In 2030 they will be teaching part of the day or night and leading as distinguished professors of education. They will be full partners in research consortia in which their ideas and experiences of teaching children and teenagers seamlessly blend into empirical analyses shaping next-generation policy and pedagogy. They will be presidents of their local and state professional guilds while still working directly with students, reaching thousands of new recruits through virtual networks that prepare them for the complex contexts in which they will teach, both in and out of cyberspace. A number of them will be the highest-paid *anybodies* in their school district.

But I no longer will be leading CTQ, with my role as CEO long jettisoned. We will have a new name for sure, and CTQ will be led by many practicing teachers throughout the Collaboratory, not by someone who has not taught in decades. After reading this book a decade and a half prior, many new recruits to teaching will have begun mapping their own trajectories as teacherpreneurs. We will become a starfish organization, with many circles operating independently and autonomously, and with classroom experts serving as catalysts of and champions for the profession that makes all other professions possible.

So how did we get to 2030?

For us at CTQ it began as school districts, associations, and state education agencies began to invest in Wave 4 of teacher leadership (as discussed in Chapter One), something that only a few progressive philanthropies had done in the past. In 2013, as this book was going to press, we were buoyed by our work in several districts and states—most prominently in Florida and Kentucky.

We had been fortunate, with support from the Bill & Melinda Gates Foundation, to work with a group of teachers and administrators in Hillsborough County Public Schools, led by its erudite and foresightful superintendent, MaryEllen Elia. Indeed, MaryEllen was well known for her serious collaboration with local union leader Jean Clements, equally open minded, in leading the transformation of a results-oriented teacher development and evaluation system embraced by classroom practitioners.

Back in 2012, after just one year of working with her team and the union in developing a virtual community of teacher leaders, she was ready to move forward. The original CTQ-Florida cadre of one hundred teacher leaders had become instrumental in making sure the district's teacher development and evaluation system would work over time and serve primarily to spread teaching capacity across the county's 250 schools. And in 2013–2014 MaryEllen called for a new brand of teacher leader, drawing on the expertise of Megan and Ryan in replicating their leadership skills among growing numbers of district teachers who would lead in hybrid roles.

We watched the numbers expand, and by 2015 there were 50 local teacherpreneurs helping their colleagues use their evaluation results to improve teaching and learning and spreading Common Core State Standards resources with teacher-vetted best practices. By 2020 the number of teacherpreneurs grew to 253, representing one in every school. Other districts took notice, as teacher effectiveness and retention soared.

At the same time Terry Holliday, state superintendent of education in Kentucky, and his agency became the first to take full advantage of the National Board Certified Teachers (NBCTs) in the commonwealth to lead Common Core State Standards reforms. Beginning with one teacherpreneur and forty other NBCTs, the Kentucky Department of Education, powered by the CTQ Collaboratory, quickly grew a virtual community that offered hundreds, and then thousands, of the state's teachers opportunities to learn from one another, share resources, and critique lessons in a highly personalized professional learning community without leaving their classroom or school.

In 2013–2014 these forty-one NBCTs connected with five hundred of their colleagues and set the stage for building bridges through offline engagement with a wider teaching corps and other key stakeholders critical to ensuring that the Common Core State Standards successfully went viral in the state. This virtual community also connected Kentucky teachers to their peers across the nation, including cohorts in Hillsborough County and throughout the state of Florida, who shared their interests, concerns, and passions for teaching and learning. The NBCTs supported a vision of teacher leadership promoted by Terry and his chief academic officer, Felicia Smith-Cummings. As we put together our work plan with Terry and Felicia and their team in Kentucky back in 2012, Felicia had sent us an e-mail:

> My heart's desire is that the public recognize that great teachers have been waiting on the opportunity to take back the profession. They want ownership! And, [our work together] will elevate the profession in ways we never could before. If the work that CTQ is doing now was around ten to twelve years ago, I would *not* have left the classroom.

By 2018 over one-half of Kentucky's forty thousand teachers were connected to a virtual community of classroom experts, fueled by four hundred teacherpreneurs (all NBCTs) who taught part of the day and served as virtual community organizers during the other portion of their assignment. These four hundred teacherpreneurs, prepared by the CTQ Collaboratory and supported by the Kentucky Department of Education, Kentucky Education Association, and the Fund for Transformig Education in Kentucky, painted a very different picture of school reform for policymakers and the public both in the commonwealth and across the nation.

But these two developments represent only a few steps, taken by one small nonprofit with a couple of state and district partners. What happened elsewhere to fuel the growth of teacherpreneurs? The nation's teachers' unions began to take the lead. And others were not far behind.

In 2013 the National Education Association (NEA) launched a serious effort to do more than just use its policy muscle, also drawing on its enormous mobilizing capacity to help teachers teach more effectively. The NEA began small, by organizing in virtual space for 30,000 members, 30 state affiliates, and 250 locals to begin building a movement to transform their union into a professional guild. The NEA turned to CTQ, as well as a number of other nonprofits, who could help it develop a comprehensive curriculum for the first 1,000 members, including a field-based practicum focused on instructional, policy, and association leadership.

At the same time, the American Federation of Teachers (AFT)—building off of its groundbreaking, results-oriented teacher evaluation reforms in New Haven (Connecticut) and Pittsburgh (Pennsylvania)—became the go-to source for school districts and policymakers on how to create a system of teacher development that fuels instructional innovations and elevates growing numbers of classroom experts from other peers, and began to market exemplars of teaching excellence directly to the public through various multimedia tools.

But this movement was not just about the teachers' unions, as a growing number of independent teachers' associations and nonprofits—staffed with teacherpreneurs to keep them grounded in teaching realities—began to proliferate and spread the policy and pedagogical expertise of those who teach. The lines of division between previously warring, competitive organizations were blurred, mirroring the lines of distinction between those who teach and those who lead. And the ease of accessibility the Internet provided spurred more organizations to connect and truly partner—and pushed the associations to transform their own operations and focus. The two largest unions reached out to the other groups seeking partnerships with them, not a fight. They began to find new ways to create common ground with those who serve students and families every day and provide direct services with a laser focus on teaching and learning.

As a result, teachers began focusing much more on what matters most. They continued to make better use of their own smartphones and tablets, assembling powerful evidence on what students were learning as well as how and why. They consistently began using new tools like those produced by Show Evidence, a second-generation e-portfolio system, as well as by diverse nonprofits, such as Better Lesson, EdSurge, the Teaching Channel, and World Teachers' TV. They started to do more as a collective, finding kindred spirits through the CTQ Collaboratory, operating in true starfish fashion as a constantly regenerating virtual community and bolstered by many other networks that developed in the early 2010s with like-minded principles about teacher leadership.

Then came the game changer. Right before President Obama's presidential term ended in 2017, a new initiative had launched to help hundreds of thousands of classroom experts virally spread their expertise. Federal incentives, supplanting those previously used in Race to the Top, were offered to states and school districts to cultivate and support teacherpreneurs. Those incentives were doubled down in local communities like Drew—because of growing political support for the federal government to incentivize states to equitably distribute school funds, with a focus on teachers and teaching, in accordance with students' needs.

And then in 2020 the AFT and the NEA merged, bringing together the best of their tools to focus first and foremost on students and those who teach them. The unions, now fully formed as a twenty-first-century professional guild, were more known for brokering the expertise of teachers than winning political campaigns. And with this evolution, independent associations found enough common ground and shared purpose to join ranks with this new guild for associations. As a result, the American Teachers' Association (ATA) emerged, representing both teachers and principals, and became very active in both preservice preparation as well as the performance-based credentialing of teacher leaders, including teacherpreneurs.

The ATA, with its combined resources and infrastructures of the former AFT, NEA, and independent associations, focused primarily on teachers' taking charge of authentic accountability with their own tools to demonstrate what was working to help their students become innovation ready (not just college ready) and why. Like their Finnish colleagues had been doing for over five decades, U.S. teachers, supported by the ATA, proved they were responsible for teaching and leading—and that they would do so without leaving the classroom. When policymakers and reformers tried to ignore them, the ATA used the Internet to reach out directly to parents and business leaders. And parents and business leaders liked what they had learned about the teaching profession and what it had become.

By 2030, legions of teachers began to systematically offer their students—from the Deep South to New York City and the middle of Iowa on to Helsinki and beyond—wondrous opportunities to learn from their peers worldwide, anytime and anywhere. And the advent of Web 3.0 and then Web 4.0 allowed teachers to connect, ready, and mobilize in ways almost unimaginable in 2013. The cracks in our divisive education policy system had been sealed. As we entered the fourth decade of the twenty-first century, we all began to see a strengthened teaching profession that was resting on solid ground, with hundreds of thousands of innovative teachers leading the way—without leaving.

Activity for Chapter Ten

Now What?

Map Your Own Path to 2030

Goal

Throughout nine chapters of reading and engagement, you have taken bold steps toward activating your learning journey toward teacherpreneurism. You have articulated where your teacher leadership has been (Chapter One), where it is going (Chapter Two), why you are headed in that direction (Chapter Three), how you know you are on the right path (Chapter Four), how your interests can be leveraged toward a broader following (Chapter Five), whom you see as the "giants" of teacher leadership on whose shoulders you stand (Chapter Six), what solutions you may apply to the obstacles you will encounter (Chapter Seven), what a proposed weekly schedule for your teacherpreneurial role might look like (Chapter Eight), and how teacherpreneurs will transform the profession in the coming decades (Chapter Nine). You have begun mapping your trajectory as a teacherpreneur. Although you have previously considered how the collective impact of teacher leaders will advance and enhance the profession, this activity asks you to reflect on what those developments will mean for *you* personally.

Think

During this chapter, we've engaged in some "futurespection" to imagine the world of teaching and learning—and our places in it—in the year 2030. Now we invite you to do the same. As you consider these questions, we encourage you to create a mindmap or write down the answers that come to the surface.

What will your leadership look like in 2030? What individuals and organizations will help you get there? What challenges will you overcome along the way? What will be your proudest and most difficult moments? What personal and professional achievements will you celebrate? What aspects of the education landscape will you directly influence?

Act

Sit down with a colleague (face-to-face or virtually)—ideally, one of the people with whom you have been talking throughout your explorations in this book—to share some of your visions for the future. What are your colleague's ideas, and where may your visions overlap? Discuss what a first step toward creating that common vision would look like, and take it.

Share

Upload your response to CTQ's virtual network (http://www.teachingquality .org) and commit to sharing your personal vision for the future with at least one colleague virtually and another face-to-face.

Although the visions shared by Ariel, Jessica, José, Lori, Noah, Renee, Shannon, and Stephen offer a helpful guide, you may also want to access the responses that other readers have uploaded on CTQ's virtual platform.

APPENDIXES

- A. Group Résumé (Chapter Two)
- B. Renee's Typical Schedule (Chapter Four)
- C. Sample Memorandum of Understanding—2011–2012 (Chapter Eight)
- D. Teacherpreneur Monthly Reflections (Chapter Eight)
- E. Sample Teacherpreneur Work Plan (Chapter Eight)

A. GROUP RÉSUMÉ (CHAPTER TWO)

Teacherpreneurs have diverse expertise and experience, allowing each individual to pursue unique leadership goals and opportunities. Nonetheless, our experience in selecting and supporting teacherpreneurs suggests that their teacher leadership "credentials" revolve around common characteristics and competencies that are outlined in the first several chapters of this book.

What does a composite picture of teacherpreneurial expertise look like? We asked the teacherpreneurs highlighted in this book each to share their résumé with us, and then combined those résumés into a snapshot of what makes the "right stuff" for teacherpreneurism. Their list of accomplishments is impressive—and we invite you to add yours to this list by completing the exercise at the end of Chapter Two.

Objective

To incubate and execute bold pedagogical and policy ideas from the classroom; to cultivate six hundred thousand teacherpreneurs by 2030.

Academic Background

A range of bachelor's, master's, doctoral, and postdoctoral degrees from the following institutions:

- Bank Street College of Education
- Brown University
- City College of New York
- Columbia University
- Delta State University
- Los Angeles Film Studies Center
- Middlebury College
- Occidental College
- Seattle Pacific University

- Syracuse University
- United States Sports Academy
- University of Colorado at Denver
- University of North Carolina at Chapel Hill
- University of Washington–Seattle
- University of Wisconsin–Madison

Degrees completed in myriad fields:

- African American studies
- Arts
- Computer science
- Cultural studies
- Curriculum and instruction
- Early childhood and families
- Education (K–12)
- Ethics
- History
- International trade
- Language arts
- Literature
- Mathematics
- Philosophy
- Religious studies
- Spanish

Well-Traveledness

Have lived in, are from, or have taught across America and in other countries throughout the globe:

- Belize
- Dominican Republic
- Ecuador

- Germany

- Mexico

- United States (Colorado, Florida, Hawaii, Iowa, Michigan, Mississippi, New Mexico, New York, North Carolina, Ohio, Virginia, and Washington)

Having the Pedagogical Right Stuff

- Conduct ongoing classroom action research

- Coplan lessons with colleagues and collaborate to create inspiring curricula and lessons across classrooms and schools

- Coteach courses for preservice teachers

- Create and implement innovative lessons in democratic citizenship, history, math, reading, science, social studies, speaking, and writing

- Design district curriculum materials with an emphasis on formative assessment and responsive instruction

- Develop local and state curricula, including Common Core assessments

- Help students to make huge gains in academics as well as to achieve personal and social growth

- Lead collaborative professional development in community colleges, faith communities, museum schools, online learning classrooms, private schools, and public elementary and secondary schools

- Provide passionate, thoughtful, and growth-focused instruction to students in K–12 classrooms as well as adults in community colleges, universities, and lifelong learning centers

Cultivating Other Teacher Leaders

- Act as "cooperating teacher," providing mentoring and other supports during student teachers' clinical experiences in classrooms prior to earning their licensure

- Coauthor policy reports, publications, and white papers to support progressive education reform

- Cofacilitate schools' arts and cultural education programs to extend learning for the whole child (for example, a Mariachi Education Program to teach students about folk music and culture in Mexico)

- Compile schoolwide data for internal school use
- Create online learning opportunities for students and teachers
- Design and open teacher-led schools
- Design teacher leadership curricula for the Center for Teaching Quality (CTQ) Collaboratory
- Envision, pilot, and champion programs to inspire students and teachers to continue pursuing learning to better themselves and their community
- Mentor and support candidates for National Board Certification
- Mentor colleagues (formally and informally), including creating a volunteer support team
- Research, develop, and support efforts to implement more positive work standards and classroom practices
- Serve as consultants to inform the systems-level decision making in education (for example, at the Institute for Student Achievement, Iowa Department of Education, and New York City Department of Education Teacher Effectiveness Pilot on Performance Based Assessments)
- Serve as members of local and regional councils to support teaching excellence within content areas (for example, the New York City Social Studies Critical Friends Group)
- Serve as Writer's Guild leaders, blog writers, and social media contributors
- Serve on state teacher and administrator certification boards and commissions, including overseeing colleges of education

Awards

- Bezos Educator Scholar
- Milken Educator Award
- National Science Teachers Association Distinguished Teaching Award
- Phillip B. Swain Excellence in Education Award
- Seattle Seahawks Hero in the Classroom
- State Teacher of the Year
- Top 20 Teacher Blog (Scholastic)
- Zora Neale Hurston Excellence in Writing Award for Social Sciences

Making Teaching Visible

- Act as Common Core State Standards curriculum consultants and assessment experts for the Bill & Melinda Gates Foundation

- Appear as guest experts on television talk and news shows

- Author more than fifty peer-reviewed papers, commissioned reports, and trade association publications

- Cochair state commissions and task forces (for example, the Iowa Model Core Curriculum and Every Learner Inquires)

- Consult for Alliance for Restructuring Education, the Council of Chief State School Officers, Iowa Public Television, the National Center for Education and the Economy, and the New Standards Project

- Deliver keynote addresses for national conferences on teachers and teaching and school reform

- Earn National Board Certification in multiple content areas

- Lead colleagues in the CTQ Collaboratory (formerly the Teacher Leaders Network)

- Present and attend conferences of such organizations as the Alliance for Excellent Education, the American Association of Colleges of Teacher Education, the City Schools Forum, the Colorado Language Arts Society, the Institute for Student Achievement, the National Conference for Teachers of English, the National Council for State Legislators, and the National Council of Teachers of Mathematics

- Serve as Citizen Education Ambassador to the Kingdom of Bahrain

- Serve on boards of directors for the National Board of Professional Teaching Standards and the Carnegie Foundation for the Advancement of Teaching

- Serve on the Bill & Melinda Gates Foundation Teacher Advisory Board, the National Education Association Commission on Effective Teaching and Teachers, and the Professional Educator Standards Board (Washington State)

- Speak at TEDx events, the Big Ideas Fest, and national school reform rallies

- Write feature and commentary articles for *Education Week*, EdNews Colorado, *GOOD Magazine*, the *Huffington Post*, and *National Journal's Education Experts* blog

- Write lessons for the U.S. Mint and PBS Online

B. RENEE'S TYPICAL SCHEDULE (CHAPTER FOUR)

Time	Mon	Tues	Wed	Thurs	Fri	Sat	Sun
6:30 a.m.				Devotional time			
7:30–8:00			Get ready for work				
8:00–9:00	• Travel to Greenville Campus (48 miles)*	• Travel to Moorhead Campus (32 miles)	• Travel to Greenville Campus	• Travel to Moorhead Campus	• No class on Fridays • Schedule out-of-town meetings on these days, speaking engagements, consultant work, etc. • Personal care time—laundry, hair, health appts, housecleaning • Check blog reader; check in on some of my networks; other prof reading • My writing projects • Grading papers, lesson planning, • Choir rehearsal, other church preparations		Church
9:25–10:40	• Class prep/ Office hours for students (120 students total this semester)†	• Freshman Comp II class (26 students)	• Class prep/ Office hours for students	• Freshman Comp II class			
10:50 a.m.–12:05 p.m.	• Freshman Comp I class (1st section—30 students)	• Brief prep or student conference • Travel to Drew Campus (26 miles)	• Freshman Comp I class (1st section)	• Office hours for students • College paperwork • Reaccreditation duties (SACS Quality Enhancement Plan Coordinator)			
12:15–1:30	• Freshman Comp I class (2nd section—10 students)	[12:15–2:30] • World Literature class (10 students)	• Freshman Comp I class (2nd section)	• Travel to Indianola (RMCA High School)			

Time					
2:00–4:00	Lunch, work-related meetings are often scheduled during this time, especially those related to my work on accreditation, or English Dept.			• Advanced Writing and Research Class (High School—17 students)	Family/Dinner
4:00–5:00	• Peer Coaching English faculty—teaching online courses (Greenville)	• Prep time—update LMS, attendance, check student e-mails	Travel home		Church-related duties
5:00–6:00	• Office hours for night students (Greenville)	• Office hours for night students (Drew)	Dinner, e-mail, other correspondence (Twitter, networks, etc.)		
6:00–8:45/ 9:00	• Freshman Comp II class (14 students)	• Freshman Comp I class (13 students)	Church Bible Study (I teach)	[7:00–9:00] Bowling League!	Prep for work
9:00–10:00	Travel home	Dinner, mail, e-mail, prep for Wed			
10:00+	Dinner, mail, e-mail, prep for Tues				

* Most of my travels are on 2-lane county highways; time depends on farm equipment.
† My office is at Moorhead Campus, so when I'm at the others, I have to find a spot to do office work or student conferences, and I have to bring my own supplies.

C. SAMPLE MEMORANDUM OF UNDERSTANDING— 2011–2012 (CHAPTER EIGHT)

MEMORANDUM OF UNDERSTANDING
between
SEATTLE PUBLIC SCHOOLS
and
CENTER FOR TEACHING QUALITY, INC.

The Center for Teaching Quality, Inc. (CTQ) and the Seattle Public Schools (SPS) hereby enter into an agreement to create a "teacherpreneurial" role for an SPS teacher in the 2011–2012 school year. CTQ will provide funding to SPS to offset the costs of one-half of that teacher's annual total compensation, in exchange for securing a .5 FTE release from that teacher's regular classroom- and school-based duties. The teacherpreneur will spend this released time in activities related to CTQ-Washington. CTQ awards this funding with understanding that the teacherpreneur remains under contract with the district during the year of his appointment and retains all rights, privileges, and obligations of a contract teacher during the 2011–2012 school year.

Contractual Agreement

This memorandum of understanding includes the rights and responsibilities of CTQ (hereafter, "Funder") and SPS (hereafter, "Recipient") in creating this role for _____ (hereafter, "Teacherpreneur") who is currently a full-time teacher at Chief Sealth International High School. The principal of Chief Sealth International High School and the Manager of Grants & Fiscal Compliance for SPS, acting with the authority and on behalf of the Recipient, agree to the following:

Funder will:

- Provide funds in the amount of $ _____ to the Recipient payable no later than August 31, 2011. This funding is to cover the costs of one-half the Teacherpreneur's annual total compensation for the 2011–2012 school year.
- Develop a scope of work for the .5 FTE of the Teacherpreneur's time, which may be shared with the Recipient upon request.
- Provide notice to Recipient or its agents (including the principal of Chief Sealth International High School) of any visits that its staff, board, or sponsoring organizations may make to the Teacherpreneur's school site, in accordance with district policy.
- Coordinate with Recipient regarding any publicity and communications work conducted in relationship to the Teacherpreneur's role and work.
- Work with the Teacherpreneur to provide work space away from the school site for his work with CTQ-Washington.

Recipient will:

- Release the Teacherpreneur from regular teaching duties on a .5 FTE basis for the 2011–2012 school year, according to a schedule codeveloped by the Teacherpreneur and relevant school and district staff.
- Use funds solely for the designated purpose. Failure to do so may jeopardize future funding.
- Identify Funder in any published pamphlet, brochure, media or press release, or related materials as "the Center for Teaching Quality."
- Coordinate with Funder regarding any publicity and communications work conducted in relationship to the Teacherpreneur's role and work, and submit to Funder electronic or printed copies of any media coverage that the Teacherpreneur or Recipient may receive.

Seattle Public Schools

_____, Principal, Chief Sealth International High School

Date: _____

Mailing address:

_____

_____

Telephone number: _____

_____, Manager, Grants & Fiscal Compliance

Date: _____

Mailing address: EIN: _____

_____

_____

Telephone number: _____

Center for Teaching Quality, Inc.

_____, Project Lead, Center for Teaching Quality

Date: _____

_____, Chief Operating Officer, Center for Teaching Quality

Date: _____

D. TEACHERPRENEUR MONTHLY REFLECTIONS (CHAPTER EIGHT)

The following is a document used by teacherpreneurs supported by the Center for Teaching Quality to record and reflect on recent accomplishments. The version that appears here shows how one teacherpreneur in 2011–2012 responded to these questions. We believe this tool has, in itself, been helpful to teacherpreneurs, but it is most important to see this as a sample of the kinds of reflective and coaching questions that should be asked of teacherpreneurs by the organizations and individuals who support them.

Teacherpreneur Monthly Reflections for March 2012

Accomplishments

Please review your individual reports on meetings and other activities over the past month. Then list one INDIVIDUAL accomplishment and one TEAM accomplishment. Tell us what the accomplishments are; why they are important in light of the goals on which you are focusing now; and what activities, meetings, and so on in which you engaged most contributed to achieving these. Please also reflect briefly on any challenges you may have addressed along the way, what strategies you used in doing so, and what learning you will take from this for the future. *(Recommended length: one to two paragraphs each)*

- **Individual accomplishment:**

    Over the past month, I began my effort to write more as part of my hybrid role. I often have ideas for blog posts, articles, editorials, etc., but rarely have the time or perhaps discipline to put them down on paper. I have nearly finalized one piece and I am reworking a second. Although my work is progressing slowly, I feel like I have broken the ice. Part of my hesitation to write during the first half of the year may have had to do with a lack of confidence in articulating my perspective on various issues. Of course, there were time and workload limitations too, but I do feel that I have gained confidence in my understanding of education policy through my hybrid role work. Attending meetings with advocacy groups, continuing discussions in our virtual community, attending conferences, and my own digestion of education news have all contributed to an increase in confidence. I still feel I have a long way to go before I fully understand complex issues like VAM [value-added measure] scores and defining teacher and teacher leader effectiveness, but I am further along than I was in September.

I have a couple of motivations for writing within my hybrid role. First, I think that it will bring our group positive exposure (hopefully) in the public sphere, which will add to our credibility both locally and nationally. Second, writing is extremely helpful in my own learning process. It forces me to consider research and the issues that I write about very carefully. It often feels like a slow process, but it gives an opportunity to solidify my understanding of ed policy issues. My strategy of reserving a block of time each week for reading and writing has not really worked yet. March has proved to be a very busy month and Fridays, the day I targeted, have been filled with other activities and responsibilities. I am optimistic that I will be able to build this time into my week in the next month.

■ **Team accomplishment:**

I am very pleased with the increase, although small, in membership in the CTQ-Washington group. We have members now from a wider range of school districts and with a nice range of experience. I am especially excited about our new members from Kent and Highline. It has been a team effort with Sarah as a virtual community organizer (VCO) and Ryan as a key player in the recruiting process. This being said, I do think that we are in a pivotal moment. If new members have success with the videos they are creating now and find meaning in the work, they will only increase their participation and will help reach out to other teachers in their districts. If we don't take advantage of this momentum, we could lose people in the rush of the spring testing season and miss out on opportunities to further strengthen our membership. I am aware of the importance of our April 10th information session and consider that a critical extension of this team accomplishment.

A challenge with recruiting has been that it is often more difficult to reach out to teachers outside of our own districts. Building relationships with union and district leadership along with prospective members takes time. The strategy that we have employed in Highline is working slowly. We have the blessing of the union president and of district leadership. We are well positioned to bring in more teacher leaders to the CTQ-Washington team. Now we just have to make that happen.

Other Reflections

We are interested in knowing more about how connected and influential you feel now—two-thirds of the way through your year in a hybrid role—compared with your sense of things before you were in this position. In Figure A.1, you'll see lines on which to mark where you are on a continuum of connectedness. Space for reflective comments is provided at the end.

Figure A.1

A note about how to use these scales: CTQ teacherpreneurs complete monthly written reflections about their successes and lessons learned through their work. Among other prompts, we explicitly ask them to reflect on how they are balancing different components of their hybrid roles so that their influence expands without detracting from their practice as teachers. Noah Zeichner's feedback below prompted conversations about how release time outside his school affected his ability to collaborate more deeply with his teaching colleagues and offer important informal supports to students. Like other teacherpreneurs, Noah has unusually high expectations about the importance of staying connected, so even a slight shift away from perfect synchronicity needed to be addressed. Together, we developed strategies (e.g., weekly lunch meetings with other teachers, working from school some afternoons to be more available to students) to bring a better balance to Noah's work.

Two points to consider: (1) As of publication, Noah will begin his third year as a teacherpreneur. (2) School organizations must be designed differently so teachers can stay connected to students and colleagues even when they are not in the building.

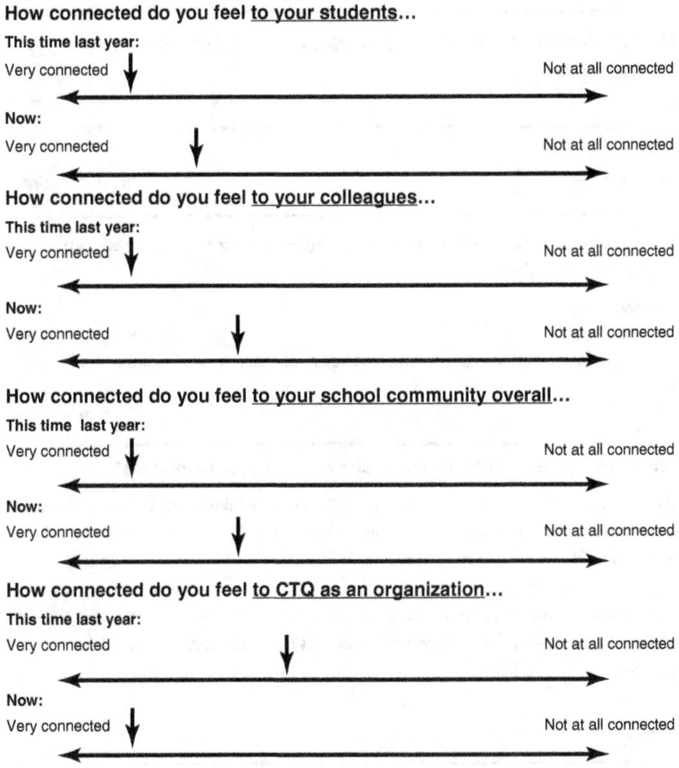

How connected do you feel <u>to your students</u>...

This time last year:

Very connected ↓   Not at all connected

←————————————————————————————————————→

Now:

Very connected   ↓   Not at all connected

←————————————————————————————————————→

How connected do you feel <u>to your colleagues</u>...

This time last year:

Very connected ↓   Not at all connected

←————————————————————————————————————→

Now:

Very connected   ↓   Not at all connected

←————————————————————————————————————→

How connected do you feel <u>to your school community overall</u>...

This time last year:

Very connected ↓   Not at all connected

←————————————————————————————————————→

Now:

Very connected   ↓   Not at all connected

←————————————————————————————————————→

How connected do you feel <u>to CTQ as an organization</u>...

This time last year:

Very connected   ↓   Not at all connected

←————————————————————————————————————→

Now:

Very connected ↓   Not at all connected

←————————————————————————————————————→

(Continued)

How connected do you feel <u>to your team of teacher leaders locally</u>...

This time last year:

Very connected ↓ Not at all connected

←————————————————————————————————→

Now:

Very connected ↓ Not at all connected

←————————————————————————————————→

How connected do you feel <u>to the national network of teacher leaders</u>...

This time last year:

Very connected ↓ Not at all connected

←————————————————————————————————→

Now:

Very connected ↓ Not at all connected

←————————————————————————————————→

How connected do you feel <u>to the process of policy change</u>...

This time last year:

Very connected ↓ Not at all connected

←————————————————————————————————→

Now:

Very connected ↓ Not at all connected

←————————————————————————————————→

How connected do you feel <u>to the national stage for teacher leadership and policy reform</u>...

This time last year:

Very connected ↓ Not at all connected

←————————————————————————————————→

Now:

Very connected ↓ Not at all connected

←————————————————————————————————→

What reflections might you like to share about your responses?

Part of my heightened awareness of and participation in the policy world is certainly due to my role on the Professional Educator Standards Board. It has definitely complemented my work with CTQ. Having just completed my fourth board meeting, I feel much more confident when speaking during board meetings than I did even a couple of months ago. For example, I have been able to connect the dots between teacher evaluation and teacher preparation because of the many conversations that I have participated in over the past 1-2 years with CTQ.

Spending Time

Like other teachers, teacherpreneurs juggle many roles and responsibilities. But unlike other teachers, you do it with a less well-defined model for how your time is allocated and when you work on specific tasks. Figure A.2 is a blank pie chart representing 100 percent of your working time. **Please draw in segments on the pie chart and label them to show how your time is spent. As you do so, think more about the *priorities and focuses* for your working time rather than sets of tasks.** For instance, think about how much time you spend on teaching, planning and grading, collaboration with teaching colleagues, collaboration with the Center for Teaching Quality virtual community colleagues on other work, outreach and collaboration with stakeholders, advocacy, special projects or leadership roles you are fulfilling this year, and so on.

Average Weekly Hours (semester 2):

Teaching: 9

Planning/grading: 15

School meetings: 2

CTQ virtual community facilitation and work: 3

CTQ webinars: 2

Other CTQ work: 10

Professional Educator Standards Board: 3

Global Education Leadership: 4

Think about what you have shared about how you spend the time you have, acknowledging that *every* professional position will require a certain amount of time spent on routine or less enjoyable tasks. Try to recall what you may have assumed about the kinds of projects or activities on which you would spend your time. **How did your imagined allocations of time as a teacherpreneur match up against the reality? What might this suggest to us about ways we could prepare and plan with the next cohort of teacherpreneurs for their roles in 2012–2013?**

When I began my teacherpreneur role last September, I imagined that I would spend half of my day teaching and planning and the other half of the day doing a variety of policy related activities: visiting other schools to meet with prospective CTQ-Washington members, reading research and writing reaction pieces, planning for meetings and webinars, and participating in CTQ webinars. I also included my PESB work (preparation and meetings) as part of my CTQ time.

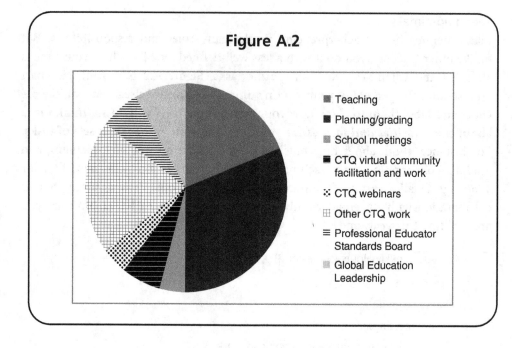

Figure A.2

- Teaching
- Planning/grading
- School meetings
- CTQ virtual community facilitation and work
- CTQ webinars
- Other CTQ work
- Professional Educator Standards Board
- Global Education Leadership

I had assumed that while I might get a good part of my planning done at school, I would still be bringing quite a bit of grading and other school-related work home. I also began the year with the assumption that I would not be giving up many of my extra responsibilities at school. I still was going to coordinate our all-school festival, I was still going to advise the environmental club, and I was still going to work with Global Visionaries. I also was anticipating several hours a week working on my global education fellowship. My goal was to keep my CTQ work within the confines of the 40% or 60% of my time while my school and extracurricular work would extend beyond the 40-hour work week (as it had before). Continuing this school-based work was important to me because I saw it as a way to maintain credibility among my colleagues and students.

My experience during the first semester this year was that I was very busy as a classroom teacher (I taught three different classes) and there was often not enough time to engage as fully in the policy work as I felt I needed to. After phone calls, emails, webinars, and recruiting work, I was often running out of time. I had demands from my fellowship or I had a PESB meeting to prepare for. I was spreading myself very thin because I was doing many different things all at the same time (not unlike how I imagine the life of a CTQ staffer must be). I did not have the time that I had anticipated to travel to other schools and to meet often with various stakeholders.

I have entered the second semester with optimism that with 60% of my time dedicated to CTQ, my time will be more flexible. During the first month of second semester I have not (yet) fallen into a routine. This is due in part, I believe, to taking four out-of-town trips during the first six weeks of the semester (2 for CTQ, 1 for my fellowship, and 1 for PESB). I am hopeful that April and May will bring more stability to my weekly schedule and I will be able to meet the goals in my work plan with more ease.

Any hybrid role is going to be complicated and will prove difficult when trying to balance one's time. My schedule could have been much more complicated if I didn't have my classes consolidated into morning periods. I would find it very challenging to have to go back and forth throughout the day between jobs. Even with my split schedule, there have been days when I had to work more hours at school or more hours for CTQ than my work plan dictated. Even with a neatly planned daily schedule, the reality is that I have had to be very flexible at times.

I have found that making weekly work plans has been helpful. I began the year trying to plan for many weeks in advance. The reality is that every week is completely different. I often cannot craft my schedule for the next week until the weekend. While I haven't accomplished every task in my weekly work plans on time, it has been an easy process to shift uncompleted tasks from one week to the next. I would recommend that future teacherpreneurs find a planning and organizational tool that works for them. I have found the Notes tool in Outlook to be especially helpful.

E. SAMPLE TEACHERPRENEUR WORK PLAN (CHAPTER EIGHT)

Noah Zeichner—Work Plan 2011–2012, Semester 2

CTQ-Washington	Center for Teaching Quality	Professional Educator Standards Board	Chief Sealth International High School	Teachers for Global Classrooms	Global Visionaries
1. Expand the team within Seattle-area districts, with special attention to building strong teams in Highline, Renton, and Kent. Invite 20–25 NBCTs to join CTQ-Washington team (work with Jim Meadows). Set up recruiting event with CTQ staff on April 10th.	1. Participate in national CTQ Steering Committee activities.	1. Prepare for PESB meetings. Develop a deep understanding of state-level policy issues.	1. Organize 2012 "ideas festival" with theme of food security (for March 2012). Build team of students, teachers, and community organizations (and delegate tasks).	1. Complete first stage of Capstone Project by February 11.	1. Serve as lead teacher on Global Leadership (GL) Curriculum Team. Mentor GL teacher at Chief Sealth.
2. Produce accessible, multimedia case studies that tell stories about what is working well and what challenge areas exist in local implementation of SB 6696 (video products).	2. Participate in the CTQ Teacher Advisory Board activities.	2. Attend PESB meetings March 8–9 and May 10–11.	2. Participate in International School Teacher Leaders PLC and facilitate International School Symposium on March 16 at Chief Sealth.	2. Attend Global Education Symposium in Washington DC February 16–18.	2. Attend Social Studies Leadership Retreat March 9–11 in Chelan, WA, to present workshop on Global Leadership class.

(continued)

Noah Zeichner—Work Plan 2011–2012, Semester 2 (*continued*)

CTQ-Washington	Center for Teaching Quality	Professional Educator Standards Board	Chief Sealth International High School	Teachers for Global Classrooms	Global Visionaries
3. Collaborate with and support efforts of the SPS Teacher Advisory Council, which will be examining issues specific to Seattle Public Schools, possibly including evaluation and assessment connected with the district's TIF and CBA implementation.	3. Ongoing learning with focus on Global Education (both curriculum and policy areas). Review webinars, articles, and other resources to further develop understanding of policy issues. Use TGC experience, both Capstone Project work and travel, to inform learning process.	3. Share knowledge of state policy with CTQ-Washington team.	3. Teach U.S. History, Global Leadership, and IB Theory of Knowledge. Work toward meeting my PG&E goals for 2011–12.	3. Travel to Brazil June 9–23. Write a travel blog pre-, during, and post-trip.	3. Submit 2012 proposal for NCSS Conference.

4. Continue to develop relationships with CBOs, education advocacy organizations, and other stakeholders to advance their sphere of influence within the Puget Sound area and later the state.

5. Update and build Washington-focused information and resources available on the CTQ Web site.

4. Produce one writing piece each month (blog posts, etc.). Some will be connected to global education work; others will be opportunity driven.

5. Increase my understanding of organizational structures of districts and unions as well as school board governance, starting with Seattle Public Schools. Use this knowledge to interact with district and union leadership more effectively.

4. Transfer learning from symposium and travel to policy work (CTQ) and school leadership (CSI).

5. Capstone Project due September 2012.

4. Coordinate 2–3 interns who are supporting the GL class at Chief Sealth.

ENDNOTES

PROLOGUE

1. Hattie, J. (2003). *Teachers make a difference: What is the research evidence?* Camberwell: Australian Council for Educational Research, pp. 6, 9.

2. Elmore, R. F. (1996). Getting to scale with good educational practice. *Harvard Education Review, 66*(1), 19, 20.

3. Ibid., p. 25.

4. Drucker, P. F. (1985). *Innovation and entrepreneurship.* New York, NY: Harper & Row, p. 28.

5. MetLife. (2013). *The MetLife survey of the American teacher: Challenges for school leadership.* New York, NY: Author, p. 50.

6. Wagner, T. (2012, August 12). Graduating all students innovation ready. *Education Week.* Retrieved from http://www.edweek.org/ew/articles/2012/08/14/01wagner.h32.html

7. Education chief's "terrorist" remark ignites fury. (2004, February 24). Retrieved from http://www.cnn.com/2004/EDUCATION/02/24/paige.terrorist.nea/index.html

8. Rittel, H. W., & Webber, M. M. (1973). Dilemmas in a general theory of planning. *Policy Sciences, 4*, 155–169.

9. MetLife, *MetLife survey*, p. 50.

10. Ibid.

CHAPTER ONE

1. York-Barr, J., & Duke, K. (2004). What do we know about teacher leadership? Findings from two decades of scholarship. *Review of Educational Research, 74*, 282.

2. Ibid., p. 260.

3. Ingersoll, R. M., & Strong, M. (2011). The impact of induction and mentoring programs for beginning teachers: A critical review of the research. *Review of Educational Research, 81*, 201–233.

4. Dewitt, P. (2012, May 24). Professional development with Andy Hargreaves [Blog post]. Retrieved from http://blogs.edweek.org/edweek/finding_common_ground/2012/05/professional_development_with_andy_hargreaves.html

5. York-Barr & Duke, What do we know, p. 288.

6. Ingersoll, R. M. (2003). *Who controls teachers' work? Power and accountability in America's schools.* Cambridge, MA: Harvard University Press.

7. Rosenholtz, S. J. (1991). *Teachers' workplace: The social organization of schools.* New York, NY: Teachers College Press, p. 68.

8. Goddard, Y. L., Goddard, R. D., & Tschannen-Moran, M. (2007). A theoretical and empirical investigation of teacher collaboration for school improvement and student achievement in public elementary schools. *Teachers College Record, 109,* 877–896.

9. Jackson, C. K., & Bruegmann, E. (2009). *Teaching students and teaching each other: The importance of peer learning for teachers* (NBER Working Paper No. 15202). Retrieved from http://www.nber.org/papers/w15202

10. MetLife. (2010). *The MetLife survey of the American teacher: Collaborating for student success.* New York, NY: Author.

11. Tough, P. (2012, August 15). What does Obama really believe in? *The New York Times Magazine.* Retrieved from http://www.nytimes.com/2012/08/19/magazine/obama-poverty.html?pagewanted=all

12. Darwish, J., Grimsley, K., & Moyer, J. (2012). World of learning: Taking action now [Blog post]. Retrieved from http://futureofed.org/world-of-learning/taking-action-now/

13. Harrison, C., & Killion, J. (2007). Ten roles for teacher leaders. *Educational Leadership, 65*(1), 74.

14. Alsop, E. (2012, September 14). Not so hot for teacher. *The New York Times Magazine.* Retrieved from http://www.nytimes.com/2012/09/16/magazine/not-so-hot-for-teacher.html?pagewanted=1&_rmoc.semityn.www&_r=2&smid=fb-share

15. Ibid.

16. Friedman, T. L. (2005). *The world is flat: A brief history of the twenty-first century.* New York, NY: Farrar, Straus and Giroux.

17. Hargreaves, A., & Fullan, M. (2012). *Professional capital: Transforming teaching in every school.* New York, NY: Teachers College Press.

18. Carnegie Forum on Education and the Economy. (1986). *A nation prepared: Teachers for the 21st century. The report of the Task Force on Teaching as a Profession.* Hyattsville, MD: Author, pp. 66–67.

19. National Research Council. (2008). *Assessing accomplished teaching: Advanced-level certification programs.* Washington DC: National Academies Press.

20. Koppich, J. E., Humphrey, D. C., & Hough, H. J. (2007). Making use of what teachers know and can do: Policy, practice, and National Board Certification. *Education Policy Analysis Archives, 15*(7), 8. Retrieved from http://epaa.asu.edu/epaa/v15n7

21. Ibid.

22. Rebora, A. (2012, October 17). National Board seeks to boost its impact on teaching profession [Blog post]. Retrieved from http://www.edweek.org/tm/articles/2012/10/17/tl_board.html

23. Luebke, B. (2011, January 26). National Board Certification in North Carolina: Time for a closer look. Retrieved from http://www.nccivitas.org/2011/national-board-certification-north-carolina-time-closer-look/

24. Rebora, National Board.

25. Berry, B., with Rasberry, M., & Williams, A. (2007). *Recruiting and retaining quality teachers for high-needs schools: Insights from NBCT summits and other policy initiatives.* Carrboro, NC: Center for Teaching Quality.

26. Wise, A. E., & Usdan, M. D. (2013, March 12). The political future of the teaching profession. *Education Week.* Retrieved from http://www.edweek.org/ew/articles/2013/03/13/24wise_ep.h32.html

27. U.S. Department of Education. (2012, February 15). Obama administration seeks to elevate teaching profession, Duncan to launch RESPECT Project: Teacher-led national conversation [Press release]. Retrieved from http://www.ed.gov/news/press-releases/obama-administration-seeks-elevate-teaching-profession-duncan-launch-respect-pro

28. Implementing the Common Core State Standards. (n.d.). Retrieved from http://www.corestandards.org

29. Frequently asked questions. (n.d.). Retrieved from http://www.corestandards.org/resources/frequently-asked-questions

30. Vilson, J. (2012, July 17). Teacher voice: How not to be a bobble-head doll [Blog post]. Retrieved from http://www.edweek.org/tm/articles/2012/07/17/tln_vilson_teachervoice.html?qs=José Vilson

CHAPTER TWO

1. Entrepreneur. (n.d.). Retrieved from http://www.merriam-webster.com/dictionary/entrepreneur

2. Vilson, J. (2011, September 27). How can Jay-Z help us remix education [Blog post]. Retrieved from http://www.edweek.org/tm/articles/2011/09/27/tln_vilson.html

3. Allen, S. (2012). Quotations from famous entrepreneurs on entrepreneurship. Retrieved from http://entrepreneurs.about.com/od/famousentrepreneurs/a/quotations.htm

4. Gallo, C. (2011, October 14). Steve Jobs and the seven rules of success. *Entrepreneur.* Retrieved from http://www.entrepreneur.com/article/220515

5. Young, J. R. (2013, March 7). At South by Southwest Education event, tensions divide entrepreneurs and educators [Blog post]. Retrieved from http://chronicle.com/blogs/wiredcampus/at-south-by-southwest-education-event-tensions-divide-entrepreneurs-and-educators/42777

6. Hess, F. M. (2007, October). *Reimagining American schooling: The case for educational entrepreneurship. Education Outlook, No. 4.* Washington DC: American Enterprise Institute for Public Policy Research, p. 6.

7. Berry, B., & TeacherSolutions 2030 Team. (2011). *Teaching 2030: What we must do for our students and our public schools . . . now and in the future.* New York, NY: Teachers College Press, p. 141.

8. Lortie, D. (1975). *Schoolteacher.* Chicago, IL: University of Chicago Press.

9. Wolf, T. (1979). *The right stuff.* New York, NY: Farrar, Straus and Giroux.

10. Zeichner, N. (2013, February-March). The next step: A hybrid teaching role. *Educational Horizons Magazine, 91.* Retrieved from http://pilambda.org/horizons/hybridrole/

11. Berry, B., & Zeichner, N. (2013, January). *The Global Cities Education Network and a virtual community for teacher leaders.* Carrboro, NC: Center for Teaching Quality.

Retrieved from http://www.teachingquality.org/content/global-cities-education-network
-gcen-and-virtual-community-teacher-leaders

CHAPTER THREE

1. Bryk, A. S., & Schneider, B. (2002). *Trust in schools: A core resource for improvement.* New York, NY: Russell Sage Foundation, p. 20.
2. Keigan, J. (2011). When teachers speak up—and policymakers listen [Blog post]. Retrieved from http://www.impatientoptimists.org/Posts/2011/12/When-Teachers -Speak-Up—And-Policymakers-Listen
3. Rocky Mountain PBS. (2011, September 16). *Colorado state of mind* [Television broadcast]. Denver, CO: Rocky Mountain Public Broadcasting Network.
4. Ibid.
5. Ibid.
6. Toppo, G. (2012, November 6). Urban middle class boosts school diversity [Blog post]. Retrieved from http://www.usatoday.com/story/news/nation/2012/10/28/schools-seek ing-diversity-get-boost-from-urban-middle-class/1661557/
7. Edutopia. (2007, November). Bank Street College of Education empowers new teachers [Video file]. Retrieved from http://www.edutopia.org/schools-of-education-bank -street-video
8. Sacks, A. (2012, March 31). What does Bank Street College know about preparing teachers? (VIDEO!) [Blog post]. Retrieved from http://www.teachingquality.org /content/what-does-bank-street-college-know-about-preparing-teachers-video
9. A brief history. (2012). Retrieved from http://bankstreet.edu/discover-bankstreet /history/
10. Anderson, M. (2011, February 21). EWA conference: The promise and pitfalls of improving the teaching profession [Blog post]. Retrieved from http://bubbler.word -press.com/2011/02/21/ewa-conference/
11. Big Ideas Fest. (2011, March 24). Ariel Sacks: Teacherpreneurs; Innovating from classrooms to communities. Podcast retrieved from http://www.youtube.com/watch ?v=wNTGET3K9Hg
12. Sacks, A. (2007). Take it from a teacher: We need merit pay. *New York Daily News.* Retrieved from http://www.nydailynews.com/opinion/teacher-merit-pay-article-1.240141
13. Sacks, A. (2012, October 17). Beyond tokenism: Toward the next stage of teacher leadership [Blog post]. Retrieved from http://www.edweek.org/tm/articles/2012/10/17 /tl_sacks.html. This article originally appeared in Education Week Teacher as part of a publishing partnership with the Center for Teaching Quality. Reprinted with permission from the author.

CHAPTER FOUR

1. Lortie, D. (1975). *Schoolteacher.* Chicago, IL: University of Chicago Press, p. 228.
2. Anderson, B. S., Berkin, C., Everdell, W. R., Gutwirth, J., Menon, R., McCullough, D., . . . Winslow, B. (2002, October 4). *Proceedings from Regents Exam Review Panel,*

Global and American History, New York, NY: Open Society Institute, p. 1. Retrieved from http://performanceassessment.org/consequences/GlobalAmericanHistory.pdf

3. Cramer, P. (2011, May 16). As Regents near teacher eval vote, researchers express concern [Blog post]. Retrieved from http://gothamschools.org/2011/05/16/as-regents -near-teacher-eval-vote-researchers-express-concern/

4. Moore, R. (2009, March 25). Test to the teach(ing)—not vice versa [Blog post]. Retrieved from http://www.teachingquality.org/content/test-teaching–not-vice-versa

5. Boyd, D., Lankford, H., Loeb, S., Rockoff, J., & Wyckoff, J. (2008, November). *The narrowing gap in New York City teacher qualifications and its implications for student achievement in high-poverty schools* (CALDER Working Paper No. 10). Retrieved from http://www.urban.org/uploadedpdf/1001268_narowinggapinnewyork.pdf; Ferguson, R. F. (1991). Paying for public education: New evidence on how and why money matters. *Harvard Journal on Legislation, 28*, 465–498; Hanushek, E. A. (1996). *School resources and achievement in Maryland.* Baltimore: Maryland State Department of Education; Rivkin, S. G., Hanushek, E. A., & Kain, J. F. (2005). Teachers, schools, and academic achievement. *Econometrica, 73*, 417–458; Rockoff, J. E. (2004). The impact of individual teachers on student achievement: Evidence from panel data. *American Economic Review, 94*, 247–252; Sanders, W. L., & Rivers, J. C. (1996). *Cumulative and residual effects of teachers on future student academic achievement.* Knoxville: University of Tennessee Value-Added Research and Assessment Center.

6. Little, J. W. (1996, April 8–12). Organizing schools for teacher learning. Paper presented at the annual meeting of the American Educational Research Association, New York, NY.

7. Campbell, J. (2012, March 21). Students look close to home for civic engagement lessons [Blog post]. Retrieved from http://gothamschools.org/2012/03/21/students-look-close -to-home-for-civic-engagement-lessons/

8. Lazar, S. (2012, October 10). Why I'm starting a school: The personal answer [Blog post]. Retrieved from http://gothamschools.org/2012/10/10/why-im-starting-a-school -the-personal-answer/

9. Payne, C. (2007). *I've got the light of freedom: The organizing tradition and the Mississippi freedom struggle.* Berkeley: University of California Press.

10. Clotfelter, C. T. (2004). *After Brown: The rise and retreat of school desegregation.* Princeton, NJ: Princeton University Press.

11. Curry, C. (1995). *Silver rights.* Chapel Hill, NC: Algonquin Books of Chapel Hill.

12. Edelman, M. W. (1995). Introduction. In C. Curry, *Silver rights* (pp. xi–xvii). Chapel Hill, NC: Algonquin Books of Chapel Hill, p. xvi.

13. Moore, R. (n.d.). My classroom organization. Retrieved from http://gallery.carnegiefoun dation.org/collections/castl_k12/rmoore/my_classroom_organization.htm

14. Hatch, T., Ahmed, D., Lieberman, A., Faigenbaum, D., White, M. E., & Pointer Mace, D. H. (Eds.). (2005). *Going public with our teaching: An anthology of practice.* New York, NY: Teachers College Press.

15. Hatch, T., White, M. E., & Faigenbaum, D. (2005). Expertise, credibility, and influence: How teachers can influence policy, advance research, and improve performance. *Teachers College Record, 107*, 1004.

16. Ibid., p. 1005.
17. Ibid., p. 1006.
18. Ibid., p. 1005.
19. Moore, R. (2010). *Teacher leaders advise on clinical preparation*. Washington DC: National Council for Accreditation of Teacher Education.
20. Moore, R. (2009, July 4). Independence Day: Ending the silence of the lambs [Blog post]. Retrieved from http://www.teachingquality.org/content/independence-day-ending -silence-lambs

CHAPTER FIVE

1. Grant, G., & Murray, C. (1999). *Teaching in America: The slow revolution*. Cambridge, MA: Harvard University Press.
2. Smith, J. (2012, July 20). The best- and worst-paying jobs for doctors [Blog post]. Retrieved from http://www.forbes.com/sites/jacquelynsmith/2012/07/20/the-best-and -worst-paying-jobs-for-doctors-2/
3. Rousmaniere, K. (2005). In search of a profession: A history of American teachers. In D. Moss, W. Glenn, & R. Schwab (Eds.), *Portraits of a profession: Teaching and teachers in the 21st century* (pp. 1–26). Westport, CT: Praeger.
4. Newsom, J. S. (2011). *Miss representation* [Motion picture]. United States: Girls' Club Entertainment.
5. About us. (n.d.). Retrieved from http://www.missrepresentation.org/about-us/
6. Ibid.
7. Odden, A., & Kelley, C. (2012). History of teacher pay. Retrieved from http://cpre .wceruw.org/tcomp/general/teacherpay.php
8. Waller, W. W. (1932). *The sociology of teaching*. Hoboken, NJ: Wiley, pp. 325–326.
9. Ibid., p. 43.
10. Lortie, D. (1975). *Schoolteacher*. Chicago, IL: University of Chicago Press.
11. National Commission on Teaching and America's Future. (1996). *What matters most: Teaching for America's future*. New York, NY: Author, p. 105.
12. Silva, E. (2009). *Teachers at work: Improving teacher quality through school design*. Washington DC: Education Sector, p. 3.
13. Vilson, J. (2010, July 20). Manna isn't falling from the sky [Blog post]. Retrieved from http://www.teachingquality.org/content/manna-isnt-falling-sky
14. Vilson, J. (2012, May 29). An open letter to NYS education commissioner John B. King [Blog post]. Retrieved from http://thejosevilson.com/2012/05/29/an-open-letter-to-nys -education-commissioner-john-b-king-testing-isnt-natural/
15. Vilson, J. (2010, September 29). The union said I couldn't wear my favorite color (and other absurd assertions in Education Nation) [Blog post]. Retrieved from http:// thejosevilson.com/2010/09/29/the-union-said-i-couldnt-wear-my-favorite-color-and -other-absurd-assertions-in-education-nation/
16. Thomas-Lester, A. (2009, July 4). Area schools face shortage of black male teachers. *The Washington Post*. Retrieved from http://www.washingtonpost.com/wpdyn/content /article/2009/07/03/AR2009070302498.html

17. C'de Baca, S. (2012, June 19). Teaching 24/7 [Blog post]. Retrieved from http://blogs
.edweek.org/teachers/teaching_ahead/2012/06/teaching_24_x_7.html
18. Cain, S. (2012). *Quiet: The power of introverts in a world that can't stop talking*. New
York, NY: Crown.
19. Waller, *Sociology of Teaching*, p. 11.

CHAPTER SIX

1. Cain, S. (2012). *Quiet: The power of introverts in a world that can't stop talking*. New
York, NY: Crown.
2. Khadaroo, S. T. (2010, September 1). School teachers in charge? Why some schools are
forgoing principals. *Christian Science Monitor*. Retrieved from http://www.csmonitor
.com/USA/Education/2010/0901/School-teachers-in-charge-Why-some-schools-are
-forgoing-principals
3. Nyamekye, A. (2012, May 12). Grassroots reform taking hold in LAUSD schools.
Huffington Post: Education. Retrieved from http://www.huffingtonpost.com/ama-nya
mekye/education-reform-_b_1536347.html
4. Khadaroo, School teachers in charge?
5. Jackson, C. K. (2012, December). *Non-cognitive ability, test scores, and teacher quality:
Evidence from 9th grade teachers in North Carolina* (NBER Working Paper No. 18624).
Retrieved from http://www.nber.org/papers/w18624
6. Humphrey, D. C., Koppich, J. E., Bland, J. A., & Bosetti, K. R. (2011). *Peer review: Getting
serious about teacher support and evaluation*. Menlo Park, CA: SRI International.
7. KUSA-TV. (2012, April 16). Education Nation: Common Core standards change
classrooms. Retrieved from http://www.9news.com/dontmiss/263226/630/Common
-Core-Standards-change-classrooms-
8. Ibid.
9. Davenport, A. (2009). Lessons from the Zone: What we can learn from Miami-Dade's
School Improvement Zone. Retrieved from http://amandadavenport.wordpress.com
/masters-thesis/
10. Gewertz, C. (2009, May 19). Miami's "Zone"—not so much improvement [Blog post].
Retrieved from http://blogs.edweek.org/edweek/high-school-connections/2009/05
/miamis_zone_not_so_much_improv.html
11. Urdegar, S. (2009). Miami-Dade County Public Schools: School Improvement Zone;
Final evaluation report. Retrieved from http://media.miamiherald.com/smedia/2009
/05/14/18/Zone.source.prod_affiliate.56.pdf
12. Keller, B. (2005, March 22). Conferees mull best uses of NBPTS teachers: Few now work
in schools that are low-performing. *Education Week*. Retrieved from http://www
.edweek.org/ew/articles/2005/03/23/28nbpts.h24.html
13. Cain, *Quiet*.
14. Lawrence, G. (1979). *People types and tiger stripes*. Gainesville, FL: Center for Application of Psychological Type.
15. Chopra, D. (2003). *The spontaneous fulfillment of desire: Harnessing the infinite power of
coincidence*. New York, NY: Harmony Books.

CHAPTER SEVEN

1. Warschawski, M. (2005). *On the border*. Cambridge, MA: South End Press, 2005, p. 48.
2. Lortie, D. (1975). *Schoolteacher*. Chicago, IL: University of Chicago Press.
3. Warschawski, *On the border*, p. xviii.
4. Broad Center. (2012, August 23). Broad Center releases "75 examples of how bureaucracy stands in the way of students and teachers" [Press release]. Retrieved from http://www.broadcenter.org/academy/newsroom/full/broad-center-releases-75-examples-resource
5. 75 Examples of how bureaucracy stands in the way of America's students and teachers. (n.d.). Retrieved from http://www.broadeducation.org/about/bureaucracy.html.
6. Organization for Economic Cooperation and Development. (2011). *PISA 2009 at a glance*. Paris, France: Author. http://dx.doi.org/10.1787/9789264095298-en
7. Hargreaves, A., Shirley, D., & National Staff Development Center. (2009). *The fourth way: The inspiring future for educational change*. Thousand Oaks, CA: Corwin.
8. Warschawski, *On the border*, p. 48.

CHAPTER EIGHT

1. Sacks, A. (2012, October 17). Beyond tokenism: Toward the next stage of teacher leadership [Blog post]. Retrieved from http://www.edweek.org/tm/articles/2012/10/17/tl_sacks.html
2. Walsh, C. (2011, November 3). A matter of principals. *Harvard Gazette*. Retrieved from http://news.harvard.edu/gazette/story/2011/11/a-matter-of-principals/
3. Arora, J. (2013, March 13). Teacherpreneur spotlight: Ryan Kinser, 8th grade English teacher [Blog post]. Retrieved from https://www.edsurge.com/n/2013–03–13-teacherpreneur-spotlight-ryan-kinser-8th-grade-english-teacher
4. Rogus, J. F. (1988). Teacher leader programming: Theoretical underpinnings. *Journal of Teacher Education, 39*, 46–52.
5. Smylie, M. A., & Denny, J. W. (1990). Teacher leadership: Tensions and ambiguities in organizational perspective. *Educational Administration Quarterly, 26*, 235–259.
6. Ibid.
7. Center for Cognitive Coaching. (2012, July 4). Overview of Cognitive Coaching. Retrieved from http://www.cognitivecoaching.com/overview.htm
8. Luke, J. S. (1998). *Catalytic leadership: Strategies for an interconnected world*. San Francisco, CA: Jossey-Bass.
9. Williams, P. (2002). The competent boundary spanner. *Public Administration, 80*, 103–124.
10. Cuthbertson, J. (2013, February 24). Searching for a superintendent [Blog post]. Retrieved from http://www.teachingquality.org/content/searching-superintendent
11. Strauss, V. (2013, February 21). It's wrong "to spend a cent less" on high-risk kids, teacher tells lawmakers [Blog post]. Retrieved from http://www.washingtonpost.com/blogs/answer-sheet/wp/2013/02/21/its-wrong-to-spend-a-cent-less-on-high-risk-kids-teacher-tells-lawmakers/
12. C-SPAN. (2013, February 21). Sequestration and the federal workforce [Video file]. Retrieved from http://www.c-spanvideo.org/clip/4363865

13. Boyd, D., Grossman, P., Lankford, H., Loeb, S., & Wyckoff, J. (2008, September). *Teacher preparation and student achievement* (NBER Working Paper No. W14314). Retrieved from http://ssrn.com/abstract=1264576

14. Center for Teaching Quality. (2013). *Teaching 2030: Leveraging teacher preparation 2.0.* Carrboro, NC: Author. Retrieved from http://www.teachingquality.org/teacher_prep_2.0

15. Pink, D. (2011, January 9). Daniel Pink on motivation. *The Washington Post.* Retrieved from http://www.washingtonpost.com/wp-dyn/content/article/2011/01/08/AR2011010800379.html

16. Elmore, R. F. (1996). Getting to scale with good educational practice. *Harvard Educational Review, 66*(1), 1–26.

17. Ibid., p. 4.

18. Ibid., p. 25.

19. Ibid., pp. 18, 20.

20. Sclafani, S. (2008). *Rethinking human capital in education: Singapore as a model for teacher development.* Washington DC: Aspen Institute, pp. 20, 21.

21. Elmore, Getting to scale, p. 25.

22. Bushaw, W. J., & Lopez, S. J. (2012). Public education in the United States: A nation divided. *Phi Delta Kappan, 94*(1), 8–25.

CHAPTER NINE

1. Gamerman, E. (2008, February 29). What makes Finnish kids so smart? *The Wall Street Journal.* Retrieved from http://online.wsj.com/article/SB120425355065601997.html

2. Friedman, T. L. (2013, March 30). Need a job? Invent it. *The New York Times.* Retrieved from http://www.nytimes.com/2013/03/31/opinion/sunday/friedman-need-a-job-invent-it.html?_r=1&

3. Partanen, A. (2011, December 29). What Americans keep ignoring about Finland's school success. *The Atlantic, 29.* Retrieved from http://www.theatlantic.com/national/archive/2011/12/what-americans-keep-ignoring-about-finlands-school-success/250564/#.TwP0KawcIAG.facebook

4. Sahlberg, P. (2010). *Finnish lessons: What can the world learn from educational change in Finland?* New York, NY: Teachers College Press.

5. Niemi, H. (2013, April 29). *Persistent work for equity and life long learning in the Finnish education system.* Paper presented at the 2013 Annual Meeting of the American Educational Research Association, San Francisco, CA, p. 11.

6. Sahlberg, *Finnish lessons.*

7. Partanen, What Americans keep.

8. Sahlberg, P. (2012, January 9). Finland's success is no miracle. *Education Week.* Retrieved from http://www.edweek.org/ew/articles/2012/01/12/16sahlberg.h31.html

9. Darling-Hammond, L. (2009, Summer). Steady work: How Finland is building a strong teaching and learning system. *Voices in Urban Education, 24,* 15–25. Retrieved from http://www.annenberginstitute.org/VUE/wp-content/pdf/VUE24_Darling.pdf

10. Hargreaves, A., Halász, G., & Pont, B. (2007). *School leadership for systemic improvement in Finland*. Paris, France: Organization for Economic Cooperation and Development, p. 16.
11. Bill & Melinda Gates Foundation. (2012). *Primary sources: America's teachers on the teaching profession*. New York, NY: Scholastic.
12. Darling-Hammond, L. (2006, May-June). Constructing 21st-century teacher education. *Journal of Teacher Education, 57*, 300–314.

CHAPTER TEN

1. Brafman, O., & Beckstrom, R. A. (2006). *The starfish and the spider: The unstoppable power of leaderless organizations* [Online version]. New York, NY: Penguin Group, p. 15.
2. Beckstrom, R. A. (n.d.). The starfish and the spider: The unstoppable power of leaderless organizations. Retrieved from http://beckstrom.com/Speaking
3. Brafman & Beckstrom, *The starfish*, p. 36.
4. Predictions made by Ray Kurzweil. (n.d.). Retrieved from http://en.wikipedia.org/wiki/Predictions_made_by_Ray_Kurzweil
5. Richmond, S. (2012, March 16). iPad: How Apple started a tablet revolution. *The Telegraph*. Retrieved from http://www.telegraph.co.uk/technology/apple/9147868/iPad-how-Apple-started-a-tablet-revolution.html
6. Dalka, D. (2007, March). Review of Don Tapscott's and Anthony Williams' *Wikinomics*. *The Wiglaf Journal*. Retrieved from http://www.wiglafjournal.com/communication/2007/03/review-of-don-tapscotts-and-anthony-williams-wikinomics/

INDEX

JB JOSSEY-BASS | Education

Jossey-Bass provides educators with practical knowledge and tools to create a positive and lifelong impact on student learning.

For more information about our resources, authors, and events please visit us at: www.josseybasseducation.com.

You may also find us on Facebook, Twitter, and Pinterest.

Jossey-Bass K–12 Education

jbeducation

Pinterest jbeducation